WOMAN
The Incredible Life Of Yoko Ono

By Alan Clayson
with Barb Jungr and Robb Johnson

A CHROME DREAMS PUBLICATION

First Edition 2004

Published By Chrome Dreams
PO BOX 230
New Malden
Surrey
KT3 6YY
UK
www.chromedreams.co.uk

ISBN 1 84240 220 X

Editorial Director   Rob Johnstone
Editor   Rob Johnstone
Cover and interior design   Mark Fuks

WOMAN

THE INCREDIBLE LIFE OF

YOKO ONO

ALAN CLAYSON

with Barb Jungr and Robb Johnson

Photographs courtesy of

Front Cover Camera Press
Inside Camera Press
Redferns
London Features International

Song lyrics courtesy of

Ono Music [BMI]
Lennono Music

Prologue ... 7

PART 1 BEFORE JOHN
  1 – **The Descendant** ... 9
  2 – **The Child** ... 18
  3 – **The Bride** ... 25
  4 – **The Divorcee** ... 32
  5 – **The Villager** ... 39
  6 – **The Visitor** ... 46

PART 2 JOHN AND YOKO
  1 – **Unfinished Paintings And Objects** ... 53
  2 – **Life With The Lions** ... 60
  3 – **Give Peace A Chance** ... 70
  4 – **Plastic Ono** ... 77
  5 – **Approximately Infinite Universe** ... 86
  6 – **Feeling The Space** ... 94
  7 – **A Heart Play** ... 100

PART 3 AFTER JOHN
  1 – **The Widow** ... 109
  2 – **The Shareholder** ... 117
  3 – **The Indweller** ... 124

PART 4 ART AND MUSIC
  1 – **Yes: An Overview of The Art Of Yoko Ono** ... 131
  2 – **From Scream to Singing** ... 139
  3 – **The Sixteen Track Voice** ... 146
  4 – **Fly and The Infinite Universe** ... 155

5 – **Double Fantasy and Season Of Glass** ... 163

6 – **Rising: Starpeace, Onobox and Blueprint For A Sunrise** ... 170

7 – **Cut Piece and The Performances** ... 178

8 – **Legacy** ... 184

9 – **Postscript. My Journey** ... 190

Epilogue ... 194

Index ... 196

Prologue

Her association with John Lennon and his Beatles will always remain central to any consideration of Yoko Ono as a figure in time's fabric. To the man–in–the–street, she appeared as if from nowhere not long after the death in 1967 of manager Brian Epstein. Quizzical eyes were soon to be raised at The Beatles' increasingly more wayward activities together – and apart for, just as US go–getter Allan Klein was to replace Epstein as Lennon's man–of–affairs in 1969, so Ono had already superceded Paul McCartney as John's artistic collaborator as she had Cynthia, the first Mrs. Lennon, in his bed.

Ono and Lennon's first album together, *Unfinished Music No. 1: Two Virgins*, was notable less for its vinyl content than the cover photographs of the pair naked. It was, they explained, an Art Statement. Joe Average was, however, too nonplussed to give an Art Reply to this and further of their bewildering pranks like the Bed–Ins, the sending of acorns to world leaders, "*Bagism*" and *Self–Portrait* a film starring John's penis.

Having thus pledged himself to Yoko more symbollically than a mere engagement ring ever could, Lennon had married her in March 1969. The ceremony was mentioned in "The Ballad Of John And Yoko", The Beatles' final British Number One. Like most of their fans, the group's authorised biographer, Hunter Davies blamed – and continues to blame – "the arrival in John's life of Yoko Ono" for The Beatles' disbandment.

Yet Yoko had amassed a qualified fame – or infamy – long before she captured Lennon's heart. In avant–garde regions of the world of Art – and music – she had been known as a performance artist of extreme strategy since the late 1950s. While this may have pointed the way to more highly–regarded achievements, much of Ono's cultural legitimacy would be lost through her affinity to The Beatles – though, conversely, it was via that uneasy liaison that her thoughts and output – much of which seemed to the uninitiated to be as devoid of ante–start agonies as an Ernie Wise play – reached a far, far wider public than they might have warranted in a more ordinary course of events. Nevertheless, since Lennon's slaying on a New York pavement in 1980, his widow has almost–but–not–quite entered an orbit separate from him and his former colleagues.

PROLOGUE

This account is, I suppose, a literary equivalent of an Ono "happening" in 1962 when a Hollywood movie was screened with her directive that viewers were to concentrate solely on the female lead. Balancing fact and researched opinion, it is written from the perspective of three very different authors. Between them, outlines dissolve only marginally as Barb Jungr analyzes Ono's artistic conduct and legacy; Alan Clayson chronicles the pre– and post–Lennon period, and Robb Johnson examines her life with the chief Beatle whilst defining the myriad political, social, economic and other undercurrents that inform this quest for the mystery–surrounding–a– puzzle–within –an–enigma that is Yoko Ono.

WOMAN

by Alan Clayson

1. **The Descendant**

'I can't present myself as a representative of any tradition'

Most families tend to claim affinity to someone at least vaguely famous, but, although Yoko Ono shared her name with countless others in Japan, her forebears included a great–grandfather, Atsushi Saisho, who traced his ancestry to a ninth century religious leader, also called Saisho, whose talents caught the attention of the emperor. With cash from the royal treasury, Saisho founded a new, and controversial, Buddhist sect, 'Tendai Lotus', in 807. After establishing a monastery, he was to be embroiled in ecclesiastical politics until his demise fifteen years later, loaded with all manner of honours. Chief among these was the title of *Daishi* – 'Great Teacher' – particularly as Saisho was the first priest in Japan to be thus known.

From Saisho, or one of his siblings, descended a dynasty so powerful that it played a leading role in the overthrow of the ancient Japanese *shogun* system of military feudal dictatorship in 1867, and the restoration of full sovereignty to the emperor. Atsushi Saisho himself was a luminary in the Imperial Household Council under the progressive Meiji, the first emperor to welcome occidentals to that chain of islands lying off the eastern coast of the Asian mainland. As well as thus kick–starting Japan's adoption of Western civilisation, Meiji was also responsible for transferring the royal court from Kyoto, the seat of the Imperial family for nearly a thousand years, to what consequently became Japan's new capital city of Tokyo.

Vocationally, Atsushi Saisho's life at the storm centre of power was a success, but his siring of one daughter, Tsuruko, and no sons was considered a mark of shame in a land that adhered strictly to the edict that male took precedent over female in matters of privilege and inheritance. Nevertheless, Saisho displayed as public a fondness of Tsuruko as he could, and didn't object when she chose to study English and music at a college in Tokyo.

She didn't leave the college with just a degree. Attracted initially by its music, she had also embraced Christianity, very much a minority faith in Japan. The eagerly–absorbed doctrines of the late convert were among considerations when Tsuroko agreed to marry Eijiro Ono, who, if a scion of a line of *samurai* warriors, was what George Bernard Shaw would have have described as a 'downstart' in that he came from a family that had once been better off. He proved, nonetheless, sound, even very able, in most school subjects and gained a place at a college of further education in Tokyo. A post–graduate course overseas at the University of Michigan resulted in a doctorate in economics and mathematics in 1890.

Returning to his homeland, Ono applied himself diligently to a demanding post as a medium–weight executive at the Bank of Japan, pondering given columns of figures and then prodding indolent colleagues and sly businessmen about where this percentage had come from, and why that interest hadn't been paid. Delighted that they'd found someone who was more than a time–server, Ono's superiors pushed him further up the ladder. He became branch manager, then was placed on the board of Directors and, finally he held a position as president of the Japan Industrial Bank before retirement and death in 1927.

Ostensibly, Eisuke, Eijiro's third son, seemed to be a chip off the old block. Yet while he earned similar academic qualifications, Eisuke, encouraged by his mother, grew fond of western Church music. Much hard listening to crackling 78 rpm records and rarer concert attendances evolved into attempts to approximate the holy sounds on the piano that stood in the front parlour. While his father lent a sour ear to his efforts, Eisuke himself was a fascinated listener when an elder brother's Russian wife made the instrument tinkle with the strains of Monteverdi, Bach and Handel during those 'musical evenings' that were a frequent occurrence in many refined households before television became an indispensable domestic fixture. Flattered by the waywardly earnest young man's interest, she taught Eisuke all she knew, delighted by his willingness to try–try again as he sweated over exercises that revealed to him that music was a science as much as an art.

If no Mozart playing blindfold, Eisuke's developing keyboard skills were a passport to entering polite society. He surfaced as a particularly wanted guest at parties in Karuizawa, a mountain village north of Tokyo, favoured as a holiday resort by young aristocrats, new money and foreign diplomats. Rather than Te Deums and Magnificats, or even Japanese popular music, he was requested more frequently to give 'em jaunty singalongs and sentimental ballads about my blue heaven and Ida, sweet as apple cider.

Most of them emanated from the United States, whose star was in the ascendant after the Great War as a haven for artistic radicalism, now that a vanguard had developed independently of those in Europe. The USA was certainly taking the lead in aspects of music, as had been exemplified glaringly on 6th March 1913 when 'jazz' was elevated from slang via its use in the *San Francisco Bulletin* in a feature concerning singer Al Jolson, whose million–selling recording of 'The Spaniard That Blighted My Life' had been released that week.

Stravinsky and classical composer *manqué* George Gershwin, were quite open about their knowledge and love of jazz, though Stravinsky's *Ebony Concerto* for Woody Herman's band lay nearly three decades in the future. So did his emigration to the States when an acceptance of a lectureship at Harvard University in the watershed year of 1939 was but one instance of European politics making an exile of one of its finest minds.

The continent's cutting of its own throat during both the previous World War and the 1917 Revolution in Russia was among the factors – among them – that spurred Marcel Duchamp to turn up on fellow artist May Ray's New York doorstep with a gift of a glass ball containing 'Parisian air'. For many of the same reasons, Edgard Varese, on a par with Stravinsky as both a figurehead and *eminence grise* of twentieth century music departed from France to New York. On the morning after his arrival, he took a tram to Greenwich Village, a district towards Lower Manhattan that he'd been assured was as vibrantly bohemian as Montparnasse, teeming with poets, painters, musicians and the like since the 1840s when Walt Whitman and an infirm Edgar Allan Poe had been near–neighbours there.

These days, when Duchamp strolled into one of its cafés, there would be an instant scraping of chairs, a pushing away of tables, in an eagerness to come across and devoutly question him on aspects of art, and accept with reverence the easy–flowing words that fell from his lips. The modern artist, he said, didn't have to produce a nice picture on a specific subject any more. Photography took care of that. A painting or sculpture no longer needed to be of anything recognisable. Representing nothing but itself, its sole purpose was to touch you in some way, perhaps for reasons you couldn't articulate.

Such ideas weren't originated entirely by Duchamp, but, following the Great War, Greenwich Village began accommodating cells of an art movement in which he was a prime mover, and that continued to grow in impetus and became more cohesive. Maybe it was almost the point, but the most formal sense of solidarity was fixed on a sect that denied both form and solidarity. There remains bitter division about Dada – alias 'anti-art,' 'the avant–garde of the avant–garde,' 'art–as–life' – but its basic premises were that all art is muck, and that anyone could create art, no matter how absurd, trivial or pretentious the end result – and there needn't necessarily be one.

By most accounts, Dada began in wartime Zurich and spread to Berlin, Hanover – where a certain Kurt Schwitters was its sole representative – Paris, New York and elsewhere. Its principal impact was on the literary and visual arts as demonstrated by such diverse resonances as the non–lexical 'sound poems' of Schwitters, the non–commital philosophical substance of Gurdjieff and the 'nothing matters' preoccupation that is the commonly–received conception about existentialism. There are elements of Dada too in today's Stuckism (or 'remodernism') that "embraces all it denounces" (1) such as the dead sheep (exhibited by Damien Hurst) and unmade bed (Tracey Emin) nominated for Turner prizes in the late 1990s.

An obvious point on one Stuckist document was that "Duchamp's work was a protest against the stale, unthinking artistic establishment of his day." (1) In unknowing acknowledgement of this, the American Society of Independent Arts refused Duchamp's entry of *Fountain* – a urinal with "R. Mutt 1917" painted on it – to its first exhibition. This overt act marked New York Dada's provocative conception.

In May 1917, Duchamp justified *Fountain* as "ready–made" art – "a polemic of materialism" – in the second edition of *The Blind Man*, a self–financed Dadaist periodical. His editorial also brought R(ichard) Mutt into existence via a biography that even specified his telephone number.

Dada was fun while it lasted. Furthermore, it had wended its way even to chit–chat at Karuizawa *soirées* by means as mysterious as a particular brand of footware had to St. Kilda, the most far–flung Hebridean island, barely a year after its acceptance in *chic* nineteenth century London.

Eisuke Ono might have chuckled at Dada's understated sardonic humour akin to his own, but he made no effort to either understand or sympathise with its underlying tenets or those of the associated Futurism, Surrealism and other modern 'isms' that induced bewilderment and frequent contempt in the Karuizawa socialite who recalled occasional paragraphs about them in the newspaper. As impenetrable as a crystal for Eisuke, therefore, were the intellectual and sonic challenges of, say, Schoenberg's now fully mobilized twelve–tone system, stubbornly chromatic Carl Ruggles or Henry Cowell, a pioneer of formal indeterminacy and pianos 'treated' with the buzzings and rattlings of nail–files, paper–clips, teaspoons and similar objects from household and office, all of which counterbalanced walk–outs by members of the audience with unrequited demands for repeat performances.

None of it reconciled either with Ono's self–picture of himself as a serious artist, even as he pounded out in mild–mannered fashion what he had lumped together derisively as 'jazz' to bow–tied tuxedos, pearly cleavages and faces tanned on the Karuizawa ski slopes.

Twenty–one year old , quietly–spoken and timorously pretty, listened to these interpretations with a crooked smile, but was enthralled when, with his digits on auto–pilot, Eisuke delved into the bits everyone knew from the classics. From having simply intrigued her, Ono was taking gradual, if unknowing, possession of Isoko, who discovered herself shivering with pleasure when a smile that showed off fine teeth was directed at her.

For his part, Eisuke was wondering whether the threshold of his thirtieth birthday wasn't a good age to look for a wife. He wasn't a bad–looking fellow, was he? He had certainly been 'talked of' with regard to cheery flirtations with some of the sillier Karuizawa ladies. Compared to them Isoko was, he decided, as a fountain pen to a stub of pencil, and a shy courtship began with feigned indifference and circuitous enquiry.

After she and Eisuke had fallen in love, Isoko's Buddhist parents were bemused when she announced that she wanted to marry the boy. They were worried about both Eisuke's Christianity and, to a greater degree, his apparent aspirations to make a living as a pianist, an unwise career choice unless you'd been born into showbusiness. Indeed, the very idea of such a well–bred lad like Eisuke venturing onto the professional stage was almost as deplorable to many Japanese gentlefolk as a girl of like status becoming a prostitute.

Mr and Mrs Yasuda kept the distressing information from the family matriarch, Isoko's maternal grandmother, whose health had been failing since Zenjiro, her husband, had been left grovelling and open–mouthed in a Tokyo street, with his life's blood puddling out of him. Labelled a conservative from earliest youth, he had been assaulted by homicidal left–wing extremists – possibly *agent provocateurs* – maddened apparently by his unspoken refusal to slot even one coin into their collection tin.

His funeral was conducted with costly Romanesque pomp, for Zenjiro Yasuda had run a tight, old–fashioned ship as founder of the Yasuda Bank, which, specialising in property investment and insurance, had thrust tentacles into Europe and North America. He was, therefore, prominent in one of Japan's wealthiest and most respected business consortiums. On such a plateau, nepotism was quite naked. Yasuda had been grooming son–in–law Iomi Teitairo, Isoko's father, as his successor, and may have pulled strings to have him elevated in 1915 to the Japanese equivalent of an earldom, albeit on condition that Iomi changed his name by deed–poll to Zensaburo Yasuda.

Isoko was the youngest of eight offspring – four males, four females – of Iomi–Zebsaburo and Teruko, Zenjiro's adored eldest child. The family dwelt within a stone's throw of the royal palace on Tokyo's loftiest hill, and possessed a motor–car long before nearly every everyone–who–was–anyone had one too. From its windows, Isoko and her siblings had noticed, but never spoken to rough boys and girls, many of them barefoot, playing in the back streets of the sprawling city of overlapping towns in which there would be more horses than cars until well into the 1920s. Isoko and her siblings' upbringing was, therefore, sheltered and genteel as epitomised by lavish incentives – gifts of diamonds sometimes for the sisters – to do well at what were, needless to say, the most exclusive and expensive of Tokyo's seats of learning. They knew few who lived much differently from themselves.

While Eisuke Ono was from a well–heeled family of high–echelon social standing like their own, why couldn't he see that a career as any kind of artist was an insecure one, a vocational back–alley? Few lasted very long. In alliance with his own parents, the Yasudas prevailed upon Eisuke to be sensible, and, with hardly a murmur, he agreed to shelve any notions about making a living as a musician, and to obey the lodged rules of bourgeois convention by following in his father's footsteps and those of his father–in–law too. So it was that Eisuke Ono came to wed Isoko Yasuda, and, if despising his innate and fastidious talent for finance, buckled down to work at the Yokohama Specie Bank. One materially appealing part of the deal was that he would commute from a comfortable home on the vast estate of his bride's lately bereaved grandmother.

It was here at 8.30am on the snowy morning of 18th February 1933, the Year of the Bird, that Eisuke and Isoko's first baby, a daughter, entered the world. It would have been more desirable if their eldest had been a son, but they were satisfied that Isoko's labour had been straightforward and that the newcomer was robust. They named her Yoko, which means 'Ocean Child,' as she was a Pisces. Of significance to Japanese parents too is a child's birth number – which in Yoko's case was nine on the basis of both the Year and $1 + 8 + 2 + 1 + 9 + 3 + 3$ adding up to twenty–seven, and two and seven equalling nine, the trinity of trinities for Christians for whom there are nine heavens, nine orders of angels and nine regions of hell.

While he had capitulated to other demands to gain Isoko's hand, Eisuke had not embraced Buddhism. Yet Zebsaburo and Teruko found him a model, if reserved, son–in–law who'd applied himself diligently to his job to the extent that he'd been stoic about an obligation to leave Japan a fortnight before Yoko's coming when sent to the bank's branch in San Francisco and instructed to remain there until further notice.

Eisuke was to be permanently away for the first three years of his daughter's life. Nevertheless, for all the opaque mystery of his framed photograph on the wall, he continued to govern family behaviour patterns *in absentia*, especially those rooted in appreciation of the value of money, and the notion that hard work and tenacity are principal keys to achievement.

Notes

1. *Stuckist pamphlet*, 11th April 2000 (Hangman Bureau of Enquiry)

2. **The Child**

"I didn't think of it as 'I'm a lonely child', because that was the only life I knew"

We would like to have the impossible: videos of scenes of whatever busied the rooms of the wooden Ono mansion, say, or to sample with our own sensory organs how a particular glance, word or gesture from Isoko affected little Yoko. In every family, there is always territory forbidden and inexplicable to outsiders, but all children are born in love with their parents. There is no God but Mummy, and Daddy is the prophet of Mummy.

However, in Yoko's case, while her father was a remote figure in her infancy, her dutiful, rather than doting, mother showed but rarely any overt emotion or physical fondness towards her ideally seen–but–not–heard daughter. Moreover, as it was with housework, Isoko trusted nappy–changing, feeding and further mundane aspects of her child's rearing to various of the thirty–odd servants, who aped the manners of those in the palace by, for example, kow–towing in and out of the mistress's presence.

That isn't to say that Isoko wasn't concerned about Yoko, far from it. Indeed, with a zeal for cleanliness that other parents might have thought excessive, she instructed the nannies to ensure that alcohol and cotton–wool were always to hand to disinfect anything Yoko was likely to touch in urchin–infested public places.

As a result, Yoko herself became fussy about hygiene, almost to the point of obsessive compulsion. While she wasn't to repeatedly wash her hands until they were chapped and sore, she would drop an object like a stone if it was still warm with the previous handler's body temperature.

She accepted too without argument that, if required for a grown–up occasion, her face would be scrubbed and her long dark hair combed until her entire scalp smarted. Then she was expected to conduct herself with nicely–spoken and fatuous affability whenever some banal platitude was addressed to her .Ostensibly, Isoko cared less about her children's happiness than the good opinion of her peers via displays of material wealth and attending social functions – stuffed–shirt suppers, say, or the kind of hushed musical recitals where the main purpose of the evening was to see and be seen during the intermission.

"Inside me, I could feel a certain rejection of my mother's show of her possessions, but I got over it as I got older" (1) was Yoko's response to a regime intended to force her to keep her own feelings in check, and not to feel bitterness or anger towards her parents, even when those feelings might be wholly justified.

Conversely, a combination of being waited on hand–and–foot and being left to her own devices much of the time began to turn Yoko into an astoundingly self–motivated, purposeful girl. Characteristics translated as 'wilfulness' by a mother who, believing that she somehow owned her child's life, seldom paused to consider not only how different Yoko's values might be to hers, but whether Yoko had even formed any of her own.

A symptom of a certain 'apartness' in Yoko would come to the fore too, whether in unsmiling family portraits or a desire to turn her back on a cosseted life to roam those parts of Tokyo where ragged children as skinny and ferocious as stray cats dwelt. The sheltered Yoko had been taught to both despise and dread them as they cat–called and scrapped in the city's coarsest intonation whilst dodging both the moving traffic and the pavement–cluttering fruit and vegetable carts standing wheel–to–wheel beneath what was visible of the sky.

Generally, however, she had little to do with a wider world to any great degree, preoccupied as it was with the aftershock of 1929's Wall Street Crash after US overseas investment dried up. So began the Great Depression: the global collapse of all sizes and manner of business enterprises with attendant multitudes suddenly unemployed.

Yet Japan was to finish the 1930s in a better situation than most other countries, thanks to rapid development of industry since the First World War. While it had been a realm of thriving tillage a century earlier, the Land of the Rising Sun was emerging as one of the planet's foremost industrial nations. City boundaries had expanded, swallowing surrounding communities in their wake as road, river and rail connections fanned out on all directions. Myriad manufactured products – reels of thread to crane–buckling steamship boilers – were being shunted daily from over–populated connurbations, haphazard and huddled with cavernous warehouses. In the years before phrases like 'environmental health' had been coined, giant chimneys of blast furnaces and factories were already belching chemical waste into the skies of Japan, and caking employees' poky dwellings with soot as indelible as Lady Macbeth's damned spot.

Any encircling depression, economic or otherwise, did not yet trouble three–year–old Yoko Ono, a–twitter with excitement as she and her mother berthed in a ship bound for San Francisco, where she was to meet her father for the first time. The voyage was not without incident as Yoko was scolded for venturing into the low–fare steerage section. "I remember playing hide–and–seek," she recalled, "I was going down, down, down, and suddenly realised that it said 'Third Tier'. You're not supposed to go in there." (2)

She stood hot–eyed at the rail of the upper deck, lost in wonder at what she could make out of California's palm–studded coastal roads and the greensward of the waterside parks against the blue curvature of the Pacific Ocean as the vessel negotiated the ingress of the trudging river that flowed beneath the Golden Gate bridge. It dropped anchor at a pier where Eisuke waved and strode towards his disembarking wife and the daughter he had never seen. Obediently, Yoko left Isoko's side and ran the few yards to her father's outstetched arms. Suddenly, she felt herself being swung off the ground by this "towering, very tall man" (1), who kissed and hugged her.

Among her next recollections of Eisuke was him measuring the span between the tips of her fingers and her thumb, and pronouncing that it wasn't long enough for her to be a keyboard player of any great merit. Nevertheless, he hired a piano teacher and was delighted to hear that he was getting his money's worth as Yoko was both keen to learn and self–contained enough to disassociate the music from the drudgery of daily practice. Soon, she was sufficiently able to be led forth, to perform pieces for visitors to both the rented house in San Francisco and, not quite a year later, back home in Tokyo.

Eisuke was more impressed with Yoko's speaking and singing voice when she acted out Japanese folk myths and narrative ballads that she had picked up from the servants, much to the disgust of her mother, who hoped that her daughter would absorb the English language as well as tap–dancing, Shakespeare and further disparate aspects of Western culture after she started at the *crème–de–la–crème Gakushuin* or Peers' School, where her classmates were to include Akihito, the Crown Prince.

Yoko hoped so too – because she was and would always be anxious about parental approval, even when she had, ostensibly, escaped from their clutches. Thus she endeavoured to exhibit no resentment when Isoko's selective and hard–won attention focussed on a new baby, Keisuke, born in December 1937, as, in the name of Akihito's father, Emperor Hirohito, Japan's involvement in the forthcoming war loomed.

The tension would climax with the Japanese assault on Pearl Harbour and, as it grew, all signposts for the Onos pointed to perhaps the last place you'd expect to find them. Isoko and the children sailed once more to San Francisco where they stowed the luggage and seated themselves in a railway carriage for a long journey to New York, where Eisuke had been ensconced for weeks in the Yokohama Specie's Manhattan outlet where he'd been so overwhelmed with work that members of his own family could only speak to him by appointment via his secretary.

Tired and foul–tempered by the time he had pulled into Grand Central Station, what nagged at Eisuke was a constant undercurrent of insecurity about what would happen if, not when, Japan, already in unofficial imperialist conflict with China, joined with the Axis powers against the Allies. Family unity counted for more than the possibility of internment at the outbreak of hostilities, but in the lull between his first day at the new bank in 1940 and the Pearl Harbour *blitzkrieg*, he grew increasingly maudlin anyway about a Tokyo he was seeing through a rosy haze as a *Noo Yawk* accent peeped out of Yoko's pronunciation of the tongue she was encouraged to speak in the classroom both in the USA and, to a lesser extent, after the Onos, in the fever of mobilisation, were able to slip away unchallenged in the New Year.

Technically, there were five of them. Isoko was pregnant again, and her final confinement would produce Setsuko just before Christmas. As it had been with Yoko, her father was a shadowy figure in Setsuko's early years. The War Office, concerned about the stalemate in the Pacific theatre, had sent for Eisuke Ono. An infinitesimal cog in the war effort, he was one of the corps that kept the Specie Bank running in Hanoi for as long as the Allies were held at arm's length by the might of Hirohito.

His empire paid for its war by turning each city into a realm of queues for items of food and clothing so scarce that you could only buy them with weeks of saved–up ration coupons or on the black market. In a protective bubble of privilege, the Onos were exempted in the first instance from having to acquire groceries via sacrifice of luxury or by illicit means, though they were pressured to donate precious keepsakes to the war effort, and were obliged to lose household staff to hospitals, munitions factories and the forces.

One constant, untouched immediately by the turmoil, was Yoko's education. She was now attending Keimei Gakuen, a newish Christian school in Tokyo, where she was instructed in the Bible by a mixture of clerics and laity, and expected to speak English in class. However, as the Allied net closed on Japan, it was decreed that all children over twelve were to work on munitions assembly lines, though, as Isoko discovered, it was easy for one such as her to circumvent such legalities, and Keimei Gakuen's principal was persuaded to subtract two years from Yoko's age on the register.

Ultimately, however, this lie didn't matter because the Onos were soon to scuttle away from Tokyo anyway after alarm bells and sirens executed a discordant threnody during the maiming of the capital city, the largest in the world, by US B–29 bombers from runways in Hawaii. Houses and theatres, shops and cinemas, public buildings and blocks of flats crumbled in a haze of smoke or else were blown more cleanly out of existence by direct hits throughout night upon night of aerial bombardment of ton after ton of death and destruction, likened by Yoko to the footsteps of grim fairy–tale giants.

The palace where Akihito used to live was no more. Ancient trees that had sprung from saplings in suburban calm snapped like twigs, and the muddy surfaces of the criss–crossing, slip–slapping canals shone with the brightness of flames that gushed like swollen rivers along the streets, consuming any obstacles in their path. Tarmac was reduced to bubbling pitch until the dousing water veins of Tokyo were slashed.

Beneath the storm, Isoko and her brood cowered in the bomb shelter into which the basement had been converted. When the hostile shadows vanished from the sky, the lull allowed the family and the rest of the human moles to emerge and find broken crockery from their cupboards, burnt mattresses from their beds and splinters from their furniture scattered across the streets.

If you could afford to go, you did. Akihito had left already for a remote woodland cottage with a sexagenarian chamberlain his only companion and, in March 1945, Isoko took the children and her one remaining servant to a distant dwelling in a cornfield near a village in the foothills round Karuizawa of romantic memory.

From the radio, Isoko gathered that Hanoi had been invested by the Allies. The post brought nothing specific about the whereabouts of Eisuke or whether he was even alive, but she shut her mind to the stomach–knotting uncertainty, and adapted as best she could to an unprecedented poverty, discovering within herself resources she had not known existed. She haggled with brutish locals during heartbreaking sales of treasured possessions to buy food. She was driven to pitching hard–luck stories at strangers who looked as if they had a pocketful of money. She had the youngsters dressed in yokel garb with the texture of a horse–blanket, and sent them to the village's state school where they were tormented in the playground for what was regarded as their hoity–toity demeanour.

The situation was so unbearable for Keisuke that he developed school phobia, but his elder sister, if placatory at first in confrontations, put up her fists, looked fierce and hoped for the best rather than swallow insults or shrug off the bullying. Furthermore, under the unimaginative and often frightening regime in class, she made steady progress. As well as betraying a flair for art and creative writing, her retentive memory and methodical tenacity helped an already advanced and sometimes encyclopaedic perception of people and places, interactions and outcomes.

This infiltrated extra–curricular activities too, notably in a then–unspoken fancy that she'd like to make her way in the world as a composer, a writer or some sort of visual artist. Was it feasible to combine all three? For hours on end, she'd tinker with fragments of verse, prose, melody and illustration for a purpose unknown apart from articulating the inner space of some private cosmos that she didn't expect anyone else, least of all her teachers, to comprehend.

Yet like every other intelligent child on the brink of adolescence, Yoko joined her mother at the wireless, following the depressing advances of the US troops, inching ever closer to Japan, and then the nuclear 'flash of a thousand suns' that turned Hiroshima and Nagasaki into deserts. This was the final straw that brought surrender in August 1945, and the subsequent non–recognition of the emperor's time–honoured divinity; the granting of votes for women and most of the agricultural land to the peasantry as part of a Westernised constitution to be imposed in 1947, and the omnipresence in the country for the next seven years of multitudinous Allied detachments whose officers began by requisitioning those hotels and evacuated private residencies where taps were still running.

When the Onos, fresh from months of mountain air, entered the distracted kingdom of queues that was Tokyo now, they rented properties to stationed GIs, who, when out of uniform, burst upon the civilian city in double–breasted suits with padded shoulders, 'spearpoint' shirt collars, two–tone shoes and hand–painted ties with Red Indians or baseball players on them. Rip–roaring sartorial visions, they acknowledged bemused, but more frequently envious, stares with waves of fat cigars. As it was in both vanquished Berlin and victorious London too, parading clusters of North Americans epitomised a new–old wonderland of opportunity, Coca–Cola, the Wild West and The Ink Spots, whose humming polyphony would enrapture Tokyo's Kokusai Theatre in 1948. Already, the coin–operated sounds of The Ink Spots and other US pop stars was pouring from nickelodeons in newly–established expresso coffee bars, thickest in city centres but penetrating many of the furthest–flung vicinities too.

Though she had tortured her hair into Western curls, such dens of iniquity were forbidden to Yoko Ono for whom the old life had been re–established within the strictures of the defeat and occupation. She and Akihito were back in class at Gakushiun again, though she sought the particular company of a younger princeling, Yoshi, who shared her interest in poetry, and was also a leading light in the school drama club.

At home, however, her father's sudden return early in 1946 from a Chinese prisoner–of–war camp removed the principal impediment to domestic stability all too briefly.

Notes

1. *John Ono Lennon* by R. Coleman (Sidgewick and Jackson, 1984)
2. To Paul Trynka

3. **The Bride**

"I was often attracted to the concept of being a wanderer"

Within weeks of beginning a job at the Bank of Tokyo, it had become clear that incarceration had not dimmed the lustre of Eisuke's diligence and ability. He found himself bound for the New York branch where he'd be recognised by a growing number of subordinates as, within his limits, a conscientious and fair–minded boss.

He was held in similar regard by his family, as instanced when he had summoned Yoko to his study to discuss her future now that she was in her final weeks at Gakushiun. Like his own father before him, he suggested with a show of kindness that she cast aside this artistic moonshine as the folly of youth. He had, for example, never heard of a successful woman composer.

Finally, after token appeals to pragmatism and common sense, he agreed to find his daughter a voice coach so that she could absorb the rudiments of opera and German *lieder*. Also, rather than start a 'proper' job, Yoko could perhaps give English lessons to those of her mother's friends that required them. There was talk too, but only talk, of Yoko enrolling at the Tokyo Music School, but Eisuke in New York conceded to Yoko's telegrammed request to apply for a degree course in philosophy, the first female to do so, at Gakushuin University.

While still living at home, she settled quickly into campus life, and, during a restless and ominivorous debauch of reading, voyaged evening after evening into the small hours with favoured authors. Gradually, Yoko's understanding of which books were worthwhile and which were not became more acute, but she would never acquire that infuriating habit some have of airing their learning in conversations beyond college tutorials.

Nevertheless, her studies at Gakushuin ended abruptly when, after two terms, the family was bound again for New York where Eisuke had bought, rather than rented, a house outside the city limits in Scarsdale. Affluent and suburban, it aligned itself more with upstate Westchester County than the Big Apple. Though soon to be swallowed in the encroaching connurbation, it was then within equally close proximity to both open countryside and the skyscrapers too close to be seen in the multi–ethnic location of *West Side Story*, then but a twinkle in Leonard Bernstein's eye.

The long saga of nineteen year old Yoko's education continued when she spent summer just over the state border in Cambridge, seat of Harvard

University, resuming her vocal training and gaining the final academic credits to qualify for beginning in September 1953 at Sarah Lawrence College. The exclusive all–girls' finishing school was spread over twenty–five wooded acres in Yonkers on the east bank of the trudging Hudson river, and within the municipal jurisdiction of New York City. It was a liberal, even permissive, establishment that, theoretically, enabled students in its small classes to follow what best suited their abilities and inclinations as they developed.

During her first months there, Yoko said as little as possible, and tended to walk by herself, lost in dreams and half–formed ambition. Perceiving her as slightly eccentric, some amused themselves by getting her to talk about, say, her notion that she was the reincarnation of Hideyoshi Toyotami, the generalissimo, who, from humble origins, rode roughshod over the civil wars in the late sixteenth century, and all but completed military dictatorship of Japan. Much exercised by Zen, his remorselessly bloody attempts at foreign conquest was exemplified by his housing in a temple of thirty thousand pairs of pickled Korean ears.

Yoko was also the subject of innumerable *bon mots* whenever her teachers compared notes in the staff room about this being apart, who homed in on details that others in a given lesson might be too lackadaisdical to consider or even notice. Yoko Ono was also more *au fait* with the historical traditions and conventions of art and philosophy than they, and was more adept than most at music transcription.

Very much knowing her own mind, she esteemed Mozart, but not "too mechanical" (1) Bach. Overall, however, she preferred composers of modern bent, especially Schoenberg, whose breakthrough *Verklarte Nacht* string sextet in 1899 had been stripped of functional harmony and all major and minor modes. Tonality was suspended altogether in 1912's semi–spoken song–cycle, *Pierrot Lunaire*, considered an aural nightmare by many, then and now, but described as "one of the most important foundations of twentieth century musical experience" by Peter Maxwell Davies. (2) Yoko was fond too of Webern whose *Passacaglia* for orchestra had ended his affable apprenticeship under Schoenberg. Of music with orthodox structure and substance, she liked Kurt Weill and his lyricist, Marxist playwright Berthold Brecht for their *Verfrtemdungtechnik* – detached comment that provokes thought rather than social validation.

Post–*bellum* popular music appears to have made little impact on Ono, even as a nod to Dada's mannered revelling in junk culture. This was exemplified by that lurid strain of musical comedy that merged burlesque, swing, mock–schmaltz and genres that defied succinct description – sometimes within the same song – when instrumental and vocal virtuosity were used to near–surreal effect in the crafted mindlessness of such as Spike Jones and his City Slickers' million–selling mangling of 'All I Want For Christmas (Is My Two Front Teeth)'.

Effusing from other students' radios, more current entries in US music trade journal *Billboard*'s disc sales charts – Al Martino's 'Here In My Heart', perhaps, or 'Mister Sandman' from The Chordettes – were treated with amused contempt by Yoko. As for rock 'n' roll's freshly–resounding thunder, "I didn't find a lot of sympathy for or interest in that in the avant–garde scene I was in – quite the opposite in fact. There was quite a pride in not becoming part of the rock scene – because it was too commercial." (3)

Caring about the opinions of others no more than a chimp in the zoo does about what people looking through the bars think, Yoko cut lectures to absorb a hidden curriculum in the library, She was also given to presenting essays with titles like 'A Grapefruit In The World Of Park', and made seemingly banal 'art statements' such as a 'Lighting Piece' i.e. striking a match and watching it burn out.

These impressed the College's bohemian set of which Yoko became very much a part. It modelled itself on the Parisian existentialists, who were about to be stereotyped by film directors as one of two types of pretentious middle–class beatnik: 'hot' (incessant rapid–fire talking and pseudo–mad stares) and 'cool' (mute, immobile and unapproachable). Yoko inclined to the latter faction, growing her hair and leaving it frizzily untamed, and dressing in black like Juliette Greco, svelte and spectral high priestess of cool, and the thinking man's French actress and recording artist. That would be Ono's 'look' for the next two decades.

She was noticed at *demi–monde* parties, held often when the host's parents were away, over on the opposite bank in Manhattan, where living rooms were transformed into dens of iniquity by dimming table lamps with headscarves and hanging prints of Man Ray on the walls. The musical entertainment might be scat–singing, bongo–tapping, a saxophone honking inanely or, surrounding the record–player, via the scattering of brittle 'seventy–eights' and the plastic 45 rpm discs that were superceding them. The eyelids of cross–legged listeners were closed in ecstasy. For some, this was a prelude to snogging and attacks of 'desert sickness'. (4)

It was in such an exotic scenario that a certain Toshi Ichiyanagi first clapped eyes on the coltish charms of Yoko, sitting amongst a prattle of her

Sarah Lawrence friends. By nonchalant enquiry of other male revellers – all berets, ten–day beards and holey pullovers – he found out her name and was provided with a thumb–nail sketch of her background. Conversely, Yoko seemed to be weighing up Toshi out of the corner of her eye.

Contact was established, and Yoko learnt that Toshi was a student at New York's Julliard School of Music where he was walking an avant–garde tightrope without a safety net. Before the evening was out, they arranged to meet again, and over the next few weeks, Toshi and Yoko crossed that impalpable barrier between inferred companionship and declared love.

The new boyfriend – Yoko's first, more or less – was, however, not a hit with her parents, mainly because he was of decidedly proletarian upbringing. Their raising of this and other objections when their daughter said that she was going to marry him, led to Yoko leaving both college and home for a period of romantic squalor – well, squalor anyway – before Eisuke and Isoko caved in. Though they absented themselves from the ceremony, they paid for the reception in a capacious city ballroom, and persuaded the Japanese consul general to make careful comment in an after–dinner speech.

They accepted too that Yoko wasn't going to return to Sarah Lawrence. Instead, she was to move into a sparsely–furnished and unheated fifth floor loft conversion along Chambers Street on downtown Manhattan's Lower West Side in the teeth of a loathsome changing of the seasons from moist gold to chill marble. The skylight iced up and gooseflesh rose in a cheerless winter of seething east winds, snow on snow still on the ground in early April, and Yoko, jerking in and out of an uneasy doze, waking shivering to her husband's open–mouthed snores.

Too soon, the compliant Toshi had become a handy peg on which to hang the vocational frustrations that marital fetters had not resolved. Interminable hours of cliff–hanging silences and the same arguments coming up over and over again built up from an irritated trace of vapour on the horizon to crockery–smashing Wagnerian thunderstorm. An evening of noisome home truths might end with an abruptly tearful reconciliation, but Toshi and Yoko were no longer an infatuated couple, holding hands around Manhattan any more. All such pretty fondnesses had swiftly gone. Both had read Nietzche, and Yoko at least had come to identify with the German philosopher of irrationalism's personal credo: that domesticity is incompatible with a life of constant creativity.

Was the *amour* over? Within hours, Yoko could be back in Scarsdale, making short work of the meal prepared for her by the cook. Then she might get lost in a film on television prior to lowering herself into the warm, scented water of the aqua–coloured bath with overhead heater before going to sleep in her own little room again. For all the 'I told you so' recriminations, the whey–faced disappointment about her throwing in college and the winkling out of exactly what she'd been up to since, it wasn't as uninviting a prospect as it might have seemed when Toshi's courtship began.

Yet she was resilient. Although her emotional allegiance to Toshi hadn't yet eroded, Yoko, probably a virgin on her wedding night, allowed herself affairs with other men after convincing him that her marriage was an 'open' relationship whereby each spouse would tolerate the other's physical infidelities. However, with the oral contraceptive Conovid – 'the Pill' – years away from US chemists' stockrooms, sexual congress outside marriage was as big a step to take as it would be when AIDS and like ailments put on the brake as the millenium neared. Condoms still burst, and 'pulling out' was less of a guarantee that you wouldn't have to either make the best of a bad job by keeping an unwanted baby, have it adopted, pay heed to perilous advice about making yourself miscarry with gin and a boiling–hot tub – or, as Yoko was to do, procure an abortion.

During frolics with either Toshi or someone else, matters had taken a serious and abandoned turn, and caution had been outweighed by the thrilling few seconds of extra–sensitive and exquisite orgasm a torn rubber afforded her. Alarmed when her period was much overdue, Yoko groped for reasons why the truth need not inflict itself on her. That she was being sick in the mornings was possibly because of extreme anxiety. That her waist was one inch bigger might be nothing either, although her wrists, ankles and armpits felt funny.

With the same questions surfacing over and over again, she'd build up a damning case against herself before concluding that she was panicking unduly. Yet as the days crawled by, there came no 'splashdown' and she was seeing prams and big–bellied women everywhere, in the streets, in public parks and on TV. She could no longer not believe it.

Yoko's first abortion was not to be her last as her espousal to Toshi muddled on when, united in play, they covered the same exhibitions, browsed in the same bookshops, guffawed knowingly at the same lines in an arthouse movie, and observed the same reverence when seated at the same concerts by modern classical composers. Varese, Penderecki and Stockhausen were the most illustrious of these, but whither Illhan Mimaroglu, Earle Browne, Adolf Weiss, Jacques de Menace and other names just as obscure then as they are now?

In the ascendant then was John Cage, formulator of chance operation, the 'prepared piano' – a development of Henry Cowell's idea – and '4' 33"', his famous 'silent' piece. Like the older Weburn, he had studied under Schoenberg, who'd insisted that "in order to write music, you have to have a feeling for harmony." At this, Cage confessed, "I have no feeling for harmony." Schoenberg then said "I would always encounter an obstacle, that it would be as though I came to a wall through which I could not pass." I said, "In that case, I will devote my life to beating my head against that wall." (5)

Lately, technology had caught up with the sounds Cage heard in his head, and he was soon to repair to Milan's Studio di Fonologia to assemble the tape collage, *Fontana Mix*, a classic of its kind. However, he was still at large in New York when Mr and Mrs Ichiyanagi stole like children to Santa's grotto into the hushed classroom in Greenwich Village's New School for Social Research where a polished and engaging Cage was presiding over a series of seminars on experimental music, replete with square wave, crossfade, white noise, EQ, envelope, tape loop, microtone and further pioneering jargon as, almost paradoxically, he sought to boil down music to its rawest state.

Among the poets, photographers and other culture vultures there were Allan Kaprow – the artist credited generally with 'inventing' 'happenings', Richard Maxfield – seen by Cage as a *protegé* of sorts, Angus MacLise – later, founder member and percussionist of The Velvet Underground, painter Frank Stella, architect and gallery owner George Maciunas and LaMonte Young, once a jazzman, but now a principal developer of a style to be known as 'minimalism', presented often in conjunction with other events such as the light shows devised by his wife, Marian Zazeela.

Exchanges of ideas during the course and afterwards led to Yoko's surfacing as frequently as rocks in the stream at correlated activities, and instigating some of her own. Traceable to her Sarah Lawrence essays, avant–garde prose in solitary paragraphs instructed participants to, for instance, spread an empty canvas on the pavement and wait for passers–by to step on it. Alternatively, you could keep dried peas about your person, dropping them periodically, one by one, as if leading a paper chase, while 'Kitchen Piece' directed you to chuck the day's leftover food onto a canvas on the wall. Creepiest of all was hammering a nail into the middle of a pane of glass, and sending each resulting fragment to a different arbitrary address.

In the huge single room that was Yoko and Toshi's apartment, such antics as well as free–association poetry, word games, shy–making soliloquys and further dialogue for the sake of dialogue precipitated six months of 'happenings', advertised mostly by word–of–mouth, and involving much audience participation. The most presigious event was the world premiere of a LaMonte Young creation in which two cellists bowed the same two notes interminably, but as memorable was Yoko hurling her peas into the audience with the swirling of her long hair serving as inaudible soundtrack.

The uninitiated didn't quite like to laugh at what could be regarded as living evidence of Yoko's own conjecture – drawn from Dada – that "You don't need talent to be an artist." (6)

Notes

1. *Yoko Ono* by J. Hopkins (Sidgwick & Jackson, 1987)
2. *Edgard Varese* by A. Clayson (Sanctuary, 2002)
3. *Record Collector*, June 1992
4. A pre–1970s euphemism for fondling (desert sickness = wandering palms)
5. *The Roaring Silence: John Cage* by D. Revill (Bloomsbury, 1992)
6. Excerpt from Yoko Ono's opening address at her exhibition at the Everson Museum of Art, 9th October 1971

4. **The Divorcee**

"I was always communicating with the highest element in each person."

Speaking of Elvis Presley, the 1950s pop star Johnnie Ray concluded, "There's nothing new – only a new way of doing it." (1) The same applied to Yoko Ono's artistic endeavours in the late 1950s. All of them could have occurred at any time since the Great War, reeking as they did of Dada, Surrealism and connected movements. Neither were they worthy of much attention beyond an invocation of passing bewilderment to the man–in–the–street – maybe on a par with him noticing a packet of corn flakes placed precisely at the foot of George M. Cohen's statue in Times Square or finding a tract from the Flat Earth Society inside his *New York Times*.

As individual stunts, therefore, Yoko's 'happenings' were lame, but, cumulatively, they were beginning to create ripples, and she was becoming a credible name to drop wherever Art was regarded as an antidote to pleasure on the principal that the more arduous the effort needed to appreciate something, the more 'artistic' it is.

George Maciunas's A'G Gallery in Canal Street, one of Greenwich Village's main thoroughfares, included Yoko's works in an exhibition by up–and–coming artists. Among her contributions were 'Painting To See The Skies' – two holes drilled through plain canvas – 'Painting To See The Room' (one hole) and the faintly sycophantic 'George Poem No. 18' – lines in Japanese which were then painted black to obscure them totally, just like Frank Stella had done already with an entire series of entirely black paintings.

Predictably, there was a small and cliquey turn–out at the A'G Gallery – notably on opening night when most visitors' purpose was to demonstrate the sheer joy of being anarchistic, free–loving and Living In The Shadow Of The Bomb – or at least being seen to sound and look as if they were. Nevertheless, no mainstream newspaper bothered to send anyone.

In the cold light of the following morning, it was painfully clear that Yoko's art wasn't going to pay the rent, and, by 1960, Toshi was tinkling piano in a cocktail bar as customers chattered, and his wife was a waitress in the Paradox, a restaurant where the richer Greenwich Villagers ate, and she was permitted to hang her paintings. She was also driven to teach calligraphy, lecture on folk music and perform secretarial duties, part–time for the Japanese Society which involved a complicated journey on the city's internal railway. However, advantaged by her cosmospolitan education, she was sent from this institute to city schools as a cultural representative – "so I would go there and show what calligraphy is like or what a tea ceremony's like etc. That paid pretty well. I did just about anything most people do in those circumstances." (2)

Yet her work for the Japanese Society wasn't a key to a fulfilling career, promoting the Japanese way of life and correlated adjustment to respectable middle–age, largely because she disregarded her pronounced gift for teaching. When such bits and pieces of employment weren't forthcoming, she sold household and personal effects to buy food, just as her mother before her had after the family had fled the bombardment of Tokyo. All the same, despite Toshi's urgings to the contrary, she would not sponge off Isoko and Eisuke.

Dogged by financial insecurity, the marriage had floated into a choppier sea than ever before. Frank exchanges in the Chambers Street loft brought to the surface the stark fact that Yoko and Toshi remained together only because neither had sufficient motivation to do otherwise. Nevertheless, a joyless partnership drifted quickly into open estrangement, and, with Yoko unwilling to fan its dull embers, Toshi quit the apartment, the city and the country to attempt a new beginning in Japan.

As there was no sign of any formal dissolution of the marriage, Yoko's worried parents, who had now revised their previously unfavourable opinion of Toshi, hoped that the emotional chasm between daughter and son–in–law wasn't too wide for either to negotiate. To oil the wheels of reconciliation, Eisuke proffered Yoko the use of an eleventh floor apartment he had maintained in Tokyo. A legitimate colour could be given to the journey to inspect it in her presence at brother Keisuke's imminent wedding.

A pivotal element in Yoko's wrestling with the decision to go or stay was that vocational success in New York might be just around the corner. On Wednesday 24th November 1961, she was to headline at Carnegie Hall, albeit not in the main auditorium, but in the adjacent recital room with its capacity of around two hundred and fifty. A booker's risk made months earlier obliged non–stop preparation for this make–or–break concert. Its programme promised what were described as 'operas'. These included 'A Piece For Strawberries And Violin' (Yoko's wordless and high–pitched wailing) and 'A Grapefruit In The World Of Park' – people shuffling about on a dimly–lit stage, among them a couple of fellows tied together trying to negotiate a path through empty bottles and cans, and dancers lugging heavy objects back and forth, their toiling grunts amplified via contact microphones. A backstage toilet was wired for sound too.

Stray paragraphs on a few newspapers' arts pages were unsympathetic with the misspelling of Ono's name by a couple adding insult to injury. A spell outside her usual orbit appeared, therefore, a fine notion to Yoko, who reunited with Toshi in Eisuke's high–rise block, an edifice of steel and reinforced concrete, praised for its ruthlessly austere aesthetic by those who didn't have to live there.

Thoroughly dispirited, Yoko gazed up from the bottom of a psychological ravine. The only strip of blue sky she saw was in summer 1962 when her poems, paintings and 'operas' were second–billed to recitals by John Cage on, not so much a tour of Japan, as a string of one–nighters. Moreover, television cameras would be in evidence when it reached Tokyo.

Yet, as it had been in New York, blink–and–you'll–miss–'em references to Yoko in reviews centred on Cage were disparaging at best. Those critics that bothered thought she was a plagiarist, reliant on gimmicks. Overall, however, no–one took much notice.

This penetrated Yoko's uneasy dozing in the crumpled bedclothes where she huddled for days afterwards, eyes open and temples throbbing. Just a gesture or a word would set off another paroxysm of sobbing despair. Bearing her self–flagellations and the drip–drip of hovering aggravations, Toshi let her fulminate and bluster without reproach from muttered trepidation to Hitlerian screech. He had learnt to keep his own feelings in check as there was room for just one tortured artist in the flat. Only Yoko was allowed to flare up, have neuroses, be unreasonable. Yet in an era when clinical depression wasn't recognised as an emotional disease, she'd been advised by others less sympathetic to snap out of it and pull herself together. She was advised to stop playing the highly–strung, misunderstood genius and do a hard day's graft for a change.

Now and then, she'd try to counteract her blackest moods by knuckling down to work almost eagerly, but the telephone would ring, a late breakfast would be getting cold or something interesting just beginning on the wireless. Maybe she would try again tomorrow.

Weeks would stagger by without a glimmer of an idea as the tacit suspicion grew that she had bitten her talent down to the quick. The hunger to create might have been sharper had a carrot of commercial urgency been dangled before her. But with nobody paying for her to survive whilst suffering for her art, hyperactivity deferred to glazed languor and, bathed in tedium, Yoko's mind would wander anywhere but to the unpaid job in hand. So she turned temporarily into my definition of an intellectual: someone who reads a lot and thinks a lot but does nothing.

Toshi feared she would do herself a mischief as she swang from dismal daytime lethargy to nocturnal contemplation of suicide. His concerns were justified as, during one particularly violent surge of self–loathing, she tried to jump out of the window. The same devil that had impelled Van Gogh to slice off his ear impelled Yoko to attempt further self–administered ends and, like Van Gogh too, she was committed to a mental hospital.

During this limbo that lasted into autumn, she confronted and grappled with her inner turmoil with the aid of the press of a buzzer whenever phantoms of eddying imaginations threatened to engulf her. Sometimes, the nurses adminstered a higher dosage of sedatives than necessary. Indeed, Yoko was drowsy with them one afternoon when a hitherto unknown well–wisher strode into the ward.

He was Tony Cox, a bespectacled twenty–three year old New Yorker with a fast mouth who, as an art student, had honked saxophone in one of Lamonte Young's jazz combos. Via Young and his associates, Cox knew all about Yoko, and one of his reasons for flying to Japan was to talk to her with a view to penning the first substantial newspaper article about her avant–gardenings.

Flattered by the solicitude of this young man – who could speak fluent Japanese and was sufficiently taken with the Fascinating Older Woman to continue visiting her – Yoko explained that she'd made no long term plans. How could she? Yet, if no Latin scholar, she was persuaded to heed Seneca's maxim *pars sanitatis velle sanari fuit.* (3) Tony thought too that it would help if her drug intake could be lowered. It was also largely through Cox's prodding of administrative nerves that Yoko was permitted to re–encounter the outside world, sooner rather than later.

He became a frequent dinner guest at the Ichyanagis, who, so he perceived, were now two old friends who used to be lovers. Yoko especially was quite frank and unashamed about a marriage that was held together only by parental pressure. There were long, dangerous moments between her and Cox whenever the husband was out of the room, but Toshi felt less anger than amusement when Tony replaced him as Yoko's bedmate. For a while, the three dwelt in the flat as a *menage à trois*, but a disagreement over financial arrangements led Toshi to seek accommodation elsewhere.

When Yoko and this Tony Cox person were seen hand–in–hand in public, Keisuke and Setsuko reported this latest folly to their parents, who, chastising and disapproving, urged Yoko to kiss and make up with Toshi, even as the *decrée nisi* was confirmed. There came a graver complication when Yoko became pregnant with Cox's child, and was not torn between resentment and panic. This time, she wanted to both give birth to and rear the baby.

An educated guess was that it had been conceived during a trip to London, a city to which she and Tony would return periodically over the next four years. In late 1962, Britain's art community was tiring of its post–war 'Angry Young Men' – Edward Middleditch, John Bratby, Derrick Greaves *et al* – whose 'kitchen sink' brushwork of domestic slumminess and sordid scenarios from the inner city wasn't quite the thing to nail over your mantelpiece. Instead, the burning question of the hour was uncertain experiments with Pop Art, foreseen by some as the coming trend, but scorned by the art establishment as a novelty.

Catching a mood of cultural radicalism that would first climax in the Swinging Sixties, its pioneers included Peter Blake, Richard Hamilton and Edinburgh–born Eduardo Paolozzi. The aim was to bring humour and topicality back into painting via the paradox of earnest fascination with the brashest of junk culture, a mannered revelling in hard–sell advertising hoardings; magazines such as *Tit–Bits*, *True Confessions* and *Everybody's Weekly*; escapist horror flicks about outer space 'Things', and further artefacts of a Coca–Cola century, usually dismissed as silly, vulgar and fake in their custard–yellows and tomato–reds.

For research purposes, Pop artists on both sides of the Atlantic listened avidly to the turn–of–the–decade Top Twenty, clogged as it was with one–shot singles, dance crazes and – just arrived this minute – the all–American piffle of insipidly handsome boys–next–door like Bobby Vinton, Bobby Vee and Bobby Rydell, all hair–spray and bashful half–smiles.

This was Yoko's fullest engrossment with pop music thus far – though that isn't saying much. But, to a degree, she'd been more than merely aware of Pop Art in general when in Chambers Street, through the 'godfather' of the US wing, Andy Warhol's soup–cans, Brillo pads, silk–screens of popular icons and comic–strip philosophy epitomised in interview when Warhol was a shallow vehicle of hardly any biographical information, weighing of experience or estimation of motive whatsover – but that was almost the point. "There's nothing to explain or understand," (4) was to be among many quotable Warhol superficialities (or perhaps not so superficial).

"Andy Warhol was using all the familiar symbols in his work," elucidated Yoko, "and Elvis was on the same level as a Campbell's soup can or Liz Taylor. Just because he used them as a symbol didn't necessarily mean he was interested in them himself." (5) Neither then was Yoko, who, however well–placed she was to do so, had chosen not to be sucked into the vortex of his Factory arts centre, his private residence two blocks away and other locations synonymous with Warhol's period of optimum impact in the early 1960s.

He was to produce interesting–but–boring films like *Couch* and *Chelsea Girls* which were, I suppose, a Pop Art parallel to the work of William Burroughs, foremost Beat Generation writer, who not so much dipped a toe as plunged headfirst into grainy movies – such as *Ghosts At No. 9* and *Towers Open Fire* – that were vaguely if mostly head–scratchingly entertaining.

During the last months of her pregnancy, Yoko planted feet in both camps when commissioned to compose incidental music to an otherwise forgettable six–minute film, *Love*, which consisted of a couple engaged in athletic sexual intercourse in tight close–up. Not meant to 'go anywhere' any more than *Ghosts At No. 9* or *Couch*, it was no better or worse than those you might see in installations at final exhibitions for Fine Art degrees at your local university. The only difference is that Burroughs, Warhol and Ono made theirs decades earlier.

Before her waters broke too, Yoko penned new poems and 'instruction pieces'. Some were along the same lines as before – notably 'Nail Piece', which was to reprised over the next few years – and, to those few in the know, there was more of a retrospective element in the re–emergence of items like 'Lighting Piece'. Nonetheless, a gentle, almost pastoral quality was embraced in such as 'Water Piece', which required you to take a bucket to a pond at night and collect the moon's reflection.

Some figured in summer performances–*cum*–exhibitions in Tokyo's Naiqua and Sogetsu Centres and Kyoto's Nanzenji Temple and Yamaichi Concert Hall. To nearly all attendees, the most captivating event was the screening of a Hollywood film starring Rock Hudson and Doris Day on the understanding that onlookers were to focus exclusively on Day. An initial print run of five hundred copies of *Grapefruit*, a self–help accumulation of Yoko's 'instruction pieces' in book form, was the only mass–market – if that is the word – merchandise for sale.

That the entire exercise came at least close to break–even point was gratifying in the light of recent domestic developments. In the 1963 week her *decrée absolute* came through, Yoko had wed Tony Cox without bothering to tell her parents. Appalled when he found out, Eisuke ordered Mr. and Mrs. Cox out of his Tokyo apartment. This was regrettable rather than disasterous as they soon found a cheap place in the aptly–named Foreigner Village in Shibuya, a suburb that attracted overseas students.

Tony kept the wolf from the door as a film extra and teaching English to native business folk – and so did Yoko for as long as she was able before the arrival of her daughter, Kyoko Chan, on 8th August 1963.

Notes

1. *Cry: The Johnnie Ray Story* by J. Whiteside (Barricade, 1994)
2. To Paul Trynka
3. The wish to be cured is the first step towards health.
4. 'Andy Warhol' by H. Geldzahler, *Art International, Vol. VIII, No. 2 (1964)*
5. *Record Collector*, June 1992

5. The Villager

"I was feeling that I was communicating with gods and goddesses. I hope it did somehow awake that element in people: that point in their brain, instead of sort of saying, 'Oh ha–ha, the girl's sitting on the stage naked,' but I don't think it was like that."

Yoko's second marriage began to follow the dismal trajectory of her first. Soon, Tony was hardly ever home, to the degree that she was spending more time with a house guest, Alfred Wunderlick, one of his pals from art school.

By the middle of 1964, a trial separation was in force. Regarding Yoko as inattentive as both a wife and mother, Tony took Kyoko half a world away to New York, specifically Greenwich Village where everything was different, everything was the same. When unfastening a thoughtful seat–belt as he left Japanese airspace, Cox couldn't help but visualise certain Village people in some fixed attitude, doing what they did when he was last there. And sure enough John Cage remained an everyday sight, shopping for groceries or watching the open air chess tournaments in Washington Square. With the removed look of a dying man, which he was, Edgard Varese still quaffed Turkish coffee in the window of Romany Marie's cafe.

If Varese was the Village's uncrowned king, Louis Thomas Hardin, alias 'Moondog', was a bastard prince, his 'image' enhanced by blindness and garb of army blankets and a sort of helmet that made him look like a cross between a Druid and a Norse jarl. A composer who made his own instruments, he and his wife Suzuko – plucking the lute–like *samisen* – busked for spare change at their customary pitch uptown in Times Square.

By all reasonable prophecies, it might have been supposed that Moondog would be a Village fixture for the rest of his natural life – and that stand–up comedian Lenny Bruce wouldn't be, even as he imbibed harder stuff than Varese's Turkish coffee nightly in Louie's Bar, a hang–out with sawdust on the floor and a juke–box.

Bruce was becoming nationally notorious for a brand of 'humor' – not humour – that hinged on talking dirty in hip restricted code throughout monologues with titles like 'White Collar Drunks', Don's Big Dago' and 'How To Relax Your Colored Friends At Parties'. He'd once been a regular at The Bitter End, a club that had come into its own when the civil rights movement had fused with folk song to be labelled 'protest'. Among genre exponents presented there and at other Village night spots were Woody Guthrie, Pete Seeger, Peter, Paul and Mary, Phil Ochs, Tim Rose and, most spectacularly in retrospect, Bob Dylan.

There was room too for the disparate likes of Bruce, beatnik bard Allen Ginsberg, The Four Seasons, Chuck Berry and Jerry Van Dyke, brother of comedy actor Dick. Unofficial entertainment was provided by Bitter End proprietor Paul Colby's telling of endless anecdotes about Dylan sniffing round the waitresses or Tim Rose "when I found he had broken into my liquor cabinet and drunk himself into a stupor" (1) – albeit related with an underlying affection and an implication that such behaviour was the prerogative of stardom, even if a stardom mostly of a type that's "about as far away from mainstream entertainment as you could get." (1)

Tony Cox, however, was less inclined to frequent The Bitter End, Louie's Bar and Romany Marie's, than to network amidst the hysterical chatter, rehearsed patter and smug backslapping at the *soirees* and first nights of the Village art coterie. As Our Man in Japan, he was quizzed about the scene over there with inevitable and specific reference to Yoko – whose imported *Grapefruit* was stocked in a few local bookshops, and whose blacked–out paintings hadn't been removed from the walls of the trendy Paradox (which had now gone macrobiotic).

Crucially, Yoko's old champion George Maciunas had stayed evangelical about her in his capacity as chief spokesman and organiser of the parochial wing of short–lived Fluxus, not so much a group as a 'collective' – in Cologne and other West German cities as well as New York – devoted to breaking down the barriers between Art and 'real life'. At its crudest level, the concepts were generally more intriguing than the executions in this rehash of Dada with pronounced overtones of Futurism, Cabaret Voltaire, action painting, Pop Art and, especially, Cage–esque chance operation.

There was also a tang of 'auto–destruction' originated by German– British artist Gustav Metzger, and beginning to insinuate itself into pop music – particularly in Britain where The Who and The Creation were to close their acts by, respectively, smashing up their equipment and splashing onto a canvas backdrop a painting that owed less to Jackson Pollock than to Tony Hancock. With Moseley Art College old boy Roy Wood at their creative helm, The Move were to impinge upon the kingdom's consciousness late in 1965 via a show that involved singer Carl Wayne charging onstage with a chopper to hack up effigies of world political figures before turning his attention to imploding televisions – and if that's not Art, then what is?

The likes of George Maciunas, Tony Cox and, when she turned up in November, Yoko Ono, were unaware apparently of any serious integration of modern art into pop – rather than Pop Art's *vice–versa* – when, after an inaugural performance in Wiesbaden in 1962 under the aegis of graphic artist Wolf Vostell, Fluxus manifested itself principally in more conspicuous 'happenings' than before – that endeavoured to involve onlookers in an unconscious rather than rational level. Nevertheless, a disaffected spectator might have shrugged them off as a bit of a laugh, now and then, but otherwise merely much babbling, shrieking of inanities, messing about with paint, making a horrible racket, and acting obscene as in, for example in at least one rumoured instance of loud and abundant defecation on stage.

Already, it was heading for the same elitist impasse as that less cohesive movement of which Yoko had been a part before that heart–sinking evening at Carnegie Hall. Personality masqueraded as principles, internal squabbles as crusades, and the riff–raff were kept in the dark, not let in on the joke because, tacitly, public acceptance was dreaded by the big fish in Fluxus's small pond. "Fluxus was the furthermost experimental group of its time," beamed Yoko with quiet pride, "Anyone doing experimental work was aware of us and took ideas from us and made them commercial. Their stuff was selling, but ours was too far–out to sell." (2)

For the time being, however, Yoko was in her element, and became rapidly, the life–and–soul of Fluxus. While she was an anonymous wanderer in a department store only two subway stops away, she was, in the immediate vicinity of Greenwich Village, 'the High Priestess of the Happening', whose comeback had been marked by a low–key collaboration with Angus MacLise, *Music For Dance*, recollected in the long term for the late MacLise's unique hand–drumming – "like poetry," according to his friend, Piero Heliczer. (3)

Drug–addled Angus's – and Yoko's – profession's peculiar exhilarations and miseries bred many insecurities among *illuminati* and small–fry alike, but the cardinal sin was to show them. Visible desperation was too nasty a reminder of the impermanence of both artistic inspiration and celebrity, even within the Village art crowd's inward–looking closed shop.

While Yoko tried not to look as if she was making an effort in public, her private woes spewed forth behind the doors of Tony and Kyoko's studio apartment where she had billeted herself before it made abrupt sense to carry on as if nothing untoward had happened back in Tokyo. There was a temporary air about the situation, but, ostensibly, they were a family again in that she shared Tony's bed, and he served as a 'house–husband' while she worked on her career, even if for every creative act, there were maybe a dozen attached mechanical processes. Much of the day was spent writing supplicatory letters to gallery managers, newspaper columnists, media 'personalities' and better–known artists.

Her badgering paid off in a lengthy interview in *The Villager* magazine plus an amused accompanying article because, as was her wont then, Yoko's grip on both budgetary and physical practicalities loosened when confiding to a newshound's notepad. Nonetheless, this triggered a feature in the arts section of the *New York Times*. This was all grist to the publicity mill of a return performance at the smallest Carnegie Hall functions room on 21st March 1965.

Aware of the chasm into which she might plunge again, a barefoot Yoko walked onto the boards, the cynosure of an unnerving stare from what looked like a gigantic photograph of silent and undemonstrative people. She carried "some anger and turbulence in my heart" (4) – and a pair of outsized scissors with which to commence 'Cut Piece', essentially the cajoling of those beyond the footlights to mount the stage, cut off a fragment of her clothing and hand the scissors to the next person in what was, ideally, an orderly queue. That was all. It wasn't exactly like being requested to join in choruses of 'The Wild Rover' by some jolly folk club ranter, but enough attendees overcame an understandable reticence to strip Yoko to her underwear, and cause her hands to cover involuntarily the deeper exposure of her cleavage.

"That was a frightening experience," she was to recall, "and a bit embarrassing. It was something that I insisted on – in the Zen tradition of doing the thing that is most embarrassing for you to do, and seeing what you come up with, and how you deal with it." (2)

'Cut Piece' *per se* was less intrinsically entertaining than audience reaction to it. What was that? Did I enjoy it? Shall I clap, or jeer? What's everybody else doing? If there wasn't so much as a faint ripple in the daily press, word–of–mouth guaranteed at least a moderate turn–out for further Ono events in less prestigious venues, and attracted the interest of agents such as Norman Seaman, whose nephew Fred was to be employed by Yoko in an unimagined future.

"For art's sake, I would do just about anything," she reflected, "That's how I felt in those days." (5) Walking another tightrope without a safety net, Yoko also found a niche in the furthest extremes of avant–garde jazz through vocal gymnastics that owed much to the free choral babbling and odd tone clusters of Schoenberg and Penderecki – whose best–known work, *Devils Of Loudon*, has Satan sniggering from within a nun's bowel – as well as *seitoha* (Japanese classical music).

Purely on the strength of sonic vibrations, some of it bore uncannily close resemblance to certain popular classical pieces. On ITV's Classical Brit Awards, broadcast on 1st June 2003, thirty–seven year old mezzo–soprano Cecilia Bartoli's excellent rendition of Vivaldi's 'Anchi'il Mar Par Che Sommerga' aria could have been lifted by time–machine from one of the milder mid–1960s recitals by Yoko Ono in the company of respected free jazzers, notably Ornette Coleman, using her voice like a front–line horn, complementing the alto saxophonist's peep–parping daredevilry with screeches, wails, nanny–goat vibrato and Nippon jabber.

Her vocal flexibility was not dissimilar either to that of Subbulaksmi, an Indian diva seen frequently on Western stages, and, more appositely, Hagiwari, the blind female *koto* virtuoso and vocalist, recipient of *Juyo–Mukei–Bunkazai*, one of the highest cultural posts that the Japanese government could assign.

While they hadn't heard of either Subbulaksmi or Hagiwari, Yoko's cult following in Greenwich Village plus a flotsam–and–jetsam of inquisitive students and weekend bohemians, knotted their foreheads in this arts centre or that hired recital room, not sure where the tuning–up ended and the first piece began. It defied succinct categorisation, but was absorbing in a knowing, nodding kind of way – though some listeners had to block out an impure King's–New–Clothes thought in the tacit question, "How could anyone like this stuff?" After clapping politely when the row ceased, the highlight of the night was the opportunity afterwards to chat about how 'interesting' it all was, this 'spontaneous music', these 'sound paintings' that were an avenue to drop names like Cage, Varese, and Berio, and assume an attitude of pitying superiority towards those who either 'didn't understand' or enjoyed it for the 'wrong' reasons.

Jazz was, laughed Frank Zappa, "the music of unemployment" and, while Yoko acquitted herself admirably with the likes of Ornette Coleman, and was a *cause celebre* as a performance artist, earnings from such ventures didn't solve the day–to–day mundanities of providing for husband and child. Gradually, she and Tony became more and more engrossed in cash–flow problems. It was nothing very tangible, just a steady gnawing away with little peaks and troughs. Yoko even swallowed sufficient pride to ask the Paradox for her old job back, and, whilst still owing rent in previous poky flats and lodgings, the family moved to cheaper and cheaper accommodation that would untidy itself in a matter of hours to look as if someone had chucked a hand–grenade into each room. Wrapped in an iron lacework of fire escapes, the buildings seemed to shiver as New York Transit Authority trains clattered by.

Finally, from a grim abode that they treated as what was called a 'crash pad' in Swinging Sixties parlance, old grievances overflowed violently during sleepless nights of repetitive, anxious talk. One morning, Yoko and Kyoko moved to the Student House at the Judson Memorial Church, stop–gap housing for academics and artists of all types and nationalities. As well as its low rent, communal facilities and a handy Village location, it was possible to contrive to stay beyond the regulated time of a year.

After settling in and taking stock, Yoko channelled her mingled vexation and wearied moodiness into developing a lucrative gimmick that might rescue her from a future as a venerable Greenwich Village 'character' like Moondog (6) or at least elevate her from surviving by perpetual mental arithmetic, and ekeing out a hand–to–mouth income that was, on aggregate, less than that of a common labourer. A brain–storming session with Tony had spawned 'Bagism' (7), which required a couple to clamber inside a huge black bag, undress and redress each other, and re–emerge. Alternatively, they could remain motionless or get up to those outside knew not what.

Like 'Cut Piece', 'Bagism' garnered Yoko another period of short–lived celebrity outside Greenwich Village, but conjured up little in the way of profit. She seemed so defeated that it seemed fanciful to look to future victories and, in some ways, the worst was yet to come. However, from this, the lowest ebb, the tide with majestic slowness, had already started to turn.

'Bagism' made just enough of a splash to tip the balance when Tony hawked two hundred shares in Yoko's art. Although the equation wasn't to be the same as that of the Wagners and King Ludwig, or Tchaikovsky and Nadezhda von Meck, Cox discovered a talent for convincing likely patrons that Yoko was a genius prior to dazzling them with a cautious confidence that he was offering opportunities to make a fortune on the ground floor of a growth industry.

The sale of thirty of these shares, worth several thousand dollars, enabled the Coxes to open their own gallery, Is–Real, in empty commercial premises in Greenwich Village, and begin the casting and shooting of a film of myriad close–ups of naked buttocks, a pair for every day of the year.

It was unfinished, but beyond pre–production when onto the Is–Real doormat fluttered an invitation for Yoko to appear at a symposium on 'Deconstruction In Art' in London, commencing on 28th September 1966.

Notes

1. *The Bitter End: Hanging Out At America's Night Club* by P. Colby and M. Fitzpatrick (Cooper Square Press, 2001)
2. *Record Collector*, June 1992
3. *The Velvet Underground Companion* ed. A. Zak (Omnibus, 1997)
4. *The Guardian, 15 September 2003*
5. To Paul Trynka
6. Although he was to uproot himself eventually to Germany, having become an internationally–acclaimed composer.
7. Conceived originally as 'Stone Piece'

6. The Visitor

"At the time, I was in New York, and it was the centre of the art world, and I just thought, 'Why do I have to go to London?'"

As it would be with Madonna and her first husband Sean Penn, Yoko was the drawing card and Tony part of the package. So it was when the ship from New York pottered along the Solent into Southampton and the two, with Kyoko, if jaded by the voyage, felt a recharge of wakefulness and a tingle of expectancy.

Before that late summer's day was out, the family were unpacking in the London home of Mario Amaya, publisher of *Art And Artists*, the periodical that was sponsoring the symposium. They were to sleep on sofas, floors and in spare bedrooms until a nine–room flat in Hanover Gate Mansions, opposite Regent's Park, became available. (1) This was the result of an easy decision to remain in England, following overtures from galleries for her to exhibit and a steady stream of callers with appetites whetted for her staging of Fluxus–like happenings. When "all this incredible art scene was presented to me," gasped Yoko, "The whole scene was, from the point of view of an American, very underground, very intimate, very high quality. There was a strange kind of shimmer in the London air, and it was beautiful. Once I breathed that, I felt, OK I'm here – and I've never looked back." (2)

There were also the mixed blessings of a more sedate pace of life, the toyland currency, the unfinished motorways, only two TV channels, cigarettes purchasable in ten–packs, no ice in your Coca–Cola, traffic wardens who called you 'love', and pubs that, unlike places like Louie's Bar back in the Village, were more than just buildings where you got drunk.

For several weeks, it was necessary for Kyoko to live apart from her parents, owing to shortage of space in the Chelsea house of painter Adrian Morris and his wife, who met Yoko at a party thrown by someone else to do with *Art And Artists*. When Morris opened the conversation by enquiring what sort of artist she was, Yoko's "I deal with music of the mind" riposte, her celebrity that was not entirely self–assumed, and the overall joviality of the occasion led Morris to invite the Coxes over for a weekend that turned into three months.

"I enjoyed their company," grinned Adrian, "and I was broadly sympathetic to what they were doing. Once, I came home and, walking towards the kitchen from the back garden, I saw her listening to a clock with a stethoscope. She was running an exhibition at the time called 'Time Piece'. Photographers were taking pictures of her, and I realised she was unique. Another day in the kitchen, I patted her playfully on the head, and called her 'Little Yoko'. I remember vividly her response: "You say *little* Yoko, but I have a universe in my head." (3) Morris was also partial to Ono's cooking – especially her steamed mackerel on a bed of beanshoots.

During their extended stay, Yoko and Tony mixed business with pleasure by soaking up the sights – St. Paul's, Big Ben, Westminster Bridge and our wonderful policemen, none of which they had seen during previous flying visits. One afternoon during that warm, sunny autumn, the two couples plus Kyoko went to London Zoo, an excursion commemorated by a photograph of Yoko alongside a row of baboons' behinds.

Naturally, the Morrises were among those welcomed into the liberty hall that was the Hanover Gate Mansions apartment after it had been furnished in minimalist fashion with white ceilings and walls. The idea being that, if your mind wasn't assaulted with colour, you could be more creative. Thus Yoko and Tony continued with the celluloid project about bottoms – which now had the working title, *Four Square*. Amongst its newer stars was *Times* correspondent Hunter Davies.

There'd been further mainstream press interest when Yoko made a British stage debut at the barn–like Roundhouse auditorium in Chalk Farm with trusty 'Bagism' and 'Cut Piece' plus newer concepts like 'Line' (draw one and erase it), 'Wall Piece' (volunteers from the audience join Yoko in banging their heads against one) and the finale, a sort of word–association game in which Ono yelled something at the paying customers, who responded by bawling back whatever flashed across their collective mind for five minutes.

Free of charge was a happening in Trafalgar Square where, recounts record sleeve designer Gene Mahon, "Yoko wanted to be in a black bag, and she called upon a guy called Ed Klein and myself to be bodyguards." (4) Another escapade at the same landmark was wrapping its lion statues in brown paper, attracting roughly the same attention as ex–civil servant Stanley Green, who paced daily back and forth along Oxford Street in a sandwich board that declared his creed of "Less Lust From Less Protein" to the few who stopped to read it.

Ono, however, was 'cool', and Green wasn't at the dawning of the age of Aquarius. Quarter–page notices heralding her activities filled regular space in the fortnightly *International Times (IT)*, London's and, by implication,

Britain's, foremost underground organ – which was to impinge on the general populace in autumn 1967 via a fuss about a centre spread of Frank Zappa seated on the toilet. Before the year was out, *IT* was leaking to back–street newsagents in Dullsville as the provincial sixth–former's vista to what Swinging London was thinking and doing. This was disturbing enough for crooner Frankie Vaughan to launch a campaign to curtail the spread of the hippy sub–culture. "Hippies are leeches on society" (5) he declared at a public meeting, spurning a flower proffered by one such leech in the audience.

With Vietnam, drugs, Che Guevara, sexual liberation, aggressive cartoons and European student protests among common denominators, *IT*'s editions dealt too with 'rock', which only the finest minds could appreciate, rather than vulgar 'pop'. As such it was rife with ga–ga statements – such as describing Love's Arthur Lee as "the only musically hip spade" and "Charlie" Manson as "just a harmless freak." One sweet flower from the typewriter of disc–jockey John Peel – then the most beautiful person who ever lived – in his regular 'Perfumed Garden' column was, "There are sparrows and fountains and roses in my head. Sometimes, I don't have enough time to think of loving you. That is very wrong." (6)

The newspaper was sped on its way with a knees–up on a cold October night in 1966 at the Roundhouse where proto–hippies milled about with celebrities like Michelangelo *'Blow Up'* Antonioni – the artiest mainstream film director of the mid–1960s, pop star Marianne Faithfull – in a cross between nun's habit and buttock–revealing mini–skirt – and other powerful friends of *IT*'s bespectacled and taper–thin editor, Barry Miles.

Thousands more than can have actually have been there were to reminisce about the free sugar–cubes that may or may not have contained LSD, the huge bathtub of jelly, the ectoplasmic light–shows that were part of the feedback–ridden act for The Pink Floyd and The Soft Machine (in days before the definite article was removed from their names) – and the latter's recital being interrupted halfway through by what amounted to an simple audience participation number by Yoko Ono. All the lights were switched off apart from tiny amplifier bulbs, and from the darkness came her amplified voice: "Touch the person next to you." Then the lights came back on, and The Soft Machine continued.

Barry Miles, who encouraged you to address him by his surname, was delighted with both the spectacular and the consequent upward turn of *IT*'s profit graph. The journal had been born in the basement of the Indica Gallery and attached Bookstore, dealing in merchandise of avant–garde and fashionably mystical bent, in Ham Yard, just off Piccadilly Circus. It had been opened in January 1966 by Miles and John Dunbar, Marianne Faithfull's first husband, who encouraged artists, talented, hopeful and hopeless, to make use of the Gallery's workshop ambience – to the degree that Eric Burdon of the Animals, who lived in the flat above, came to regard it as "Yoko Ono's place of business." (7)

In this 'Arts Lab', Russell Hunter, drummer with The Social Deviants, noticed "this very intense, bossy Japanese woman tearing about, ordering people around, and Chris Rowley sitting in a corner with a teapot, a teacup, a chair, maybe a cushion. He had this cutter, and he was sawing everything in half. Yoko was mounting one of her exhibitions, and he had to saw all these incredibly commonplace household objects in half: half a table with half a tea–set and so on. He was sawing it up, and she was being incredibly bossy. It's difficult to saw a cushion in half. It kept fraying, and she was very upset." (4)

Rowley, another stalwart of the underground press, was also instructed to paint certain objects white or black. He remembered particularly "black jars in which she'd drop people's messages – 'Have a nice day', that sort of thing – and she charged two hundred pounds for the jars. She also had a glass hammer." (4)

As such items weren't expected to allure many folk with more money than sense, Ono and Cox economised with weeks of an unvaried diet of either junk food or brown rice and vegetables, costing half–a–crown (12½p) at Notting Hall Gate's Macrobiotic Restaurant, patronised by so many of a particular type of diner that it provoked raids by Scotland Yard officers and sniffer dogs, and led the proprietors to insist that all guests sign a written statement that they were not in possession of controlled substances, contrary to the provision of the 1966 Dangerous Drugs Act, section 42.

Yoko knew marijuana and amphetamines well, and was becoming aware that the surreal perceptions of LSD varied from trip to trip. It was usually a stimulating experience, whether you plunged into nonsensical frenzy, emerged from a quagmire of horror, withdrew into extreme spiritual reverie or ascended untold heights of creativity.

If full of chemically–induced glimpses of the eternal, Yoko was responsible enough not to bring them home – or, at least, not until Kyoko was asleep. As it had been in New York, it was Tony more often than his busy wife who ministered to the meals and general well–being of a daughter who seemed desperate for affection and attention to some outsiders. "I went there one evening," said Gene Mahon, "and Kyoko was clinging to my hand because I made conversation with her, and not wanting me to leave. She was a sad little kid, and I didn't know how to deal with this." (4)

Kyoko's parents supported themselves and her partly by writing articles for *Art And Artists* and *IT*. Moreover, at the Anti–University, an 'alternative' seat of learning in Shoreditch, financed by a Peace Foundation established by philosopher and nuclear disarmament campaigner Bertrand Russell, Yoko ran a course similar to the one once hosted by John Cage at the New School for Social Research. Her students grew fond of her for her musicians' slang, her Japanese accent from which a strong *Noo Yawk* twang protruded – and, crucially, her infectious enthusiasm for her subject.

Nevertheless, a well–concealed ledger in Yoko's artistic accounts was, purportedly, what might have been a more–than–cursory attempt to maximise such public exposure as she'd garnered by putting herself forward as a potential chart contender like Marianne Faithfull. Demonstration tapes – probably made on a domestic reel–to–reel in the most acoustically–sympathetic corner of Hanover Gate Mansions – of what might be described as verse–chorus pop songs were mailed to Island, an independent record label that went in for oddball "ethnic" material.

What Island's artists–and–repertoire department made of this effort, if it ever existed, is not known, but such a pot–shot at Top Twenty fame wasn't as far–fetched a notion at a time when recording contracts were to be offered to the disparate likes of ineffable Tiny Tim – all castrati warble and doe–eyed eccentricity, Moondog and Los Angeles' Wild Man Fischer, a hoarse and psychotic street singer.

In the months clotted round 1967's Summer of Love too, the proferring of sex and marijuana 'joints' became a gesture of free–spirited friendliness, while the mind–warping effects of the soon–to–be outlawed LSD possessed venues like New York's Fillmore East, Amsterdam's Paradiso and London's Middle Earth where *berserkers* with eyes like catherine–wheels, cavorted, shrouded by flickering strobes, tinted incense fumes and further audio–visual aids that were part–and–parcel of simulated psychedelic experience.

This was surpassed at bigger events such as the inauguration of *IT* at the Roundhouse, and, another *IT* benefit, the Fourteen Hour Technicolor Dream at Alexandra Palace on 29th April 1967 with *son et lumière* on the cavernous walls as well as stages where 'bands' – not groups anymore – playing on and on and on and on. One after another, they appeared on platforms erected at either end of the massive exhibition centre – The Pink Floyd, The Move, Tomorrow, John's Children, The Flies (who 'apparently' urinated over the front row), The Soft Machine, you name 'em, entertained tranced hippies and other updated beatniks, either cross–legged or 'idiot dancing'.

Promenading onlookers were treated also to a female model, rendered supine by some narcotic or other, seated on a step–ladder with a blazing spotlight shining on her. In a variation of 'Cut Piece', audience members were handed a pair of scissors each, outfitted with a microphone plugged into the sound system, and directed by the ubiquitous Yoko to cut away the woman's garments.

"There was violence towards Yoko quite often when she performed those pieces," groaned Keith Rowe of AMM – an outfit that had more to do with John Cage than The Move – "I found it quite unpleasant, a quite powerful emotion. The violence shown to her was quite out of order. She had racism and sexism against her. Even today, it would probably be illegal to go on–stage and take someone's clothes off, but with a pair of amplified scissors, it's possible." (8)

Not everyone was impressed with either Yoko's talent or her courage in remaining true to her strange star. "Yoko Ono's happenings were boring," grimaced another *IT* associate, John Hopkins, "She was the most boring artist I'd ever met." (8)

Yet, to quote one of Picasso's homespun homilies, "It doesn't matter what people say about you as long as they are talking about you." (9) Certainly, there'd been much debate about Yoko since her arrival in London – and there remains bitter division about her impact during this period. Was she a Tracey Emin *du jour* – or to Art what the late Screaming Lord Sutch was to British politics? Food for such thoughts was digested during an expedition to Liverpool's Bluecoat Chambers in 1967 where she'd had an audience innocent of the capital's *sang froid*, picking up pieces of a jug she'd just smashed. She also brushed the stage, masticated sandwiches and invited people to jump off ladders. Spencer Leigh – awaiting his destiny as a BBC Radio Merseyside presenter – was asked to wrap up Yoko in bandages. However, when she was thus covered, John Gorman of multi–media aggregation, Scaffold, shouted out, "You're wanted on the telephone." Everybody laughed.

Back at the Indica the previous November, however, some found nothing amusing about, say, an all–white chess set, an apple with a £200 price tag and further puzzling 'Unfinished Paintings And Objects' by Yoko

Ono, who, at the preview, had been on the look–out for a mug with a pocketful of money.

Notes

1. Today, the building is a mosque.
2. To Paul Trynka
3. *John Ono Lennon* by R. Coleman (Sidgewick and Jackson, 1984)
4. *Days In The Life: Voices From The English Underground 1961–1971* by Jonathon Green (Heinemann, 1988))
5. *Playpower* by R. Neville (Jonathan Cape, 1970)
6. *International Times*, 17 May 1967
7. *Don't Let Me Be Misunderstood* by E. Burdon and J. Marshall Craig (Thunder's Mouth, 2001)
8. *Lost In The Woods: Syd Barrett And The Pink Floyd* by J. Palacios (Boxtree, 1998)
9. *Edgard Varese* by A. Clayson (Sanctuary, 2002)

PART 2 JOHN AND YOKO

WOMAN

by Robb Johnson

1. Unfinished Paintings And Objects

Yoko Ono first met John Lennon on November 9th, 1966. She was a minor cultural celebrity, like most Artists, impinging on the general cultural landscape of the latter half of the twentieth century primarily only when the media found her entertaining. Lennon, as a Beatle, was a primary iconic element in the process whereby pop culture assumed a hegemonic position with regard to that general cultural landscape. Their subsequent relationship not only ensured that Yoko was immediately promoted to a position of major mainstream cultural importance, it also created a first template for the post–modern cult of Celebrity.

Their subsequent relationship enabled Yoko's previous work, confined beforehand to the lofts, galleries and concepts of the marginal Fluxus movement, to have an unimagined effect upon mainstream culture.

The relationship also afforded Yoko the security with which to examine fully and to confront the demons and the forces that oppressed her as an individual and as an Asian woman, and the opportunity publicly to fight back. And in the process, the relationship effectively exhausted her ability to work as an artist, steadily narrowing her creativity into the limited conventions of pop culture.

When they first met, on that November day in 1966, Yoko's creativity was at full conceptual play. She was preparing an exhibition of her work, entitled *Unfinished Paintings And Objects,* at the Indica Gallery, when the owner of the gallery, John Dunbar, arrived with John Lennon for a preview visit. Dunbar often invited Lennon and his Beatles songwriting partner Paul McCartney to exhibitions at the Indica. Dunbar had phoned John and excited his interest by telling him about Yoko's 'Bag Piece', whereby Yoko climbed into a bag with a friend while the audience wondered whether they were having sex or not. In the event, John enjoyed the playful imagination and wit of Yoko's work, and would always retell in interviews how delighted he was with the positivity of 'Ceiling Painting (YES Painting)', where visitors climbed a ladder to examine a black canvas in a frame, looked through a magnifying glass, and found the white dot in the centre was actually the word "YES" painted there.

John was looking at Yoko's 'Hammer A Nail In' piece, which invited the viewer to hammer a nail into the canvas, when they were first introduced to each other by Dunbar. Yoko was still preoccupied with ensuring the exhibition was ready for the public opening. When John wanted to hammer a nail into the canvas, Yoko, who wanted her canvas to stay blank until the exhibition officially opened, said it would cost him five shillings. Fortunately John never carried any money, so he paid her an imaginary five shillings, hammered in an imaginary nail and the canvas remained in pristine condition. John, however, hadn't given up hope of a bag event taking place, and asked her "Where's this happening event?" Yoko presented him with a card with the instruction "Breathe" on it; he responded by leaning forward and panting like a dog. Although Yoko found John's exuberant behaviour worrying, she was, nonetheless, impressed both by Lennon's physical presence and by his ability to play conceptual games.

On his way out, John passed an apple on a pedestal with a £200 price tag attached to it. He looked at it, picked it up, took a bite from it. Yoko's face registered instinctive displeasure. John giggled sheepishly and put the apple back. Yoko later said, "The first impression I had of him, looking at the hammer and nail painting like as if it's a portrait of the Mona Lisa was he looked very beautiful...It would be nice to have an affair or something with somebody like this...When he did the apple –'Oh well, forget it'."

After the Indica exhibition, Yoko's next project was a film, *Bottoms,* co–produced with her husband Tony. Yoko later said she had noticed how, unlike faces, people are unable to control the movement of their buttocks. "Cabinet ministers and labourers, beautiful women and ugly women are all equal when they take their clothes off. Their bottoms all have innocent looks beyond their control," she explained. Over two days of filming, the various bottoms that answered a newspaper advertisement produced a film that lasted over two hours, with each bottom receiving twenty seconds of film time. Unfortunately the British Board of Film Censors noted that other more controversial parts of the human anatomy also featured in some of the sections and refused to give the film a certificate for distribution. Yoko and Tony picketed the offices of the BBFC, which ensured some typically condescending coverage in the press. An application for a permit to show the film at the Royal Albert Hall was refused. When Fleet Street critics finally did have an opportunity to review the film, they were generally unsympathetic, prompting Yoko to write in defence of her work in *International Times,* emphasising the playful, humorous and participatory elements of the film.

Yoko and Tony continued to attract press attention throughout the summer of 1967. They were arrested for dancing naked in Belgium, and in August, Yoko tied herself in a bag to a lion in Trafalgar Square, "using the press for peace" as she later said. Meanwhile, Yoko had also been meeting

John Lennon again. He, in the company of Paul McCartney, was at the opening of an exhibition by Claes Oldenburg that Yoko went to, and he also attended her performance at the *Fourteen Hour Technicolour Dream* event at Alexandra Palace in April. As part of her continuing programme of self–promotion, Yoko sent out copies of her book *Grapefruit* to various media figures, including a copy to John whilst he was in the Abbey Road studios recording *Sgt. Pepper's Lonely Hearts Club Band.*

He was intrigued by the book, which consists of instructions that begin with the imperative "imagine...." He invited her to his mock–Tudor house, Kenwood, in Weybridge, and asked if he could purchase a 'Light House', one of the imaginary articles included in the list of conceptual merchandise included with the book. Despite this instance of John's apparent complete misunderstanding of conceptual art, their friendship continued to develop, initially through phone calls. On one occasion, Yoko telephoned him to ask if he would contribute to a book of twentieth century music scores being compiled by her fellow avant–garde artist John Cage. John responded by inviting her to the studio, and in the course of the evening they further explored their intellectual similarities and differences, discovering they both admired each other's writing, but found each other's musical tastes incomprehensible.

Of more immediate significance was John's promise of financial support for Yoko's next exhibition, *Half A Wind.* In the past, it had been husband Tony who had hustled for the money to stage or exhibit Yoko's works, but by now their marriage, and, therefore, their working relationship was beginning to show signs of strain, and Yoko decided to ask John directly for patronage. His promise of support enabled Yoko to approach the Lisson Gallery, and once assured of Lennon's backing, the proprietor Nicholas Logsdail agreed to stage the exhibition the following October.

Yoko threw herself whole–heartedly into preparing for the exhibition. Tony's role became more and more that of both assistant – Yoko's idea of the perfect male partner – and lone parent. People began to notice how Yoko was effectively replicating with her daughter Kyoko the same condition of maternal indifference and neglect that she described when talking of her own childhood.

The exhibition commenced with a *13 Days Do–It–Yourself Dance Festival* that involved subscribers receiving daily cards of dance instructions. Yoko also sent cards to John, and started calling in person at his home. John's wife Cynthia began to complain about Yoko's presence in their lives, which she was now finding suspiciously intrusive. When the exhibition proper opened, John didn't attend. Those who did found the three floors of the Lisson Gallery occupied by a comprehensive representation of the diversity of Yoko's work. The first floor was entitled 'Yoko And Me' ("Me" referring to John Lennon), and presented half a bedroom, with the objects of an ordinary bedroom all cut perfectly in half and painted white. The other half, at John's suggestion, had been put into bottles. The ground floor gathered together a variety of old and new conceptual exhibits and the basement was focussed on Yoko's 'Bag Piece'. Yoko later said that whilst the Lisson exhibition was on, John made it clear that he was attracted to her more than just intellectually; Yoko, however, decided not to respond.

Yoko's next important creative venture came about partly out of a wish to distance herself from John's attentions. After attending the 1968 Knokke film festival in Belgium for a screening of *Bottoms,* she decided to avoid returning to London, and Lennon, by accepting an invitation to go to Paris. She arrived in a city gearing up for insurrection, an insurrection that would involve students, factory workers and cultural workers too. On February 15th there was evidence of the extent of popular discontent when cultural workers, including Jean–Luc Godard, Simone Signoret, Luis Bunuel, Marlene Dietrich and Jeanne Moreau took part in a demonstration protesting the Ministry Of Culture's sacking of cineaste Henri Langlois.

Back in England, Yoko's personal situation was temporarily eased when Lennon, along with the rest of the Beatles and their wives, left on February 18th, to travel to Rishikesh in India, in order to study transcendental meditation with the Maharishi Mahesh Yogi. Still in Paris, Yoko met up with the highly regarded avant–garde jazz saxophonist Ornette Coleman, who asked her to perform with him at his forthcoming concert at the Albert Hall on February 29th. Yoko insisted on performing her own composition, and Coleman agreed. Also, perhaps of more long–term significance, it was whilst in Paris that Yoko and Tony, their relationship on the point of collapse, went to the party where Yoko was to have her first experience of snorting heroin.

Returning to Britain for the concert Yoko discovered a pile of letters waiting for her from John who was still in India. For her part, she also continued to maintain contact by sending him occasional instructions. Of more immediate concern, however, were the rehearsals for the Albert Hall. In order to convey her ideas to the musicians, Coleman suggested Yoko write out her ideas as a set of prose instructions, that Coleman then attempted to translate into terms the musicians would understand. Coleman also suggested these instructions be included in the programme for the concert. However, the management of the Albert Hall took exception to the notes on the grounds of their scatological content, and set about confiscating the programmes, and told the box office to stop selling tickets. Eventually, under pressure from the audience, the concert went ahead, with Yoko's vocalising duetting perfectly with Coleman's saxophone style.

In the month following the Albert Hall concert, it was clear that the breakdown of her relationship with Tony was irreversible, and Yoko moved out of the family flat into a hotel, leaving Tony to look after Kyoko. Lennon returned from India in April disillusioned with the Maharishi's purported inability to overcome the temptations of the flesh. Yoko and John resumed their close contact, their communications becoming lengthier, more frequent, and more openly expressive of a mutual attraction.

The long cautious process of their courtship came to an end one night in May, the month when the barricades went up in Paris and the insurrection initiated by students all but brought the Gaullist French state to its knees. Cynthia was on holiday in Greece, which was then controlled by the right wing Colonel's Junta. The military had seized power in the April 1967 coup, the anniversary of which had been the occasion for a recent protest march in London led by Greek actress Merlina Mercouri.

On May 19th John telephoned Yoko, inviting her to Kenwood, telling her to take a taxi that he paid for on her arrival. John said they could chat or go up to the home recording studio he had set up in the attic. Yoko opted for the latter option. Assisted by the effects of LSD, they spent all night collaging the diverse sounds and elements – birdsong, white noise, Yoko's avant–garde vocalising, John's surreal sub–*Goon Show* humour – that they later released as the *Unfinished Music No. 1: Two Virgins* album.

In Paris, the Sorbonne was occupied and two million workers were on strike. And in Weybridge, as the night ended and the sun rose, John and Yoko made love for the first time.

2. **Life With The Lions**

Yoko maintains that Cynthia was informed of the development in their relationship by John's driver and by the nanny of Julian, John and Cynthia's child. She refutes the story that Cynthia returned to Kenwood and was shocked to find Yoko sitting there drinking Cynthia's breakfast tea dressed in Cynthia's kimono and that, although tense, the first meeting between John, Yoko and Cynthia was not as dramatic as it has been represented. "We were all civil, like the flower children we were," says Yoko. Cynthia also recognised that the marriage with John had run its course: "I knew at the time there was nothing I could do to stop what was happening," she said later. "He was hell–bent on something. And it happened to end up he was hell–bent on Yoko." John was always extremely effusive about the nature and extent of his attraction to Yoko. "I'd never known love like this before, and it hit me so hard that I had to halt my marriage to Cyn...With Yoko I really knew love for the first time. Our attraction was a mental one, but it happened physically, too." And even in the last interview he gave, talking with Andy Peebles from BBC Radio 1, John still dwelt on the unique nature of Yoko's attractiveness to him: "I realised somebody else was as kind of barmy as me..." he enthused, ".. a wife with sort of freaky sounds."

By comparison, Yoko has remained noticeably more reticent about this particular stage in their relationship. In *Uncut* in 2003, she described the situation retrospectively from her point of view. "I was ready to be independent from my marriage, and I thought, well, OK then, I would probably live in a loft by myself or something like that. John didn't like that idea. And so we came together that first time and we finally got together in May – we started living together."

Across the Channel, the student revolt had so encouraged the confidence of people in their discontent that by 23rd May, ten million workers were on strike, and even the Cannes Film Festival had to be abandoned in the face of action by technicians and film directors. At the same time, the debates about the nature and role of art and the artist that were taking place provided an important critique which would consequentially influence and inform both Yoko and John's work in the future. Whilst ostensibly endorsing the radical, imagination–centred and democratic participation–orientated elements of the Fluxus movement that had animated Yoko's past work, these debates were severely critical of other characteristics of the movement, whereby the artist "does what he wants to do, he believes that everything is possible, he is accountable only to himself or to Art... he invents something unique, whose value will be permanent, and beyond historical reality.... Let us make it clear that it is not the establishment of better contracts between artists and modern technology that will bind them closer to all the other categories of workers, but opening their eyes to the problems of workers, that is to say of the historical reality of the world in which we live."

A week later, interviewed by student leader Daniel Cohn–Bendit in *Le Nouvel Observateur,* Jean–Paul Sartre commented approvingly, "What is interesting about your action is that it puts imagination in the seats of power. You have a limited imagination like everyone else, but you have a great many more ideas than your elders... The working class has often imagined new means of struggle, but always as a function of the precise situation in which it found itself... You have an imagination that is much more rich and the slogans chalked up on the walls of the Sorbonne prove it. Something has emerged from you which surprises, which astonishes and which denies everything which has made our society what it is today. That is what I call the extension of the field of possibility."

"The extension of the field of possibility" is also a very appropriate description of the effect Yoko was to have upon John's creativity. Art critic Anthony Fawcett wrote, "What Yoko was doing for John was changing his attitude about art, and everything else, by showing him that anything was possible, and more importantly that all ideas he had in his head should be brought out into the open and followed through, not just left as fantasies."

Yoko began to accompany John to the Abbey Road studios, when, at the end of May, the Beatles were starting to record the *White Album.* Previously, it had been taken for granted by the Beatles that girlfriends and wives were left at home during recordings, and the other members of the closely male–bonded group were at first surprised and then angered by Yoko's presence.

They began to be seen in public during the first week of June, lunching together in matching white kaftans and then going to the new Apple offices together. They also undertook their first public joint creative work together when they participated in the National Sculpture Exhibition at Coventry. One of the organisers was Anthony Fawcett. He had become a close friend of Yoko and a sympathetic advocate of her work since the Indica Gallery exhibition, and this connection facilitated the inclusion of a piece by John and Yoko in the exhibition programme, despite the conceptual nature of their proposed contribution. Yoko wanted to represent symbolically her relationship with John by planting two acorns, one facing east, one west, in the churchyard where the exhibition was taking place. Fawcett considered, "The concept of acorns as 'living art' was original." The other organisers were less convinced, and the cathedral authorities refused permission because the acorns be planted in consecrated ground. Eventually the acorns were planted on a lawn near the cathedral – where they were subsequently dug up and stolen. A second pair was sent, and a security guard employed to protect 'Acorn Piece' whilst the exhibition was on.

On June 18th, John and Yoko attended the premiere of *In His Own Write,* an adaptation of John's book, at The Old Vic theatre. The press demanded to know where his wife was, and John said he had no idea. The next day most newspapers carried a photograph of John and Yoko arriving at the theatre together, and their relationship effectively became public property and front–page news. Meanwhile, they both set in motion processes intended to extricate themselves officially from their previous relationships, both of which involved issues of custody over young children.

John filed for divorce on the grounds of adultery, hoping to gain custody of five–year old Julian. Yoko negotiated her separation from Tony directly, and he continued to look after four–year old Kyoko. Cynthia, who countersued for divorce on the grounds of adultery, stayed in Kenwood with Julian, and Tony and Kyoko moved to the south of France. John and Yoko set up home together in a one–bedroom basement flat that Ringo Starr owned, in Montague Square. The flat had an interesting list of recent tenants that included Cynthia's mother, Jimi Hendrix and William Burroughs.

The couple again attracted massive press attention when John's first complete art exhibition *You Are Here* opened at the Robert Fraser Gallery in Duke Street on July 1st. The catalogue contained the dedication "To Yoko from John, with love," and the exhibition's central piece, a white circular canvas with the words "You are here" painted in small letters at the centre, bore a certain conceptual similarity to Yoko's 'Ceiling Painting (YES Painting)'. Yoko later recalled, "We came out of the car and there were tons of reporters there, and the photographers, and my first instinct was, 'Let's immediately rush into the back room.'" But John insisted they face the press, and in answer to their questions he simply stated: "I'm in love with her."

Part of the event was the release of three hundred and sixty five white helium balloons, each with a note attached asking the finder to write to John Lennon, c/o The Robert Fraser Gallery. The letters that resulted from this event contained a response that was overwhelmingly critical of John's relationship with Yoko, including several letters that were overtly racist. The antipathy indicates the true extent of the deeply embedded racism in Britain that Yoko had to deal with, a racism endorsed by the frequent incidence of blatant hostility and the constant, barely concealed subtext of dislike that has characterised the mainstream media's treatment of her, and which lingers on, even today.

Even the traditionally liberal *Guardian* newspaper still can't resist using headlines that sneer, "Ono! It's her again" (February 1997), and "Yoko bares all for peace – again" (September 2003), and dismisses what she has to say as "bullshit" (*The Guide,* September 2003). In the superficially progressive atmosphere of the 60s, it was possible for an Asian woman to appear in concert with a black African–American jazz musician at the Royal Albert Hall. But this was in front of an audience of a thousand; the Beatles numbered their audiences by the millions, and the popular response to Yoko is a good index of just how far the progressive social revolution in 60s Britain had actually progressed. And the response to Yoko within the Beatles and their Apple organisation was no different, with hostility again frequently being articulated in racist terms.

Initially, publicly at least, Yoko and John attempted to respond positively. Yoko made *Film No.5,* whereby a high–speed film of John smiling for three minutes was replayed at normal speed, thereby lasting an hour and a half. It was first screened on July 17th. Yoko explained, "We call it our smile movie because John smiles in it and sometimes says, 'Don't worry, love'. Originally, I wanted to make a movie of everybody in the world smiling, but then I realised this was impossible, so I just let John represent everybody and send out vibrations. I think people in five hundred years' time will watch it and just feel the vibrations."

But privately they were finding it increasingly difficult to maintain that positivity. Ostensibly as a celebration of their success as artists, but in retrospect also partly as a response to the stress they felt themselves subject to, they began using heroin in July. John later told *Rolling Stone's* Jann Wenner, "We took H because of what the Beatles and their pals were doing to us." According to Apple director Peter Brown, Yoko said, "John was very curious. He asked me if I had ever tried it. I told him that while he was in India with the Maharishi, I had a sniff of it in a party situation. I didn't know what it was. They just gave me something and I said, 'What was that?' It was a beautiful feeling. I think because the amount was small I didn't even get sick. It was just a nice feeling. So I told him that...I think maybe because I said it wasn't a bad experience, that had something to do with John taking it."

Of course, John had a long history of drug use and drug experimentation, stretching back to his consumption of Preludin in Hamburg. What was significant about his heroin use was that it was something that he did with Yoko. It simultaneously strengthened their relationship and distanced them from the rest of the world. This was particularly important with regard to the internal dynamics of the Beatles. As recordings of the *White Album* continued, the other members found it increasingly difficult to work with John because working with John involved working with Yoko too, who insisted on offering her opinions and her vocalisings during the recording sessions, providing the first instance of a solo female voice on a Beatles song with her contribution to 'Bungalow Bill.' Together, John and Yoko, with some minor assistance from George Harrison, created the track 'Revolution 9', an avant–garde collage of sounds that had a great influence on listeners as diverse as the American mass–murderer Charles Manson and post–Prague Spring anti–Stalinist radicals in Czechoslovakia. John later explained that it was inspired solely by Yoko's creative pieces; "Once I heard her stuff, I got intrigued, so I wanted to do one. I spent more time on 'Revolution 9' than I did on half the other songs I ever wrote."

Although the revolutions of 'Revolution 9' are more in terms of form and concept than in terms of an explicit engaging with the current historical reality, it was, nonetheless, an apposite title for a song in 1968. That summer, in Czechoslovakia, the attempt to achieve 'socialism with a human face', the 'Prague Spring', was crushed when Soviet tanks entered the city on August 21st, in an intervention that had great significance for the development of The Revolution as historically represented by Russia and the Marxist–Leninist Communist world. And in sleepy London Town, Yoko and John appeared on the flagship London Weekend Television programme *Frost On Saturday,* advocating a more democratic and inclusive understanding of what constitutes art, demonstrating the concept of participation with a version of Yoko's 'Hammer A Nail In' piece. Also in August, the satirical magazine *Private Eye* began the first of a long series of vicious satires ridiculing Yoko and John, with the usual racist assumptions frequently surfacing in their treatment of Yoko.

In defiance of such continued hostility, Yoko and John decided to release the recordings they had made together on May 19th. They called the album *Unfinished Music No 1: Two Virgins,* and they wanted to use as a cover a photograph of themselves naked. The album was intended to be the new Apple label's first release, but the proposed cover caused such controversy that the its release was delayed for months, with printers refusing to reproduce the photographs, EMI refusing to distribute the album and magazines refusing to carry advertisements for it.

Yoko had also discovered that she was four months pregnant. Because of the sensitivity of John's divorce proceedings, the couple were advised to keep this fact secret, although, in the light of Yoko's pregnancy, John felt it wise to drop the adultery allegation from his suit. To make matters worse, on October 18th, their flat in Montague Square was raided by police searching for drugs. Nevertheless, the couple had been warned that a raid was imminent, and Yoko and John had thoroughly cleaned the flat, concerned both to eliminate evidence both of their own drug use and also any traces of illegal substances left behind by previous tenants, when the police arrived with sniffer dogs at noon, a small quantity of cannabis resin was finally detected, after an hour of determined searching,

Yoko and John always maintained that it was planted by the police. They were released on bail, but a few hours after their release, Yoko had to be taken to Queen Charlotte Maternity Hospital. In the hospital, she nearly suffered a miscarriage and had to be given several blood transfusions. Doctors told her that she had to stay in hospital for the foreseeable future. While Yoko remained in hospital, John's first marriage was officially ended when Cynthia's decrée nisi was granted on November 8th. Negotiations with Tony with regard to Yoko's marriage also finally reached a conclusion. John repaid Tony's debts, and it was agreed that Tony and Kyoko would move to the Virgin Islands where the divorce would finally take place, with both parents sharing custody of their daughter. However, on November 21st, Yoko was told that she was going to lose the baby she was carrying. John recorded the child's dying heartbeats, and named the dead child John Ono Lennon II.

On November 27th, John pleaded guilty to the charge of possessing hashish. He was fined £150, with two guineas costs, and the charges against Yoko were dropped. The popular press, however, were not so lenient: by now *Unfinished Music No1* was finally distributed, and it was Yoko who again attracted the particularly nasty headlines. Whilst the cover of *Private*

Eye that reproduced the *Two Virgins* photograph had John saying, "It won't stand up in court," *The News Of The World* headline simply sneered "Oh, oh, Yoko!"

Significantly, their next two public appearances were characterised by physical concealment. In December, Yoko appeared again on stage at the Royal Albert Hall as part of the 'Alchemical Wedding' event, but this time it was with John and both were concealed in a bag. And for their appearance on the Rolling Stones television concert, *Rock'n'Roll Circus,* John was dressed in a striped leotard with ostentatious ruffs at the neck and hip, while Yoko dressed as a witch with a pointed hat.

Elsewhere, in France the year ended with the right–wing Gaullist state re–established after a massive electoral victory, with a programme of essentially left–wing reforms, and in Northern Ireland with the first civil rights marches, and a BBC TV camera crew, being attacked by the police. And on the mainland, in December the radical newspaper *Black Dwarf* carried an article by Sheila Rowbotham entitled, 'Women: A Call To Revolt', which stated: "Revolutions are made about little things. Little things which happen to you all the time, every day, wherever you go, all your life...[women's] 'emancipation' has often been merely the struggle of the privileged to improve and consolidate its superiority – the women of the working class remain the exploited of the exploited, oppressed as workers and oppressed as women.... But subordination is not an affair of economics and institutions only... It is an assumed secondariness which dwells in a whole complex of inarticulate attitudes... It is located in a structure in which both sexes are tragically trapped... It is only women who can dissolve the assumptions. It is only women who can say what they feel because the experience is unique to them."

Articulating that experience was something that would become a dominant feature of Yoko's work in the future. There is a degree of ambiguity to Yoko's conceptual conceit 'Cut Piece'; this is much less the case in her overtly feminist work in the 1970s, which effects a clear separation between a critique of male domination ('What A Bastard The World Is', 'Coffin Car') and an assertion of her own, female sexuality ('Men Men Men', 'Kiss Kiss Kiss').

In January 1969, the Beatles began work on another album, provisionally entitled *Get Back.* The song itself is notorious for affording Paul McCartney the opportunity to express his hostility to Yoko, with stories of him looking directly at her when recording the chorus vocals in the studio. But by now, antipathy towards Yoko, whether from the fans shouting abuse to her outside the Apple offices, the fans sending her hate mail, or from the employees working inside, had reached almost hysterical levels; memoirs abound with fiercely negative anecdotes about her, always interpreting her actions in the worst possible light, most having no respect whatsoever for her as a creative artist, and many depicting her as humourless and arrogant.

Apple employee Richard DiLello provides a rare, more objective perspective: "There was already a lot going against Yoko Ono when she walked into the goldfish bowl. She was over–educated, spoke several languages, was highly proficient in the culinary arts, and a writer of verse and a creator of sculpture. She was well–versed in history and a survivor of the New York avant–garde scrap race. She was also an older woman and Japanese. Somehow she managed to carry it all with ease, as she did her hair, as part of the terrain." Apple was after all the corporate expression of the Beatles, an essentially lower–middle class phenomenon that fabricated a socially mobile, classless identity by cherry–picking attributes from both working class and aristocratic cultures. Its 60s British popmusic mindset was about sometimes being a bit arty, but it was not about Art.

Memoirs of people from outside the pop world are often very different in tone. Underground writer Mick Farren, in his autobiography *Give The Anarchist A Cigarette,* has an anecdote about phoning unsuspecting "leading lights of the underground and the avant–garde" and recording them talking to a delayed echo of their own voice for possible use on The Deviants first album. "The only one who twigged and turned the mystery into an impromptu performance, was Yoko Ono; when I later got on the line and explained what we were doing, Yoko – who even then, had a formidable reputation as a hard–nosed businesswoman – was more than agreeable to us using the tape."

Nonetheless, the attrition of such constant hostility, and the condition of a shared, mutual isolation with John, was impacting upon Yoko's creativity. Whereas once her sense of isolation found expression in processes of objectification and imagination, now her creativity became much more reactive and consciously, obsessively self–referential and biographical. And unrealised – there were a profusion of ideas for films that were never carried out. However, the dying heartbeats of their unborn baby were used in several pieces: in a project for the American Aspern Arts Society, as a possible contribution to a magazine's giveaway floppy disc, and finally appearing as a track on their next album, *Life With The Lions.* It was followed by a two minutes silence, the length of silence usually associated with the commemoration of Armistice Day.

One film idea that was seen through was *Rape.* A cameraman filmed people in Hyde Park, showed Yoko and John the results and they eventually selected an Austrian tourist, who was then followed everywhere and filmed by their camera crew, without explanation. "It was just a filmic idea about just following a girl, and to keep following and just filming her, and what would happen to somebody who's totally exposed all the time, you know," explained Yoko "That filmic idea was something I thought before I really got together with John... But it was very interesting that in a way the Beatles were in that position." And so, of course, was Yoko.

Whilst the Beatles struggled on with recording the album that would eventually be entitled *Let It Be,* they were also struggling to agree on a manager who could rescue their Apple organisation, which was by now in serious financial difficulty. John, and Yoko, favoured a New York accountant called Allen Klein, who had a history of effective management in rock music. Paul McCartney favoured the lawyer Lee Eastman, father of his current partner and future wife, Linda. Although Yoko and Linda had never had a particularly strong friendship, Linda's understandable antipathy towards Klein effectively ended any chance of amicability between them.

A welcome distraction from these tensions was an appearance at *A Natural Music Nothing Doing In London Concert,* on March 2nd at Lady Mitchell Hall, Cambridge. Yoko had been asked to perform, and she assembled a band that included drummer John Stevens, who had played at her Albert Hall concert with Ornette Coleman, saxophonist John Tchai , and John on guitar. Yoko's piece, entitled 'Cambridge 1969', was recorded and later released as the first side of *Life With The Lions.* Essentially a duet between Yoko's vocalisings and John's feedback guitar, with none of the quirky humour of *Unfinished Music No. 1,* it expressed abstractly and intensely their condition of trauma and pain, a condition compounded of long–term personal histories and present circumstances.

Perhaps, given the complex nature of the relationship between John and Paul McCartney, Yoko and John's decision to formalise their relationship with a wedding ceremony was given impetus by Paul and Linda's marriage on March 12th. But whereas Paul and Linda's wedding had been a quiet, private event, Yoko and John initially wanted to be married by the Archbishop of Canterbury. When the Archbishop claimed to be too busy with other previous engagements, Yoko and John investigated a number of other characteristically idiosyncratic options – marriage at sea, for example, on a car ferry, or a cruise ship – and eventually settled for a marriage service conducted by the British Consul in Gibraltar, on March 20th. Both bride and groom wore white, and both wore tennis shoes. After the ceremony, they flew first to Paris, then on to the Amsterdam Hilton, where they invited the world's press to participate in their honeymoon.

3. **Give Peace A Chance**

For their honeymoon, they proposed to stay in bed at Amsterdam Hilton for a week. The press's interest in the Bed–In was initially excited, like John's interest in the Indica Gallery, by the prospect of sex, or at least a little fashionably shocking nudity. What they found were two people who wanted to talk about world peace, at a time when the world was witnessing two serious conflicts, both of which were having terrible effects on civilian populations. One was the war between Nigeria and Biafra, a post–colonial conflict in which British interests were implicitly engaged, and which was in effect an act of genocide against the people of Biafra, and the other was the US's continued escalation of its aggression in south east Asia in the face of impending military defeat by the guerrilla armies of Vietnam.

For ten hours every day for the next seven days, in a double bed, wearing white pyjamas, Yoko and John disappointed and deconstructed media expectations by promoting peace and answering questions with patient good humour. "What we want is for people to stay in bed or grow their hair instead of getting involved in violence," announced John. "Hair is nice. Hair is peaceful." The mainstream press responded with its customary affected shock, abhorrence and derision, but alongside this there was a grudging amusement starting to emerge and a recognition that the event had a serious intent.

John later said that the Bed–In concept, with its characteristic surreal wit, was Yoko's creation, not his. Lennon's biographers have noticed a considerable discrepancy between his previous, more youthful behaviour, which was notable for its tendency towards arrogance and aggression, and his promotion of peace and pacifism after his marriage to Yoko. In Hamburg, he had often replicated towards German people the same sort of populist post–war xenophobic stereotyping with which much of the hostility towards Yoko was animated, but Lennon's arrogance and aggression weren't exclusively youthful and anti–German. Although in a *Melody Maker* 'Pop think–in' interview in 1966, Lennon claimed that 'punch–ups' "aren't there any more with me. It all happened when I was eighteen and nineteen." Lennon never quite lost his reputation for aggression amongst other musicians, particularly when drunk, and May Pang's generally affectionate account of her relationship with Lennon in the 1970s, *Loving John,* alleges both continued violent behaviour and unreconstructed xenophobic stereo–typing.

Interviews from the mid–sixties, however, do show the Beatles, and Lennon in particular, in the process of growing up, moving through dismissive flippancy towards considered sincerity, in response to the historical events taking place during the decade. In an interview in 1965, John says, "I don't suppose I think much about the future. I don't really give a damn. Though now we've made it, it would be a pity to get bombed. It's selfish, but I don't care too much about humanity," and Paul adds, "It's disturbing that people should go around blowing up, but if an atom bomb should explode I'd say, 'Oh well'. No point in saying anything else, is there? People are so crackers. I know the bomb is ethically wrong, but I won't go around crying."

But a year later, John is insisting, "All our songs are anti–war." When asked, "What do you think of the Vietnam war?" he replies, "We think of it every day. We don't like it. We don't agree with it. We think it is wrong. But there is not much we can do about it." "Anybody who feels fighting is wrong has the right not to go in the army," says Paul. Then in June 1967, the Beatles release 'All You Need Is Love', a song that, however generalised and rhetorical its lyric, is, nonetheless, intent on making a clear and considered social statement.

But it was not until the relationship with Yoko started, that John became an active advocate of the more politically charged concept of peace as a radical position capable of changing the current condition of historical reality. By contrast, Yoko had arrived at a position of activism by a different, more internal process. Whilst her previous work reflected a commitment to radical forms of creativity, her subsequent, post–1968 work has admitted more and more of a consistent deeply–felt commitment to peace that is a consequence of her first–hand childhood experience of war, and a similarly emotional commitment to issues of social justice that is a consequence of her adult experience, as an Asian woman, of racism and sexism.

1968 provided the personal and the historical catalytic experiences that determined their subsequent creativity, an idiosyncratic blend of autobiography and activism. And in January 1969, in response to *Unfinished Music No.1,* 30,000 copies of which were confiscated in New Jersey alone, the FBI opened a file on Yoko and John as dangerous subversives.

After Amsterdam, Yoko and John flew to Vienna for the television premiere of *Rape,* which they promoted at a press conference on March 31st from inside a black bag. When reporters asked if it really was the famous couple inside the bag, John sang them 'Maggie May'. Yoko, however, sang Japanese folk songs, an interesting choice of personal identification, and a resource whose influence would become more manifest in her work during the next few years.

When they returned to London, they held a press conference at Heathrow where they announced a new initiative, their 'Acorns For Peace' campaign, whereby they planned to send one hundred acorns to one hundred world leaders to plant for peace. On their return they also found that television magnate Sir Lew Grade was on the point of buying up 37% of the Beatles' publishing rights. Yoko began to accompany John and Allen Klein to the various meetings that took place in an attempt to organise an effective counter–bid. This was her first experience of music business 'business', and the start of the process whereby she acquired the skills to become a very efficient professional business woman later in the 70s, capable even of out–negotiating Klein himself, while John was the house–husband who looked after their child.

On April 22nd John changed his middle name (Winston) to Ono, and recorded "The Ballad Of John and Yoko," the most pop–audience friendly of the couple's next three releases, all of which were focussed with obsessive fascination on the development of their relationship. As well as that single, there was *Unfinished Music No.2* (its subtitle *Life With The Lions* both echoes the popular television programme and also suggests pride and defiance), and *The Wedding Album,* all released in the same month. Both albums were primarily continuations of their avant–garde explorations, collecting and collaging sounds, in order to record an abstract portrait of their relationship.

In May, Yoko and John at last decided on a house to live in, buying Tittenhurst Park, a Georgian mansion in seventy–four acres of ground near Ascot. They then set off for America, to stage another Bed–In for peace. Although refused entry to the US on the grounds of John's drug conviction, and having first tried the Bahamas, Yoko and John eventually gained entry to Canada, where in Montreal they had a ten day Bed–In that allowed them more direct contact with the US media and the US New Left, including student demonstrators defending People's Park in San Francisco from development by Berkeley University. The Bed–In also saw them produce their first single. Recorded on June 1st, in their bedroom in the Queen Elizabeth Hotel, with a cast of counter–culture icons joining in the chorus, the song 'Give Peace A Chance' consciously utilised their personal mythology for the purpose of making a clear political statement. Although songwriting credits were 'Lennon–McCartney', the performance was credited to The Plastic Ono Band.

Returning to England, on June 14th Yoko and John were again interviewed by David Frost in a programme that was to be broadcast in the US. After an initial frivolous discussion about 'bagism', Frost asked John and Yoko about their recent Bed–Ins. John replied that their purpose was to "advertise" peace. "We're trying to sell peace, like a product, you know, and sell it like people sell soap or soft drinks, you know...People just accept (war and violence)'oh they did it, or Harold Wilson did it, or Nixon did it,' they're always scapegoating people. And it isn't Nixon's fault, we're all responsible for everything that goes on, you know, we're all responsible for Biafra and Hitler and everything. So we're just saying SELL PEACE, anybody interested in peace just stick it in the window, it's simple but it lets somebody else know that you want peace too, because you feel alone if you're the only one thinking 'wouldn't it be nice if there was peace and nobody was getting killed', so advertise yourself that you're for peace if you believe in it."

Later that month, Yoko and John collected their children and set off for a family vacation in Scotland in a hired car. The holiday was curtailed when John failed to negotiate a curve in the road and the car went into a ditch. All four occupants had to be taken to hospital in Glasgow, where all but Julian needed stitches as a result of the accident. Yoko later had the car crushed and installed as a cubic sculpture at Tittenhurst. After leaving hospital, they went to Liverpool to recover with some of John's relatives. The accident caused them to miss a press conference on July 3rd to promote the release of the single 'Give Peace A Chance', an event further over–shadowed by the death earlier that same day of Rolling Stone guitarist Brian Jones.

Despite this unpromising start, the single reached number 2 in the British pop charts, and number 14 in the US, and Yoko and John further developed Yoko's concept of an imaginary band by putting full–page advertisements in the music press announcing "YOU are the Plastic Ono Band." The first advertisement featured the "Jones" page out of the London telephone directory. Subsequent publicity and press conferences featured a sculptural work commissioned by Yoko consisting of four pieces of perspex of differing dimensions, that contained respectively a tape–recorder and amplifier, a closed circuit television, a record player and amplifier, and a miniature light show and loudspeaker.

Apple publicist Derek Taylor, writing in the July 26th issue of *Disc and Music Echo,* proclaimed, "The band may be the property of Apple, but it also belongs to everyone, because what it represents is freedom, freedom for performers to be themselves, taking no heed of who they are or what they look like or where they have been or what their music is supposed to be. It could be children in a playground screaming their release from the bondage of the classroom or it could be John and Yoko screaming their love for one another."

The following week, DJ John Peel wrote an article in the same magazine about how nice it was to be a member of the Plastic Ono Band, particularly when confronted by "the cruelty, the stupidity and the selfishness of a great number of those with whom we share the planet. They will take it from us if we don't stop them." The Plastic Ono Band concept is a reminder of "the good and thoughtful people...you'll never see or meet or know – but they're there and you'd like them, love them if you did meet them. John Lennon and Yoko are two of them."

For Yoko and John, however, although there were welcome proposals to screen her films at the Edinburgh Film Festival and the ICA in London, the latter programme consisting of *Rape* and a new film *Self-Portrait* (which spent fifteen minutes showing John's penis achieving erection), and John was working on the Beatles *Abbey Road* album, the summer of 1969 was overshadowed by the problem of their increased heroin use. Yoko said it was a way of easing the pain resulting from the car crash – Piaf had also blamed her serious use of the pre–heroin narcotic morphine on the pain caused by a car crash. They decided to stop using the drug, to retreat to their bedroom in Tittenhurst and go through the process of "cold turkey," to deny the body the drug it was attuned to, and to cure themselves of their addiction. When the ICA screening occurred, they sent two Hari Krishna devotees instead in a bag purporting to contain John and Yoko. The ICA nonetheless wanted to screen another evening of their work, which encouraged Yoko and John to make the film *Apotheosis,* whereby a camera is attached to a hot air balloon as it leaves the earth behind.

Eventually Yoko and John did manage to beat their addiction to heroin, but only by replacing it with methadone use. Something of the agony of that experience was subsequently captured by Lennon in the song 'Cold Turkey'. It was premiered at the first official Plastic Ono Band live performance when John and Yoko, along with Eric Clapton, Klaus Voorman and Andy White appeared at the Rock'n'Roll Revival Concert in Toronto on September 13th. The event was originally intended to showcase the 50s rockers booked to perform there, but after some backstage arguments, the promoters decided to headline the show with the Plastic Ono Band, as it would represent the first concert appearance by a solo Beatle. Having had no opportunity to rehearse, the band started their set with some rock'n'roll standards, before launching into 'Give Peace A Chance' and 'Cold Turkey'. Then Yoko moved to the microphone and performed 'Don't Worry, Kyoko, (Mummy's Only Looking for Her Hand in the Snow)'. The song nominally referred back to that summer's car accident. Yoko hadn't seen or heard from her six year old daughter since she put her on a plane to Tony and New York shortly after the accident, but although generated by her personal biography, the performance allowed the expression of an intensity of anguish and loss that evokes the recent Asian history of devastation from Hiroshima to Hanoi. The song, and the band's performance, ended with a wall of guitar feedback; Lennon and Clapton leant their instruments against their amps and the musicians left the stage.

A month later, on October 9th, John's 29th birthday, Yoko again miscarried, and was informed by doctors she would never be able to have children. Nonetheless, all that autumn Yoko and John continued to become increasingly active politically. Their films were screened to raise money for Biafra, they appeared in a bag at Hyde Park Corner to protest the innocence of James Hanratty, hanged in 1962, and on November 26th Yoko accompanied John to the servants' entrance of Buckingham Palace, where he handed back his MBE "in protest against Britain's involvement in the Nigeria–Biafra thing, against our support of America in Vietnam, and against 'Cold Turkey' slipping down the charts."

In December, they created an Anti–War Room in the Apple offices, and from there continued to advertise peace by paying for billboards in major western cities to display their Christmas message, "War Is Over – If You Want It – Happy Christmas, John And Yoko." On the 15th they performed 'Cold Turkey', 'Give Peace A Chance' and 'Don't Worry, Kyoko' with an enlarged Plastic Ono Band at the Peace For Christmas benefit concert for the United Nations Children's Fund at the Lyceum Theatre, and the next day flew to Canada to discuss the possibility of staging a peace festival with John Brower, who had been involved in the Rock'n'Roll Revival festival. They spent Christmas back in London then flew to Denmark on December 29th to stay with Tony, Kyoko and Tony's new wife, Melinda. Tony had become fascinated with Christianity, and given up tobacco, alcohol and all other drugs. Yoko and John symbolically burned their cigarettes in the snow and cut off their hair, in a gesture that was both conciliatory towards Tony and his new lifestyle and an expression of their hope for a new beginning. It was, after all, the start of the 70s, as their New Year's Eve press statement had acknowledged, declaring 1970 to be

75

"Year 1 AP (After Peace)." "We believe that the last decade was the end of the old machine crumbling to pieces," they said, "And we think we can get it together, with your help. We have great hope for the new year."

And it was also, of course, the end of the 60s.

4. **Plastic Ono**

"A lot of fence–sitting, quasi hip pundits have always made a big deal of the exact point at which the Sixties ended, and the spirit of peace and love slunk off snarling," notes Mick Farren, "and the establishment we'd so carelessly challenged looked for payback." This process could already be seen in the nature of Yoko and John's political commitment, and their increased involvement in particular and specific issues. Evidence of establishment desire for payback was provided on January 16th, when police raided the London Art Gallery, which was holding an exhibition of John's lithographs, and confiscated eight of them on the grounds of obscenity. In response, Yoko and John wrote and recorded the song 'Instant Karma' in a day, working with the legendary producer Phil Spector. They promoted its February release with an appearance on *Top Of The Pops;* John sang and Yoko knitted a scarf. They donated their cut hair to an auction to raise funds for the Black House community centre, a project organised by black radical Michael X. Although the press attended the auction, they chose not to report it the next day.

The plans for the Toronto Peace Festival finally collapsed in March, and in April, Paul McCartney released the first solo Beatle album, and a statement saying he had left the group. Although in a subsequent interview he insisted no one person was to blame for the break–up of the Beatles, he implied that it was John's love for Yoko that had been a major factor. Hunter Davies, the group's official biographer, endorsed this analysis when he wrote in the *Sunday Times* that after Yoko, "the rest of the Beatles didn't matter any more" for John. Later on, John himself appeared to confirm this when he said, "That old gang of mine was over the moment I met her." Although the truth is more complex, nonetheless the result of Paul McCartney's announcement of his solo career was that Yoko was identified as the person responsible for the break–up of the Fab Four.

In April, Yoko and John received through the post a book entitled *The Primal Scream,* by Los Angeles psychotherapist Arthur Janov. They both became fascinated by the possibilities Janov's techniques seemed to offer with regard to freeing them from the psychological consequences of their past experiences, particularly their unhappy, isolated childhoods. They contacted Janov who, delighted at the prospect of having such famous patients, travelled to England with his wife Vivian to begin their treatment. Initially this was carried out at Tittenhurst, then in hotels in London, and then Janov decided to approach the US Immigration and Naturalization

Service to grant Yoko and John visas that would allow them to continue receiving therapy with him in California.

The application on medical grounds was successful, and Yoko and John returned to the US with Janov where they continued to receive treatment, that also involved attending group sessions at the Primal Institute in West Hollywood. But after a while it was here that John began to fall out with Janov, objecting to being filmed at a group session. Yoko also became more and more sceptical about Janov's theories. The experience was useful in terms of their songwriting, having a marked influence on John's *John Lennon/Plastic Ono Band* album, but as therapy it was ultimately inconclusive; the US government refused to renew John's visa, and so in July they returned to England.

The England they returned to was showing little sign that Yoko and John's designation of it as "Year 1 AP" was in any way justified. On the day 'Instant Karma' entered the charts, February 20th, three Essex University students had been arrested for attempting to firebomb a Barclays Bank to protest the bank's support for the apartheid South African regime. In May, there were more bombings, including an attempt to bomb the site of the proposed new Paddington Green Police station, which became known as the first Angry Brigade bombing. In June, just before the Conservatives assumed office, the magazine *Oz* had been closed down by the police for its "Schoolkids" issue.

Against this background, John and Yoko recorded a *Plastic Ono Band* album each in London. John's album reflected both the experience of Primal Scream therapy – 'Mother' – and the current radical focus on class–based politics – 'Working Class Hero'. Yoko's album was dominated by her radical vocalising, with John, Klaus Voorman and Ringo providing a rock–underground style backing track for her voice on the first two tracks, 'Why' and 'Why Not'. There is a continued use of autobiography to initiate direction ('Greenfield Morning I Pushed An Empty Baby Carriage All Over The City') and of avant–garde techniques – the album utilises recorded sounds, birdsong, the sound of trains, and Yoko reprises her orgasmic duetting with Ornette Coleman. There was also a problem between the intrinsic qualities of the avant–garde and the somewhat less flexible requirements of the copyright laws. It proved impossible to copyright the lyric to the song 'Why', because the law stipulated a lyric had to be at least eight lines long, and the lyric to 'Why' simply consisted of Yoko's repetition of the title.

When the albums were finished, Yoko decided she wanted to return to New York. Perhaps she was finding their particular celebrity lifestyle restrictive. In England, she was almost always treated as the subordinate partner, and recently her creativity had been expressed primarily through music, where she was always very much overshadowed by John. In an interview at the start of the year, when John had been asked about infidelity, Yoko's answer dealt more with what she perceived as the practicalities of their creative relationship. "Before we met," she said, "we were both too free. I always felt I was the creative one in the family and so I had to have my freedom. Now John and I have made a match. We don't really have close friends...we try to keep a slight distance from everybody, even with our own children. We know that if we love our children too much, then it will draw us slightly apart."

Again, the answer reflects how important emotional distance is for Yoko's creativity, although it assumes that the "match" with John, where they are paradoxically alone together, will still enable her to work creatively. John's answer had been, "We wouldn't mind going to see a bit of a sex show, you know."

Eventually, Allen Klein managed to persuade the US Immigration and Naturalization Service to grant Yoko and John new visas, and Yoko arrived in New York with John on November 26th. She immediately started work on two new film projects, with her old friend Jonas Mekas and a new recruit, Steve Gebhart, who had shown *Bottoms* whilst in charge of the Cincinnati Film Society and, thereby, awarded Yoko her first prize money, $50. One film, *Up Your Legs Forever,* was similar in concept and form to *Bottoms,* only with a different anatomical focus. The other, *Fly,* was to feature a fly crawling over a woman's naked body. "The idea of the film came to me when I thought about that joke where someone says to a man, 'Did you notice that woman's hat?' and he's looking at her bosom instead," explained Yoko. "I wondered how many people would look at the fly or the body."

To assist with organising the production of these films, Allen Klein's New York office detailed an efficient young secretary May Pang to work with Yoko and John. Her job was to help find three hundred and sixty five people who would allow their legs to be filmed – "And make sure you tell them it's for peace," insisted Yoko – and a woman who would lie still while a fly crawled over her, and a fly that would do what it was told. The filming of the first project presented relatively few problems. *Fly* was another matter. A woman had been found who could lie absolutely still for as long as required, apparently due to her ingestion of large quantities of illegal substances. Flies proved more of a problem. Filming was taking place in December, and as with 'Acorn Piece', this was the wrong time of year for the eponymous element involved in the project. Even when supplies of flies were located, despite the film crew coating the woman with honey, then coating the woman with a sugar and water solution, the flies all simply flew away. Eventually Yoko's friend Dan Richter suggested dousing a fly in liquid carbon dioxide, which slowed the fly's movements to a filmable crawl. Even so, they were unable to film the ending Yoko wanted, whereby the fly flew away out of a window and into the sunrise, so they had to suggest this conclusion by having the camera track the route of the fly's escape.

Whilst Yoko and John were working on these projects, John also gave a succession of interviews to various magazines. He was always an enthusiastic advocate of Yoko's work, and its influence on his creativity, in particular, his guitar playing. He told *Rolling Stone* that Yoko was disliked because she was a woman, Japanese and held responsible for the demise of the Beatles. Yoko was also always with John during these interviews, but even in New York she was rarely questioned by the interviewers. She did, however, on one occasion, tell another *Rolling Stone* journalist, "An artist couple is the most difficult thing... The fact is that we both paint, compose and write poetry and on that basis I think we're doing pretty well."

The films were only just completed, literally at the last minute, in time for screening at a special event at the Elgin Theatre. Unfortunately, the audience was less than appreciative, and discontent became more and more audible during the eighty minutes of *Up Your Legs Forever.* Yoko and John, however, hadn't attended the screening; they had left New York to fly to Japan to visit her parents. It was the first time she had seen them since 1962, and Yoko hadn't warned her parents in advance, instead telephoning them from the Tokyo Hilton to announce their presence in Japan. But John was at his most charming, and generally the six–week visit passed off pleasantly enough. But again, when Yoko's mother talked to the press during the visit, the focus of their attention was on John, not Yoko.

They arrived back in England in March 1971. The police had just made their first wave of arrests in response to the activities of the Angry Brigade, but the bombings still continued, targeting high profile property representing the state and the forces of capital. In some respects, the Angry Brigade with its leaderless, participatory character, was the armed struggle's realised equivalent of the theoretical concept of the Plastic Ono Band: "THE ANGRY BRIGADE IS THE MAN OR WOMAN SITTING NEXT TO YOU" ("Comminique 9"), "YOU ARE YOUR OWN LEADERS. HAVE YOUR OWN TACTICS. CONTROL YOUR OWN

STRUGGLE" ("Comminique 11"), and always ending with the slogan, "POWER TO THE PEOPLE." "Personally I found the Angry Brigade a total pain in the arse," said Mick Farren, "they had as much of an effect on the early Seventies as a marginally significant rock album... After the Brigade's first detonation, my friends and I found ourselves with the heavy–duty security services of the nation running all over our creaking little alternative society in their size thirteens, learning far more than they needed to know."

On March 19th, a bomb devastated the Ford Motor Company offices at Gant's Hill, coinciding with a nationwide strike by Ford workers. The following Angry Brigade manifesto, "Communique 7," ended with the declaration: "WE BELIEVE IN THE AUTONOMOUS WORKING CLASS. WE ARE PART OF IT. AND WE ARE READY TO GIVE OUR LIVES FOR OUR LIBERATION. POWER TO THE PEOPLE." And coincidentally, the next day, March 20th, the Plastic Ono Band single 'Power To The People' entered the charts.

Although the title reflected perfectly the sloganised position, character and aspirations of post–68 early 70s radicalism, the lyrics didn't advocate a bombing campaign. What it did have was a proto–feminist verse that demanded that comrades and brothers consider their oppression of their female partners. That same month there was a lengthy interview in the left magazine *Red Mole,* with Yoko and John talking to Robin Blackburn and Tariq Ali. John had previously engaged in an exchange of letters, "a classic New Left/psychedelic left dialogue," published in Tariq Ali's newspaper, *Black Dwarf.* In the *Red Mole* interview John gave the impression that he was now committed to the radical leftist politics that he had argued with in the earlier correspondence. John asserts that he is working class, a claim not actually born out by the economic circumstances of his childhood, and that he'd always been political. He sums up his personal experience of the success of the Beatles as "a complete oppression. I mean we had to go through humiliation upon humiliation with the middle classes and showbiz and Lord Mayors and all that."

Yoko's assessment of their position as highly successful cultural workers has a somewhat different perspective: "We are very lucky really, because we can create our own reality, John and me, but we know the important thing is to communicate with other people." John name–drops various left states and left leaders – "obviously Mao is aware of this problem and keeps the ball rolling" – while Tariq Ali and Robin Blackburn provide an accompanying ideological commentary and explain the ideologically correct answers. Yoko, however, refuses to accept the interview's shared ideology, and talks about wanting "to incite people to loosen their oppression by giving them something to work with, to build on...people who have been demoralised, who have no confidence in themselves because they have been told they have no creative ability, but must just take orders. The Establishment likes people who take no responsibility and cannot respect themselves...even after the revolution, if people don't have any trust in themselves, they'll get new problems."

Yoko also refuses to accept Blackburn's insistence on the necessity for "popular force." "Violence isn't just a conceptual thing...it could happen to your kids," she insists. Blackburn, however, sticks to his position: "Popular violence against their oppressors is always justified. It cannot be avoided." Towards the end of the interview, John introduces the subject of women's liberation: "And the women are very important too, we can't have a revolution that doesn't involve and liberate women... (Yoko's) a red hot liberationist and was quick to show me where I was going wrong... How can you talk about power to the people unless you realise the people is both sexes?" Yoko states quite simply, "You can't love someone unless you are in an equal position with them...if you have a slave around the house how can you expect to make a revolution outside it?"

The interview ends with Tariq Ali asking, "How do you think we can destroy the capitalist system here in Britain, John?" "Only by making the workers aware of the really unhappy position they are in, breaking the dream they are surrounded by," says John. "As soon as they start being aware...the workers can start to take over."

In the last interview he gave in 1980, when the subject of 'Power To The People' came up, John gave a somewhat different impression of his political engagement. He tells Andy Peebles, "I remember that was the expression going round those days... Tariq Ali had kept coming round wanting money for the *Red Mole* or some magazine or other and I used to give anybody – it was sort of Left Field, avant–garde or sort of in the Art field or political field – money kind of out of guilt, as well, because I was thinking, well, I'm working class and I am not one of them, but I am rich so therefore...I would fork out... and I kind of wrote 'Power To The People' in a way kind of as a guilt song." Yoko adds, "But...it's very heavy, very good." "Yeah, not bad," agreed John, "to me it's like a newspaper song, you know, when you write about something instant that's going on right now... the news headline with the misprints and everything but the B side was 'Open Your Box' which is worth a play, Yoko Ono in all her finery." "And which was banned at the time," says Yoko, because 'box' is American sexual slang for vagina. The US B–side was eventually changed to 'Touch Me', from her *Plastic Ono Band* album.

Having effected a reconciliation with her parents, Yoko was also concerned to develop a better relationship with her daughter, but Tony, new wife Melinda and Kyoko had left Denmark and Yoko had no idea of their whereabouts. John hired private detectives and eventually they were located in Majorca, attending a meditation course. On April 23rd, Yoko and John then travelled to the school Kyoko attended and took her away from the playground, back to their hotel, intending to fly with her back to London. When Tony found that Kyoko was missing, he went to the police saying his daughter had been kidnapped. At the hotel, Kyoko became feverish. John called the hotel doctor, and this in turn alerted the police. Yoko insisted that the Virgin Islands divorce had not given either parent custody. A temporary solution was arrived at; Kyoko was returned to Tony pending a court judgement and Yoko and John set about gathering lawyers and evidence. On May 5th, the Palma court dropped all charges against Yoko and John, and Allen Klein then brokered a meeting between both couples where a "joint custody" agreement was arrived at. Yoko and John returned to London on May 8th, not knowing that Tony, Melinda and Kyoko, in defiance of the custody agreement, would immediately vanish with no trace.

Later that month, *Apotheosis* and *Fly* were shown at the Filmmakers' Fortnight Festival in Cannes, which was an underground festival that ran alongside the official Cannes Film Festival. The audience response was similar to that of the Elgin theatre; unfortunately, this time, Yoko and John were in the audience too. At the start of June, they were back in New York and guesting at Frank Zappa's Mothers Of Invention concert at the Filmore East on June 6th. Their performance was recorded and later appeared on John's 1972 album, *Sometime In New York City*.

Back in the UK, the summer of 1971 saw the first Glastonbury Festival (a free festival then). This was counterbalanced by a revivalist Christian Festival Of Light. The Old Bailey *Oz* obscenity trial began, and the size thirteens of the heavy–duty security services of the nation were still very much hard at work. Yoko and John wrote and recorded a benefit single, 'God Save Oz', which was released on July 16th. John decided to have singer Bill Elliott perform the vocals on the A side, but the B–side 'Do The Oz' featured both Yoko and John's vocals. Underground writer Charles Shaar Murray was at the initial recording session strumming an acoustic guitar; in *Days In The Life,* he remembered the single with little enthusiasm: "Apple put out the record but nobody played it on the radio and two weeks later it was totally forgotten. It was one of Lennon's radical gestures of the time: we've done one for the Irish, now we'll do one for *Oz:* 'From Bill Haley to the Old Bailey / Freedom's arrow flies...' Some bullshit like that."

Yoko and John had also both started work on new albums in their recording studio in Tittenhurst. Yoko's was entitled *Fly.* As well as having used that insect in her recent film, Yoko also saw in the small creature's incessant buzz of activity and its capacity to annoy parallels with her own work. *Fly* is a double album that continues to explore sound but which also sees Yoko experimenting with conventional song structures. The second album is the more traditionally avant–garde, containing two soundtracks 'Airmale', from John's film *Erection,* and the soundtrack of *Fly,* and also sounds produced by Joe Jones and the Tone Deaf Music Co, eight instruments constructed by Fluxus friend and artist Joe Jones that all but played themselves. The album also produced the first solo Yoko Ono single, using the blues–rock 'Midsummer New York', which actually starts off with the standard blues convention about waking up in the morning, and the acoustic ballad 'Mrs Lennon'. As always, Yoko's creative endeavour was overshadowed by John's work, but that overshadowing was even greater than usual this time, because the album he was working on that summer was *Imagine.*

The album itself, however, actually reflected a great deal of creative input from Yoko. She was always acknowledged as providing the melody for the song 'Oh My Love'. Later, however, John admitted on several occasions how important Yoko was to the creation of the title song, which has often been cited as the most popular song of the twentieth century. Talking with Andy Peebles, he said that the song should really be credited "Lennon/Ono." "A lot of it – the lyric and the concept – came from Yoko, but those days I was a bit more selfish, a bit more macho and I sort of omitted to mention her contribution, but it was right out of *Grapefruit,* her book, there's a whole pile of pieces about imagine this and imagine that and I have given her credit now long overdue."

Although started in Tittenhurst, both albums were finished in New York. Yoko and John flew there because Tony and Kyoko were seen visiting his parents on Long Island. They carried on working on their albums at the Record Plant, while their private detectives tried unsuccessfully to locate the whereabouts of Yoko's daughter. When the recordings were finished, they returned to Tittenhurst with the intention of making a film soundtracked by the songs from their two new albums.

The filming was interrupted, like the recording, by the sudden appearance of Tony Cox. This time, it was in July in Houston, where Tony, through lawyers, instigated legal action to establish his custody over Kyoko. To add to the stress on their relationship, George Harrison invited John to appear at his August 1st fundraising concert for Bangladesh, but refused point blank to allow Yoko to appear. Also in July *Grapefruit* was issued in paperback, and Yoko and John undertook various promotional interviews and book signings. In August they joined a London demonstration protesting the sentencing of the defendants in the *Oz* trial. When sentenced, *Oz* editor Richard Neville observed "There is only an inch of difference between Labour and Conservative, it is, however, the inch in which we work and live."

On August 13th, Yoko and John booked into the St. Regis Hotel in New York. With this move the couple were effectively saying goodbye to England. They were intending henceforth to make the US, and New York in particular, their place of residence.

5. **Approximately Infinite Universe**

It was partly to be able to pursue the custody battle with Tony more effectively that Yoko and John had decided to move to the US. But there were other factors influencing this move; there was John's genuine delight in New York as a city, and Yoko's increasing problematic relationship with her own creativity. New York to Yoko represented artistic success in the past and increased artistic possibilities in the future, and the chance to re–establish an artistic identity that was not dependent upon the fact of her being attached to a Beatle. She began by mounting what was supposed to be a retrospective exhibition of her work at the Everson Museum of Art in Syracuse, entitled *This Is Not Here,* scheduled to open on John's 31st birthday. The month of September therefore saw the couple engaged in three separate significant projects – the promotion of their albums *Fly* and *Imagine,* the preparations for the Everson exhibition, and the continuing custody battle with Tony. After nearly a month of acrimonious allegations by Tony Cox, alleging violent behaviour on Yoko's part, drug abuse and nudity on John's part, the judge gave Tony and Melinda temporary custody and awarded Yoko extensive visiting rights, with a provision specifically allowing Yoko to have Kyoko for ten days at Christmas.

When *Fly* and *Imagine* were released, it was the latter that received most attention, and the title track that has achieved subsequent iconic status, becoming, according to an article in December 1999 in *The Independent On Sunday* "a non–denominational anthem for world humanism." Yoko, without whom the song would probably never have been written, recalled in the article, "It was a genuine wish, a dream for the future. It had a naivety about it, even on the level of the very simple chords. Actually, other songwriters have said that it's 'so simplistic', or things like that, and of course we can all be artistic snobs. But this was one song which John really wanted to communicate to the world, and so he dispensed with his artistic snobbery and really made it very sweet and simple – to get the message across." The article suggests that the song was also an expression of Lennon's dissatisfaction with the New Left in Britain, but this revisionist assessment ignores the statements John made at the time of the release of this "anti–religious, anti–nationalistic, anti–conventional, anti–capitalistic song." In a letter to the *Melody Maker,* he wrote, "So you think *Imagine* ain't political? It's 'Working Class Hero' with sugar on it for conservatives like yourself!"

The album also contained many songs – 'Oh Yoko', 'Jealous Guy' – that celebrated in a more conventional way John's love for Yoko. Yoko's fulfilling of the role of traditional muse, inspiring and informing John's work, has always been complicated both by the reluctance of the media and the audience to accept that Beatle John would fall so completely in love with their stereotype of Yoko as an Asian woman eight years older than he was, and the extremely direct, naked nature of much of the work their relationship provoked. From the cover of *Two Virgins,* through his lithographs of their sexual intimacy, Lennon celebrated all aspects of their relationship with a particular obsessive intensity that up till 'Imagine' generally avoided the sugar–coatings of romance and sentimentality. Yoko's work was always less interested in the details of their physicality, and gives a different emphasis to the dynamics of their relationship to the one that might be inferred from John's actual representations of it.

Looking back, she was quoted recently in the *Daily Telegraph* as saying, "As John put it, our attraction was a spiritual one. But, just by the way, physically it was OK too. But it was true, we were very 'head' people. Our work was very important for both of us. It was an artistic relationship."

Yoko decided that it wasn't possible to organise a retrospective in the space of a month, so she decided instead to invite five hundred friends and celebrities to contribute a piece of work on the theme of water to the exhibition. Yoko's piece was an installation featuring water dripping from a balcony into a miked–up saxophone, and John contributed 'Napoleon's Bladder', which was a plastic bag with something pink inside it. Many contributions gave the impression of striving to be self–consciously avant–garde. Yoko introduced the exhibition by saying, "In this show here, I'd like to prove the fact that you don't need talent to be an artist. 'Artist' is just a frame of mind. Anybody can be an artist, anybody can communicate if they are desperate enough. There is no such thing as imagination of artist. Imagination, if you are desperate enough, will come out of necessity, you will start to get all kind of imagination. Even the best artist, if they don't have the necessity, they will be dried up and they won't have any imagination."

It is the first part of her speech, ending with the claim that anybody can be an artist, that is the most often quoted. But perhaps it is the last sentence that was, for Yoko, more significant; she stages an exhibition of water pieces, three rooms of work contributed by other people, produces one piece herself that involves only drips, and talks about artists becoming dried up.... When the exhibition opened, much of it was ruined within a matter of hours. Nonetheless, the general critical response was very favourable, and *Newsweek* and the *Nation* taking this as an opportunity to review her previous body of work. That autumn also saw a revival of the theatrical piece 'A Grapefruit in the World of Park', an appearance on Channel 13 with Jonas Mekas discussing conceptual art, and an imaginary show outside the Museum of Modern Art involving a man carrying a sandwich board advertising the release of a collection of flies sprayed with Yoko's favourite perfume, and a book of photographs recording their subsequent adventures.

Yoko and John also continued their commitment to radical politics, although there was a significant difference between the politics of the US radicals they associated with and the class–based ideology of Trotskyite politics they had been increasingly involved with in Britain. On arrival in New York, they had been contacted by counter–culture activists Jerry Rubin and Abbie Hoffman, two founder members of the Youth International Party ("Yippies") and two of the Chicago Seven (convicted of "crossing statelines with intention to riot" for their part in organising the protests at the 1968 Democratic Party convention in Chicago). Yippies disparaged the "ideological left". Rubin's book *Do It!* declared, "There's a thousand miles between their actions and their ideology...Their theories don't explain us – a revolutionary movement that has come out of affluence, not poverty...The Yippies see white middle–class youth a revolutionary class...Capitalism will die because it cannot satisfy its own children." The book expresses the Yippie manifesto with a plethora of sloganistic aphorisms, "We gotta reduce politics to the simplicity of a rock'n'roll lyric...Politics is how you live your life, not whom you vote for...(in Yippieland) People will farm in the morning, make music in the afternoon and fuck wherever and whenever they want to." Rubin later said, "I felt that yippie was Beatles music put to politics, and John was the most politically aware of the Beatles."

Accompanied by street musician David Peel, they met Yoko and John in Washington Square, and immediately established a rapport. When Yoko and John moved into a small flat in Bank Street, in the traditionally bohemian Greenwich Village area, Rubin and Hoffman became frequent visitors, and an important means of their introduction to leading members of the wide spectrum of US counterculture, and the causes and issues which were then current.

In November, Yoko and John appeared at the Apollo Theatre in Harlem, in a benefit for the relatives of black prisoners killed by guards in the Attica prison uprising. Yoko performed her new feminist song

'Sisters, Oh Sisters', and John performed 'Attica State'. Their appearance further added to the reports being compiled against them by the security services. On December 10th, Yoko and John, accompanied by David Peel and Jerry Rubin, appeared at a benefit concert in Ann Arbor for White Panther Minister of Information John Sinclair, one–time manager of the MC5, a band who had travelled to Chicago to play as part of the protests in 1968. The following year Sinclair had announced, "The MC5 is totally committed to the revolution. With our music and our economic genius we plunder the unsuspecting straight world for money and the means to carry out our program, and revolutionize its children at the same time... We don't have guns yet – not all of us anyway – because we have more powerful weapons – direct access to millions of teenagers is one of our most potent, and their belief in us is another. But we will use guns if we have to – we will do anything – if we have to. We have no illusions."

By 1971, he was serving a ten year sentence for selling two spliffs to an undercover policeman. Commenting on the sentence, Sinclair observed, "You get nine and a half – ten years for smoking weed and promoting revolutionary culture, but for taking part in a demonstration you get ninety days. A demonstration is not a threat." Rubin described Sinclair's release from prison three days after the Ann Arbor concert – albeit as a result of a previously arranged Appeal Court hearing – as "a stunning victory for the merger of music and politics."

Yoko worked particularly hard on the organisation of the benefit. A negative review of the concert in the *Village Voice* prompted Yoko to write in its defence: "Both in the West and the East music was once separated into two forms. One was court music, to entertain the aristocrats. The other was folk songs, sung by the people to express their emotions and their political opinions... Aristocrats of our age, critics, reviewed the Ann Arbor Rally and criticised the musical quality for not coming up to their expectations. That was because they lost the ears to understand the type of music that was played there...We went back to the original concept of folk music. Like a newspaper, the function was to present the message accurately and quickly... Also it is supposed to stimulate people among the audience and to make them think, 'Oh, it's so simple, even I could do it.' It should not alienate the audience with its professionalism but communicate to the audience the fact that they, the audience, can be just as creative as the performers on the stage..."

In December, Yoko and John's Christmas song 'Happy Christmas (War Is Over)' was released. Ostensibly a politicised contemporary antidote to the self–satisfied sentimentality of "traditional festive songs – "What we wanted was to have something besides 'White Christmas'," said John later, it came to represent" for Yoko and John a more personal message when, after having told her mother she didn't want to see her, and despite the court order allowing Yoko access over the Christmas period, Kyoko and Tony suddenly disappeared again.

Throughout the winter of 1971–72, Yoko and John continued to meet with US radicals, and the US security services continued to monitor their activities. Rubin and Hoffman cherished plans of Yoko and John spearheading a "musical–political caravan (to) tour the United States, raise money to feed the poor and free prisoners from jail," culminating in San Diego to coincide with the Republican convention. John later insisted in a 1980 interview with *Playboy* magazine that he responded to the San Diego idea by adopting the same position on "popular violence" that Yoko had expressed in the *Red Mole* interview. "When they described their plans...It was the poets and the straight politicals divided. Ginsberg was with us. He kept saying, 'What are we trying to do, create another Chicago?' That's what they wanted. We said, 'We ain't buying this. We're not going to draw children into a situation to create violence.' But then the story got out that we *were* going to San Diego. That was enough to get the Immigration on us."

There are still persistent allegations that the FBI asked for and received a file on Yoko and John's activities in Britain from MI5. According to *The Guardian,* in an article printed in February 2000, "The MI5 file is believed to contain claims that Lennon helped to fund the Workers Revolutionary Party in Britain, paying £46,000 to the Trotskyist group whose supporters included the actress Vanessa Redgrave, and also gave money to *Red Mole*, a Marxist magazine edited by Tariq Ali, the former leftwing student leader...According to the former MI5 officer, David Shayler, the British security service files also say that Lennon gave money to the official IRA, before it split in the early 1970s, when the Provisional IRA – responsible for the subsequent terrorist campaign – was formed."

Ironically, as they became the targets of increased surveillance, Yoko and John began appearing regularly on that staple of US mainstream Middle America culture, the television talk show. These appearances culminated in their co–hosting the Mike Douglas Show for a week in February 1972. On the songs they sang they were backed by local New York underground band, Elephant's Memory, to whom they had been introduced by Jerry Rubin in January. They invited Rubin and Black Panther Bobby Seale on to the show, and performed a couple of songs with Chuck Berry. Yoko explained, "We tried to show that we're working to change the world, not with dollars but with love...we tried to show that we're not just freaks shouting and screaming about it, but we're thinking in terms of a balanced life."

Yoko performed 'Midsummer New York', 'Sisters, Oh Sisters', and also, on the final show, a traditional Japanese folk song, 'Sakura'. With Elephant's Memory providing most of the backing musicians, John and Yoko were also spending much of February in the studio, with Phil Spector, recording their recent "newspaper" songs. To underline the urgent, contemporary nature of these songs, the resultant double album *Sometime In New York City* was presented with a mock newspaper cover. The first two sides contained the songs previewed at benefits or on the Mike Douglas Show, while the second album contained two older live recordings. The new songs were mainly credited Lennon/Ono, and three were credited to Yoko alone, and two to John.

February also saw the *New York Times* publish Yoko's article 'The Feminisation of Society', and Yoko and John also maintained their contacts with the radical press, contributing articles to the underground magazine *Sundance*. Their political position here was also a clear articulation of Yoko's feminism; "In two–thousand years of effort, men have demonstrated to us their failure in running the world. Instead of falling into the same trap as men, women can offer something that society never, because of male dominance, had before. That is feminine direction... We can now change the society with the feminine touch, or rather with feminine intelligence and awareness, into a basically organic, non–competitive one based on love rather than reasoning. The result will be balance, peace and contentment."

With their visas about to expire at the end of February, Yoko and John hired attorney Leon Wildes to apply for an extension. Their application, usually a formality, was refused point blank, the New York Immigration Services citing the1968 conviction for cannabis as a reason for their refusal. But it rapidly became clear that the US authorities had no intention of allowing the Lennons to remain in the US because of their political activities. Ironically, on March 3rd, two days after the Immigration Services declared Yoko and John had 15 days in which to leave the country, the courts in Houston granted Yoko temporary custody of Kyoko within the USA. Wildes then attempted to change the category of Yoko and John's visa applications to that of "third–preference immigrant" status, which was reserved for people whose "exceptional ability in the sciences or arts" would be of benefit to "the national economy, cultural interests or welfare of the United States." He advised Yoko and John to distance themselves from their activist friends, advice they only partly followed.

They stopped seeing Jerry Rubin so regularly, possibly also as a result of the FBI spreading a rumour that he was a CIA agent. In April, they released the single 'Woman Is The Nigger Of The World', a feminist song John elaborated from a remark Yoko made when interviewed several years before for the magazine *Nova*. Although it was promptly banned because of its use of the 'N' word, it still failed to chart. They also held a press conference to announce the creation of Nutopia, a country with no borders or passports. As two of its ambassadors, they said, they claimed diplomatic immunity. But it was more the hard work of Wildes that delayed their deportations, and allowed them time to assemble a stellar cast of witnesses willing to testify as to their exceptional abilities in the arts. They made a public appearance at the National Peace Rally in New York, protesting against the escalation of the Vietnam war, and on June 12th *Sometime in New York City* was released. It was hardly an album likely to support the claim that they possessed exceptional abilities in the arts that would benefit the United States; many of the songs focussed on cases of injustice within the US, and what was worse, nobody liked it, and it sold very badly.

Their appeal against their deportations, however, was going slightly better. Yoko discovered that her marriage to Tony Cox had provided her with her 'green card' permanent resident status, and the court was presented with petitions, statements and speeches by cultural workers supporting their appeal. Partly as a break from the stress of the legal process, and partly to lessen their use of methadone, which John had become particularly dependent upon, they set off to travel across America to California in a chauffeur driven car.

In California, they finally met Elliot Mintz, a radio broadcaster with whom they had previously developed a friendship by phone, and who would become one of their closest associates as the decade wore on. They visited an acupuncturist who helped cure them of their methadone use. John said that he also gave them advice that eventually helped them conceive a child together: "Eat well and behave yourself. No drugs, no drink, eat well. You have a child in eighteen months."

Upon returning to New York, they were approached to appear at a benefit concert on August 29th at Madison Square gardens for the One To One Foundation. The foundation had been set up to support people with learning difficulties following a documentary by TV journalist Geraldo Rivera, revealing the appalling way they were being treated in a New York institution. Yoko and John rehearsed with Elephant's Memory, and the concert raised one and a half million dollars for the foundation. However, when the concert was later shown on television, Yoko had been entirely edited out, as had Rivera.

In October, Yoko began recording a solo album. Again, Elephant's Memory provided the musicians, and again the finished work was presented as a double album. But *Approximately Infinite Universe* was a double album composed of twenty–two songs credited entirely to Yoko, songs that contained radical, mainly feminist messages, but which were characterised by the conventions of 70s rock rather than by the conventions of the avant–garde. Recordings continued into November, the month of the Presidential elections, with Nixon seeking re–election, challenged by the Democrat McGovern. Yoko and John went to watch the result at Jerry Rubin's apartment. What happened that night was ostensibly of great political significance; despite the best efforts of the revolution, the election result represented yet another victory for the establishment. In retrospect, it put a last final full stop to John's radicalism and political activism. But what happened that night in Rubin's apartment would also prove a significant watershed in John and Yoko's personal relationship too.

6. Feeling The Space

In an interview in *The Daily Telegraph* in 1998, Yoko recalled that, as it became apparent that Nixon had won, "John became totally drunk and pulled a woman into the next room and started to make love. Nobody could leave because all the coats were in that room...The wall was paper–thin and you could hear the noise...In the middle of all this, a New York celeb woman chose to make conversation with me (saying of John) 'He's a great man...he is a wonderful man.'...with an angry look as if to blame me for not rejoicing for what was happening in that room...Something was lost that night for me."

Jerry Rubin's insensitive attempts to excuse John's reversion to rock star behaviour –"McGovern lost. All of us were totally devastated. You can imagine how John felt about it. It was a real blow to us." – is actually a very revealing index of how exhausted the radical movement John had espoused had become. It was an interesting trajectory, from love, to peace, to people power, through Trotskyites in London and Yippies in New York, to relying on a Democratic victory in the Presidential elections.

Rubin, in his book *Growing (Up) at 37,* analyses the defeat of the youth revolution. Part of the problem was the downside of basing a revolution on the issue of generation rather than class. Rubin himself was publicly 'retired' from the movement by young activists in July 1972 when he became thirty. But he also identifies the 1970 Kent State shootings of four white student protesters as a significant moment; as State reaction gathered momentum and force "there was tremendous pressure on all activists to translate their radical talk into action – shoot a gun or plant a bomb."

In May 1972, a Weathermen bomb exploded in a Pentagon washroom, but what brought Nixon down was not the revolution, but the scandal following on months later from Republican attempts to bug the offices of the Democrats in the Watergate building. In Britain, again it wasn't the underground or the Angry Brigade that brought down the Conservative government, but trade union action spearheaded by a miners' strike. Even John's support for Michael X added to the pervading climate of failure, when in August 1972 the black radical was sentenced to death for murder in Port of Spain. Rubin attempted to evaluate the situation in 1972 positively: "The movement ended when its particular historical task was over. We curtailed US involvement in Vietnam and created the atmosphere that led to Watergate and the fall of Nixon. Some people feel that because the movement ended, it failed. That is not true. The 1960s transformed

America's consciousness in immeasurable ways. Then we discovered that although we had exposed the hypocrisy and inequality of American society...We were as chauvinistic as the society itself, radicals as far as Vietnam and blacks were concerned, but imitation John Waynes in our personal lives...we ourselves had been conditioned by that society, and we had to release ourselves from that conditioning. This led to the Inner Revolution of the 1970s."

But if the revolution no longer provided an organising principle for John's daily existence by the end of 1972, this was not the case for Yoko; the feminism continued to animate both her life and her work.

'Happy Christmas (War Is Over)' was released in Britain in December, but Kyoko remained missing. The deportation issue was not likely to be resolved until the new year. That winter John watched television, and Yoko gave interviews promoting *Approximately Infinite Universe,* released in January 1973. The album was generally well–received, one review concluding, "she writes better music than Sylvia Plath and better poetry than Dory Previn." Although dedicated to "my best friend John of the second sex," and including the statement of friendship 'Song For John', and the mawkish sympathy of 'I Want My Love To Rest Tonight', in reality, there was now increasing distance and arguments between Yoko and John.

In an attempt to ease the tension in their relationship, in February they moved into a much larger apartment in the prestigious Dakota Building overlooking Central Park. Yoko was finally awarded permanent custody of Kyoko, but the private detectives were still unable to find her. In May, Yoko, minus John but backed by Elephant's Memory, headlined a benefit concert for a listener–sponsored New York radio station. In June, Yoko and John briefly returned to politics when they attended the Watergate hearings in Washington, and took part in a demonstration at the South Vietnamese embassy. Yoko accompanied by a somewhat subdued John on guitar, also performed at a conference organised by the National Organisation for Women.

Perhaps due to the relative critical success of *Approximately Infinite Universe,* Yoko was also recording a new album of songs that continued to promote a feminist perspective. Not wanting to use Elephant's Memory again, she had asked drummer Jim Keltner to assemble a backing band, the mainstays of which were guitarist David Spinozza, bass player Gordon Edwards, and Kenny Ascher on keyboards. John had also resumed songwriting and by August he had completed the songs for a new, determinedly non–political album, *Mind Games,* and he was so impressed by Yoko's band, he decided to use them on his record too. Production assistant on both recordings was May Pang, who by the summer of 1973 was working full time for John and Yoko. During the period John was mixing *Mind Games,* he began an affair with May; they would finish work at the studio, have sex in her flat, then John would return to Yoko and the Dakota, where May would arrive in the morning for work. In her memoir, May insists that Yoko engineered the affair because of the tensions in their relationship, as a way of controlling John's increasing tendency towards infidelity.

Yoko insists, "It's more delicate than that." She considered John's behaviour on the night of Nixon's re–election "unforgettable," and months later she was aware that he was still "thinking about other girls, or looking around...I didn't want somebody thinking about things like that when they're sitting with me. It's very unflattering, isn't it?" So she says, "I told John that I thought a trial separation would be a good idea: 'We're both young and attractive – it's crazy to stay together just because we're married...That's not what we were about, was it?" Yoko says she suggested John might like to move to Los Angeles, because he had had a good time there when he was with the Beatles, and that she suggested several travelling companions, including May Pang. In 1980 John glossed over the details by simply asserting, "The feminist side of me died slightly and (Yoko) said, 'Get the hell out' and kicked me out." In fact, it wasn't until October that John finally left for Los Angeles with May Pang, whilst Yoko was away in Chicago at a feminist conference.

John's absence gave the title of Yoko's new album, *Feeling The Space,* released in November, and "dedicated to the sisters who died in pain and sorrow and those who are now in prisons and in mental hospitals for being unable to survive in the male society," an added element of autobiographical irony. The sleeve contained a prose piece originally published in the *New York Times,* that made reference to Yoko's childhood, racism, sexism, survival, and the beauty and fragility of existence, concluding with, "All we have to do is just admire each other and love each other twenty–four hours a day until we vanish. The rest is just foreplay...In my mind I'm really an eternal sphinx. Shake my hand for what it's worth. There is a wind that never dies."

But although the tracks were primarily very polished exemplars of 70s studio rock music as performed by highly efficient studio session players, rather than great songs in themselves, they did soundtrack some of Yoko's best conventional rock vocals to date. The musicians are also adept at the pastiche jazz used on the humorous 'Men, Men', but completely at a loss when Yoko uses a melody that derives from Japanese cultural models, resorting unsuccessfully to country music in an attempt to accompany her. Nonetheless, it is immediately obvious that the proud female persona the songs present was incompatible with the oafish rocker persona John presented during his eighteen month 'lost weekend' in Los Angeles with the long–suffering May Pang. However, Yoko and John couldn't entirely let go of each other, and kept in touch by phone. Yoko recalls that "John was incredibly ecstatic for four days. He called me to thank me... After four days, he called me with a totally different voice: 'I've had enough. I want to come home.' I laughed it off. It was too soon."

In an interview with David Sheff for *Playboy* in 1980, Yoko described their separation as resulting primarily from "pressure" and her creative frustrations. "I think I really needed some space because I was used to being an artist and free and all that, and when I got together with John, because we're always in the public eye, I lost the freedom. And also, both of us were together all the time...twenty–four hours a day. And the pressure was particularly strong on me because of being the one who stole John Lennon from the public or something...and I think my artwork suffered." She said, "I'm what I call a 'moving on' girl. Rather than deal with problems in relationships, I've always moved on... I thought I had to move on again because I was suffering being with John. I thought I wanted to be free from being Mrs Lennon. Society doesn't understand that women can be castrated. I felt castrated. Before that I was doing all right, thank you..."

Unfortunately, when rid of Mr Lennon and the necessity of being Mrs Lennon, Yoko found herself unable to recover the level of creativity she had enjoyed before they met, when her highly imaginative work had mediated her acute sense of isolation. She maintained that she didn't take the opportunity to "look around" for other relationships. "What I found out is that for guys, it's very easy. You go somewhere and everybody arranges so you can have fun. With a woman or a wife of a person, I think it's a different situation," she said in an interview in *UNCUT*. "Nobody's going to suggest or help you. You're just sitting in the corner. I went to a Buddhist lecture and learnt a new mantra. I went through all different religious organisations to check out things. All different kinds of philosophy I got into, new age philosophy more than the old ones."

She also continued to develop her understanding of the business world, attending meetings with their lawyers, and in John's absence, taking a more active part in these proceedings. In 1974, she also started talking openly about wanting to divorce John.

But as far as new work was concerned, despite renewing old friendships with Andy Warhol, Allen Ginsberg and Ornette Coleman, there was no Yoko renaissance. Yoko's imagination seemed to have reduced itself to fit within the conventions of the 70s rock album. She worked on a new set of songs, entitled *A Story,* and started to record them with the same nucleus of musicians she had used on the previous album. Unreleased until 1997, the predominant atmosphere of the album is one of loss, loneliness and longing. The front cover image suggests autobiography, with a photograph of Yoko as a small child, sitting in a lifebelt. The back cover shows her again as a child, dressed as Shirley Temple, "winning the first prize at the costume party." Significantly, with the recording of *Rock And Roll*, John also made an album that looked back longingly at the past, again packaged with a nostalgic cover image.

In August 1974, Yoko and her band toured Japan. The Japanese press, and the Japanese public, received her unsympathetically, and treated her as a foreigner. In October she had a week's residency at Kenny's Castaways, in Greenwich Village, which again failed to receive much in the way of a positive response. John, meanwhile, had been affecting the lifestyle of the professional 70s rock star. As well as tiresome behaviour in public and being obnoxious to the working class people who had to put up with it, this included making guest contributions on other rock star's albums, and having other rock stars make guest appearances on his own recordings. Elton John had played piano on John's 'Whatever Gets You Through The Night', and exacted a promise from John that if the song reached number one, John would join Elton onstage at his next New York concert. The song did indeed become a US number one, so on November 28th John joined Elton onstage at Madison Square Gardens and performed three songs with him.

Yoko had maintained contact with John throughout their separation; as well as frequent telephone calls, she had visited him in Los Angeles, and he had seen her in New York. On the day of Elton's Madison Square concert, a friend who owned a gallery asked her if she wanted to go. Yoko says she was initially reluctant, but had her secretary send John and Elton each a gardenia. Her friend persisted in asking her to go to the gig "So at the last minute, I decided to go as a favour to this guy...John came out at the end as a surprise guest. People were so excited that the whole Garden was shaking. I looked at him and tears ran down my cheek. He was looking lonely. He was looking scared. He bowed once too often. This was not the John I knew."

When Yoko went backstage "John couldn't believe his eyes. We looked at each other for the longest time...We couldn't take our eyes off each other. It was terrible. Oh, God, please don't do this to me, again, I said to myself. I want a life, remember? 'You're looking very good,' John said...That's how we came back together again."

7. **A Heart Play**

For both Yoko and John, the reality was that they had exhausted their language of and their capacity for meaningful creativity; in the course of their relationship they had outlived, outworn, and grown tired of the loneliness and the demons and the delights that had previously animated their work. All they had left was that shared history, and each other.

May Pang gives a somewhat different account of Yoko and John's meeting after the concert, and says the reconciliation wasn't completed until the following January, when Yoko arranged a meeting for John at the Dakota to cure his nicotine addiction, and she maintains she continued to see John secretly for some time after he announced to her, "Yoko has allowed me to come home." Yoko and John's account also describes the reconciliation as a process. In 1980, Yoko said that after the Madison Square meeting "We dated...It was really like starting to know each other again. I wasn't sure yet. I was thinking, Am I ready to go back to that – um – pandemonium...Some moments when we really felt, Ah, we'd be crazy *not* to be together, I would think about it all and finally say, 'All right, you'd better go now.'...But we were *crying* about it. It was very difficult...We had to clean our aura."

In the major 1980 interviews with David Sheff and Andy Peebles, tactfully, no–one refers to May Pang at all. Ironically, what happened to her was what had happened all too often to Yoko as an Asian woman having a relationship with Beatle John; she became invisible.

At the start of March, Yoko told John she was pregnant. Yoko was over forty; she had been told after her last miscarriage that she wouldn't be able to have any more children, and John had been told there was a problem with his sperm. They, therefore, made sure that the pregnancy was prioritised, and that Yoko did nothing to exert herself. With the Beatles finally officially dissolved, a lot of the business issues that had occupied their attention disappeared. John cancelled work on a new album, and spent all his time in tending to Yoko's needs. On October 7th, John's appeal against his deportation order was finally successful, and the Judge instructed the Immigration and Naturalisation Service to review his application for permanent resident status. Then two days later, on John's 35th birthday, their child, a boy, was born. It was a Caesarean birth, not without problems, "not because of her age, but because of a screw–up in the hospital and the fucking price of fame," said John. "Somebody had made a transfusion of the wrong blood type into Yoko...she starts to go rigid, and then shake from the pain and trauma. I run up to this nurse and say, 'Go get the doctor!' ...He walks in, hardly notices that Yoko is going through fucking *convulsions,* goes straight for me, smiles, shakes my hand and says, 'I've always wanted to meet you, Mr. Lennon, I always enjoyed your music.'"

They called their son Sean Ono Lennon, and went home to their Dakota apartment and tried to become what neither of them had known themselves, a close and loving family. With the luxury of wealth, Yoko and John were able to use the birth to redefine and recreate themselves. Paradoxically, that redefinition and recreation involved both of them ceasing to work as creative artists, but gave new meaning to their idea "our life is our art"; Yoko recreated herself as a business person, and John recreated himself as a househusband. Yoko made money and John made bread. They made few public appearances. On July 27th 1976, John and Yoko finally collected John's 'green card'. When asked what his plans were, John answered, "I hope to continue living here with my family and make music."

Perhaps it was just as well that he didn't carry out the latter intention. In 1976, the important music was being made not by rock stars like Lennon, but by a motley collection of disaffected British youth, in groups with generally a higher percentage of working class heroes in them than was actually the case with the Beatles. The day before Sean's first birthday, The Sex Pistols, the group spearheading punk rock, masterminded by a manager whose manifesto included fond memories of the Situationists and 1968, signed a £40,000 two year contract with the Beatles old record label, EMI. In 1977, Yoko negotiated a very favourable settlement that severed the connection with Allen Klein, and the family flew to Japan for a visit to Yoko's parents that lasted several months. Back in England, The Clash song '1977' kicked off with the defiantly iconoclastic "No Elvis, no Beatles, no Rolling Stones" (though singer Joe Strummer would later sometimes add, "Except John Lennon!" after "no Beatles" when performing the song live). After returning to New York, Yoko invested in farms and dairy livestock in Delaware County (in 1980 one of the cows resulting from this venture would be sold for $265,000). She began to collect artefacts from ancient Egypt (an interest that was already manifest on the cover of 1973's *Feeling The Space*) and visited the pyramids with John. Also in 1977, her work as a creative artist was recognised by an entry about her being included in the highly respected publication *Contemporary Artists, 1977.*

But with the absence of any actual creative work to focus upon, the media, whose attention they had so long excited, redefined Yoko and John simply as a celebrity couple, famous for being famously eccentric. Stories, rumours and leaks by insiders within the Dakota came increasingly to characterise the way Yoko and John were perceived during the latter half of the decade. Many of them ranged from the ludicrous to the scurrilous, and almost all of them were negative and uncorroborated. "The fun of when we weren't doing anything was all these amazing stories," said John. "They had in the *Daily Mail, Daily Express* that I'd gone bald...and the other one was that I'd made this extraordinary statement (saying) I've made my contribution to society...and I'll no longer work again."

Yoko's interest in guidance systems like numerology, the tarot and astrology receive exaggerated importance, often presented in sinister terms as a devotion to and manipulation of the occult for her own ends, subtly perpetuating the negative image of the scheming, acquisitive oriental who had destroyed the nice Fab Four. Her achievement in becoming an efficient administrator of their business interests is also often presented in a similar light. It has been a standard criticism of 'Imagine' that its Nutopian sentiments about imagining no possessions are undermined by the fact of it having been written by a rich hippy on an expensive grand piano in a manor house near Ascot.

In an article entitled 'You may say I'm a charlatan' published in the deeply conservative *Sunday Telegraph* in September 2003, Robert Elms wrote, "In our small north London council house, my mum struggling as a single parent to bring up three sons, we didn't have to imagine, we just had to look round the living–room, certainly no possessions that weren't on hire purchase." His article further lampoons Lennon by sneering "This is the man who dreamed up the idea that it was a profound political act to sit in a bag," a statement that both misunderstands the nature of the Fluxus movement and in its misattribution renders Yoko once again invisible. Only recently have some journalists started treating Yoko's talk about the Buddhist concept of non–attachment seriously.

As well as the prurient press interest, Yoko and John were also aware of other consequences of their celebrity; they received a succession of anonymous telephone calls threatening the family and demanding money, and every day there was the constant presence of the fans, faithfully, obsessively waiting for them outside the Dakota building.

John and Yoko broke their silence with a full–page advertisement in the *New York Times* on May 27th 1979, entitled 'A Love Letter from John and Yoko to People Who Ask Us What, When, and Why'. It explained that their silence was a silence of love, and reinforced the impression of them as being two complacent, affluent boring old farts who had entirely lost touch with the punk rock realities of everybody else's daily existence. It is therefore ironic that it was after listening to a cassette of post–punk new wave bands just over a year later in Bermuda that Lennon decided to start writing and recording again. John saw a clear link between the Plastic Ono Band, particularly in regard to Yoko's performances, and the new groups like the B52's. He was adamant that Yoko should have an equal input into the project, with their songs forming a male – female dialogue.

Once started, the project proceeded at a rapid pace, and in August twenty–two songs were recorded in ten days at the Hit Factory and the Record Plant studios. Fourteen were selected for the album, entitled *Double Fantasy (A Heart Play)*, which was to be released on the Geffen Records label. Of Yoko's seven songs, two had been written in 1973, and one, 'Hard Times Are Over' had actually been recorded for the unreleased album *A Story*. In keeping with the male–female dialogue structure of the album they are largely conventional songs about relationships, but nonetheless several of her tracks are characterised by an idiosyncratic approach to form, that isn't so much avant–garde anymore, more an imaginative use of sound that anticipates subsequent developments in sampling.

When the album was released on 17th November, although it immediately sold well, critical reaction to Yoko's contribution was mixed. However, Charles Shaar Murray, who in the mid 70s had become one of the most authoritative rock critics with his work for the *New Musical Express* (despite writing in 1976 that The Clash were "the kind of garage band who should be speedily returned to their garage, preferably with the motor running"), thought Yoko's songs were the strongest feature of the album. Yoko and John promoted their new album with photo–sessions and in–depth interviews, in which they answered questions with an apparent frankness about all aspects of their life together. In fact, they used the opportunity to present a carefully airbrushed revision of their shared history. Drug use was discussed safely distanced in the past of 'Cold Turkey', John admitted Yoko's importance in the writing of 'Imagine', but May Pang was conspicuous by her absence, and Lennon did his best to smooth over and downplay his past political commitments.

Yoko was more consistent in her continued feminism, and also reiterated and developed the ideas she had expressed in defence of the John Sinclair benefit. "Pop music is the people's form," she told David Sheff. "Intellectuals trying to communicate with the people usually fail...Forget all the intellectual garbage, all the ritual of that, and get down to the real feeling – simple, good human feeling – and express it in a sort of simple language that reaches people. No bullshit. If I want to communicate with people I should use their language. Pop songs are that language."

But both Yoko and John were intent on presenting the image of a relationship that had survived. John is open about his dependence on Yoko, who he also calls "Mother," and acknowledges how much she has taught him. And she speaks of him with both affection for the person and respect for the work. The album is deeply autobiographical, but unlike their earliest, determinedly avant–garde, collaborations together, Yoko and John were ambitiously asserting that their particular personal history distilled and reflected the general social condition. In the Sheff interview Yoko makes the point clearly: "OK, we had the energy in the Sixties, in the seventies we separated, but let's start over in the eighties...I believe we will blossom in the eighties."

Unfortunately, the couple whose relationship would best represent the coming decade wasn't the new–age Yoko and John, but the New Right Maggie and Ron. In Britain, Thatcher was already planning to ensure there would be no more working class heroes; never again would miners bring down a conservative government, because within five years time, she would close all their mines down, with the aid of a police force acting as the armed wing of the Tory Party. In the US, Reagan was embarking on a programme of barely covert military operations that would brutally put down the revolutionary movements attempting to give genuine power to the people of Central America. Punk rock was also something else that wouldn't be allowed to happen again. Domestic populations were to be kept docile by an increased and all pervasive media culture that would feed them a dumbed–down diet of trivia and celebrity. "I'm amazed that people can be so concerned about someone else's life," said Yoko in the *Playboy* interview. "I mean, what about their *own* lives? *Every* life is interesting. Every life can be a huge encyclopaedia. There's not that much difference between our lives and somebody else's. You can pick a person on a street and start asking questions, and you'll find that it's full of miracles. It's a pity somebody has to think his life is less interesting than ours, and put his mind onto our lives."

At the end of the interview, asked about 'Hard Times Are Over (For A While)', Yoko had said, "It's a prayer...What inspired me, though, was remembering when John and I went cross country from New York to San Francisco in a car and we had to stop for gas or something in a sort of like nowhere city. While our driver was getting gas, John and I were standing on the corner of the street looking at each other. I didn't know the name of the city or anything. It didn't matter where we were when we looked into each other's eye

On December 6th, Andy Peebles concluded his interview by asking John, "One final question to you. What about your private life and your own sense of security these days?" John replied, "(Yoko) told me that, yes, you can walk on the street. You know. She says, You will be able to walk here...I can go right out this door now and go in a restaurant. You want to know how great that is?"

Two days later, returning from the studio with a remix of Yoko's 'Walking On Thin Ice', Yoko and John step out of their limousine outside the Dakota building. They walk past the usual collection of fans waiting there. One of them calls out, "Mr. Lennon." John stops to turn round, and is shot four times in the back by an obsessive fan who feels Lennon has let him down.

There is one long scream, and it sounds like it will never end.

Sources

Listed below are the main sources used for *John and Yoko*.
The all–important human resources were provided by my fellow writers Barb and Alan, researcher Ian Drummond, who never minded when I phoned him or how obscure my question was, and conversations with my friends Ken Hunt, who lent me his Yoko Ono cuttings and CDs, and Boff Whalley, who gave me the benefit of his magnificent Beatles obsession.
Most important though, was Yoko Ono herself. I met her when I visited her *Women's Room* exhibition in the Musée d'Art Moderne de la Ville de Paris, in September 2003. Yoko: thank you.

Books

Ali, Tariq and Watson, Susan: *1968 Marching In The Streets* (Bloomsbury 1998)
Clayson, Alan: *John Lennon* (Sanctuary 2003)
Clayson, Alan and Leigh, Spencer: *The Walrus Was Ringo – 101 Beatles Myths Debunked* (Chrome Dreams 2003)
Farren, Mick: *Give The Anarchist A Cigarette* (Pimlico 2002)
Farren, Mick and Barker, Edward: *Watch Out Kids* (Open Gate Books 1972)
Green, Jonathan: *Days in the Life* (Heineman 1988)
Giuliano, Geoffrey: *The Lost Beatles Interviews* (Virgin 1995)
Giuliano, Geoffrey: *Lennon In America* (Robson Books 2001)
Hopkins, Jerry: *Yoko Ono A Biography* (Sidgwick and Jackson 1987)
Neville, Richard: *Playpower* (Paladin 1971)
Pang, May and Edwards, Henry: *Loving John* (Warner Books 1983)
Peebles, Andy, Lennon, John and Ono, Yoko: *The Lennon Tapes* (BBC 1981)
Rubin, Jerry: *Do It!* (Simon and Schuster 1970)
Rubin, Jerry: *Growing (Up) At 37* (M Evans 1976)
Seale, Patrick and McConville, Maureen: *Red Flag Black Flag* (Ballantine 1968)
Sheff, David: *Last Interview* (Pan Books 2001)
Vague, Tom: *Anarchy In The UK The Angry Brigade* (AK Press 1997)
Records:
Yoko Ono: *Ono Box* (Ryko 1992)
Yoko Ono/John Lennon: *Unfinished Music No.1. Two Virgins* (Ryko RCD 10411)

Yoko Ono/John Lennon: *Unfinished Music No. 2. Life With The Lions* (Ryko RCD 10412)
John & Yoko: *Wedding Album* (Ryko RCD 10413)
Yoko Ono/Plastic Ono Band (Ryko RCD 10414)
Yoko Ono with Plastic Ono Band: *Fly* (Ryko RCD 10415/16)
Yoko Ono with Plastic Ono Band: *Approximately Infinite Universe* (Ryko RCD 10417/18)
Yoko Ono with Plastic Ono Band: *Feeling The Space* (Ryko RCD 10419)
Yoko Ono: *A Story* (Ryko RCD 10420)

Articles
Daily Telegraph, Ono, Yoko: Just Like Starting Over (October 1998)
Daily Telegraph, Elms, Robert: You May Say I'm A Charlatan (September 2003)
Daily Telegraph, Brown, Mick: You may say he was a dreamer (September 2003)
Disc and Music Echo, Taylor, Derek: Congratulations on a hit, everybody! (July 1969)
Guradian, Bracewell, Michael: *Give Yoko a chance* (January 1996)
Independent On Sunday, Hilton, Tim: Ono, Yoko's got a new show (December 1997)
Independent On Sunday, Bracewell, Michael: Imagine Yoko's own story (December 1999)
Melody Maker: Pop think–in, John Lennon (January 1966)
Mojo, Trynka, Paul: The Mojo Interview (2003)
Red Mole: Power to the people: John Lennon and Yoko Ono talk to Robin Blackburn and Tariq Ali (March 1971)
Rolling Stone, Flippo, Chet: The Private Years (October 1982)
Sounds, Pulin, Chuck: Talking straight to America (February 1972)
Uncut, Clerk, Carol: All You Need Is Love (September 2003)

Websites
http://www.bagism.com/library/lennonwall–timeline.html
http://homepage.ntlworld.com/carousel/pob07.html
http://homepage.ntlworld.com/carousel/pob00.html
http://www.guardian.co.uk/print/0,3858,3965739–103690,00.html

WOMAN

by Alan Clayson

1. The Widow

"John and I were so exclusive to each other that we didn't really have many friends – and that's what I noticed."

When the world woke up, John Lennon had not recovered from being dead. As it was with the early demise of Hollywood heart–throb Rudolph Valentino in 1926, the slaying sparked off suicides. In an attempt to nip others in the bud, Yoko issued a statement via the *New York Daily News*, stressing that "when something like this happens, each one of us must go on." (1)

This was more considered than Paul McCartney's "It's a drag," uttered when accosted by a television camera crew and a stick–mike thrust towards his mouth. (2) Unlike Paul, George Harrison cancelled the day's recording session, and didn't venture beyond the confines of his country estate until the dust had settled.

If as fearful as George and Paul – and, with sounder reason, Yoko – of a copycat killing, Ringo Starr made a grand gesture on his late colleague's behalf by catching an immediate flight to New York to offer condolences, even if he was heard to murmur "It was her who started all this" (3) as he and fiancée Barbara Bach waited in a Dakota ante–room for an audience with the widow.

A hasty cremation at Hartsdale, a city mortuary, had already been arranged, even as Ringo and Barbara were being shepherded through the tightest security net to a purring Cadillac. Through its one–way windows, they glanced at chalked headlines on newspaper stands and electronically–transmitted images of Lennon and Ono on TV sets in appliance shops pocking the stop–starting drive from Kennedy airport to the city centre.

Suntanned amidst the cold, they were self–contained spectators with no stake in the tragedy until, with no parking space in the Dakota forecourt, shock impinged itself on them as they hastened past clutching hands, some flapping autograph books, winced at the pitiless *woomph* of flashbulbs, and stepped over the self–same paving stones that had been wet with Lennon's gore. Though he apprehended the massed grief behind that corridor of police barricades, Ringo "was not very happy with the vigil. Those people showed very little respect for either John nor Yoko. It was disgusting." (4)

Once inside, the seemingly compulsory journey appeared even more foolhardy when Ono insisted at first on speaking only to Starr. Biting back on his anger, Ringo persuaded Yoko gently that as she and John had been – sorry, still were – one, so it was with him and Barbara now. After defusing what might have developed into an untimely flare–up, Ringo played for a while with Sean, bringing a smile to the five year old's face before leaving. But, commented one of her friends, "Yoko was not forgiven. Oh, Ringo was nice. He always was nice." (5) All the same, Yoko would be conspicuously absent from Starr and Bach's wedding in London a few months later.

Yet, for a while, the manner of a wider world, if not genial exactly, was at least grimly sympathetic towards one still derided by punks and hippies alike as the most "breadhead" half of a rich, refined couple, long detached from the everyday. Yet Mrs. Lennon's announcement that she intended to tithe some of her millions to worthy causes, because that's the way John would have wanted it, was noted. Moreover, at her request, many sent donations to the Spirit Foundation, a multi–purpose charity organisation set up by her and her late spouse in 1978. Far greater multitudes across the globe observed a ten minute silence to pray for John's soul at the same time on the Sunday after the shooting, and accepted Yoko's syndicated message of thanks: "Bless you for your tears and prayers. I saw John smiling in the sky. I saw sorrow changing into clarity. I saw all of us becoming one mind. Thank you. Love. Yoko." (6)

The more credulous had also paid heed to the theories that had been flying up and down when flags were still at half–mast, and the wireless was broadcasting the dead man's music continuously in place of listed programmes. Had it been a rite by which the 'Beatle generation' – if rendered wrinkled, balding and old by the speed of events – had been saved by the sacrifice of its leader in his prime? Was it an Art Statement more surreal than anything John and Yoko had done in the dear, dead Swinging Sixties? Had Yoko reneged on an elaborate suicide pact? One particularly powerful rumour was that Ono had eaten Lennon's ashes.

For all the mystical, arty and political analogies that went the rounds, most people reckoned that John Lennon had been killed simply because Mark David Chapman, who'd been sighted sniffing round Bob Dylan too, was as nutty as a fruitcake. Although he was to be confined, not to a mental institution, but New York's Attica Correctional Facility – the setting of 'Attica State' from *Sometime In New York City* he'd be separated from other prisoners for the sake of his own safety, particularly when he seemed to be becoming something of a celebrity as the focal point of a video documentary and numerous magazine features.

When Mark Chapman first began acquiring this purportedly unlooked–for immortality, John's side of the tragedy had bequeathed unto *Double Fantasy* an undeserved "beautiful sadness," thus reversing its fall – and that of the '(Just Like) Starting Over' spin–off single – from their respective listings as that creepy Christmas petered out. Indeed, universal grief and an element of ghoulish Beatlemania enabled Lennon to score a hat–trick of British Number Ones within weeks, an achievement that matched that of his Beatles when the world was young. Out of sympathy too, Yoko notched up her first solo chart entry – with 'Walking On Thin Ice – For John' at Number 35 in Britain and 58 in the US *Hot 100* in February 1981. It was also to be nominated for a Grammy award, thus lending creedence to the cruel old joke: death is a good career move.

You didn't quite like to laugh either when a *New Musical Express* reader's letter had bawled "The leader of the band's arrived!" back in the aftershock. (7) This was based on a presumption that John was being conducted to the table head in some pop Valhalla. A spiritualist *au fait* with Lennon's afterlife adventures knew of his affair with a long–departed Hollywood screen idol – intelligence that did not inflame Yoko as much as the bursting of a commercial dam of such force that John Lennon's name would continue to sell almost anything.

A particular wellspring of much anguish here resulted from publishers liaising with biographers while the corpse was still warm. One team of writers had a life of Lennon, entitled *Strawberry Fields Forever,* in the shops inside a fortnight, and Mark David Chapman let it be known that he wanted to write his version of events, but wouldn't do so if Yoko didn't wish it. That must have been a great comfort to her.

Books by former associates like May Pang and Fred Seaman were swiftly in the pipeline, but worse was to follow with US journalist Albert Goldman's brief to portray Lennon as being as sectionable a lunatic as Chapman, and Yoko as a cross between pop's Wallis Simpson and Beryl Formby, who watched her hen–pecked husband, George, the Lancashire music–hall entertainer, like a hawk, and ruled him with an "iron petticoat."

The surviving Beatles were united with Yoko in condemning this ignoble account by Goldman who, having dished the dirt already on Elvis Presley, was as twisted in his way as Chapman, but morbid inquisitiveness ensured, nevertheless, a mammoth return for his *The Lives Of John Lennon*. This was in spite of a prototypical protest from George Harrison

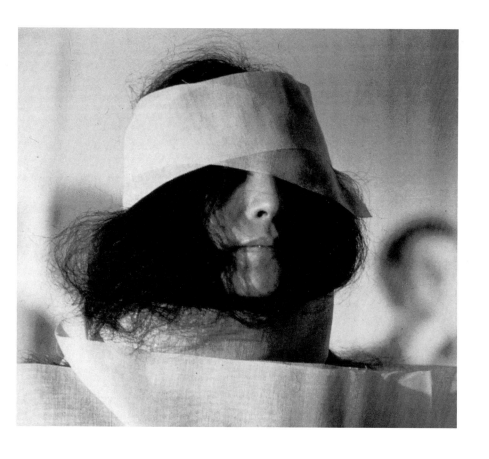

WOMAN

WOMAN

WOMAN

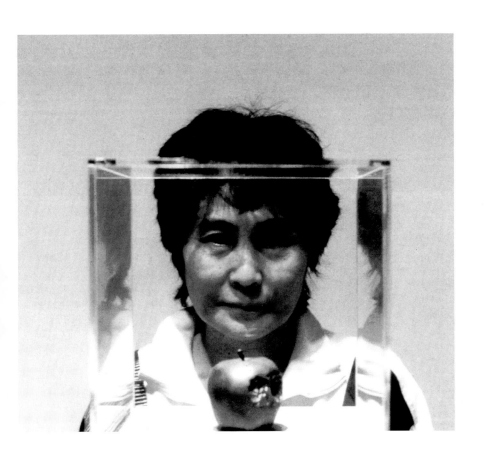

WOMAN

WOMAN

that its purchasers "don't realise it's the same old clap–trap, and that the Goldmans of this world can make a hell of a living, a lot of money, for slagging off someone who's dead." (8)

Yet Harrison had been sufficiently thick–skinned, or inspired, to start work on a Lennon tribute disc within days of the news breaking. While it's futile to hypothesize about John's beyond–the–grave verdict on 'All Those Years Ago', George's first big hit since 1973 – not to mention 'It Was Nice To Know You John', 'Elegy For The Walrus' and like chart–shy efforts by other artistes, he might have shared the dismay of Sean's godfather, Elton John, whose 'Empty Garden' oblation climbed no further than Number 51 in 1982. Though he procrastinated for even longer, Mike "Tubular Bells" Oldfield – with sister Sally on lead vocals – slummed it on *Top Of The Pops* with 1983's 'Moonlight Shadow' which addressed itself to the horror outside the Dakota on the night it happened.

However, the principal subject of Oldfield's ditty was not John but Yoko, who was by then returning to her pre–Chapman status as a subject of barbed invective. Some of it was prompted by what had been understood about her grip on the purse–strings of John's fortune and her interrelated attitude towards both longtime employees and his blood relations. For instance, her and Lennon's tarot reader, albeit ineffectual in the light of what occurred on 9th December 1980, was directed to vacate his apartment in the Dakota, and Julian Lennon was to receive assorted and, according to him, long overdue, monies only after much to–ing and fro–ing of solicitor's letters.

There was no love lost between him and his father's relict. While noting her and Sean's attendance at the funeral of Lennon's eighty–eight year old aunt, Mary "Mimi" Smith in December 1991, others from John's side of the family felt the same. "Dad bought his half–sister Julia and her family a house to live in," snarled Julian by way of example, "As soon as Dad passed away, Yoko went and took their home that had been given them by him, and then gave it to charity with no compensation for them." (9)

The ease with which Yoko's embittered step–son secured a British Top Ten hit in 1984 might be the most renowned instance of affinity to The Beatles kick–starting a musical career. In April the following year, Julian and his backing musicians played three nights in a theatre in New York. During this brief residency, he and his mother were spotted at a dining table, sharing the proverbial joke with his half–brother and Yoko Ono. "It was after Julian's first appearance in New York," clarified Cynthia Lennon, "and he and I, Yoko and Sean were there – so for the photographers, it was a classic coup, but though we both wed the same man and both had a child by him, we were, and still are, worlds apart."

Ono and Sean had had no qualms either about walking onstage after Elton John sang 'Empty Sky' at a Madison Square Garden concert in August 1982, but there'd been an earlier, if less conspicuous, indication that Yoko was rising from a half–death of Dakota seclusion, comfort eating and, as a newly–bereaved Japanese wife was supposed to do, scissoring off thirty inches of the black frizz that had hung like a cloak over her shoulders since God knows when.

When an invitation arrived for her to collect a Grammy for *Double Fantasy* at the National Academy Of Recording Arts and Sciences, Yoko laid out an all–white trouser suit, made the most of what was left of her hair and performed a cosmetic miracle on a careworn face. She wouldn't let John down. In the summer of 1981 too, she'd become actively involved in the creation of Strawberry Fields, a two–and–half–acre garden memorial to John in Central Park (which was to open formally in 1984), and had undertaken her first media interviews since *Double Fantasy*.

When going through such motions, she revealed the existence of a boyfriend in Sam Havadtoy, a Hungarian interior decorator and antiques dealer, twenty years her junior. Not long after John's death, Havadtoy had been commissioned to renovate Yoko's properties in New York and Florida. With Sean's approval a key point in his favour, Havadtoy was to be Yoko's "constant companion" for longer than all of her three husbands put together.

She was also back in the office, doing deals on the telephone and in the studio recording a new album, *Season Of Glass*, with most of the crew who'd been on *Double Fantasy*, though they weren't as willing participants as they'd been when John had been there too. Yoko also hired and then dispensed with the services of Phil Spector who'd only agreed to help for old times' sake.

"I really wanted to make everything stark and raw," explained Ono, "which was diametrically opposed to what Phil believed in. He helped me to create the basic tracks, but when he started arranging extensive overdubs, I sort of had a talk with him. I just chucked out all the overdubs and did a very drastic remix. I had to do it from scratch. Even the basic tracks were completely removed from the Spector tradition. Then I felt I was being unfair to Phil, standing there in front of him and taking charge like that – so that's when I said, well, maybe we should not work together any more on this project." (10)

After Yoko had seized the reins of production, and sleeve design, herself, *Season Of Glass* garnered mixed reviews from the *New Musical Express*'s "trivial...banal" (11) to the *Los Angeles Times* putting Ono on a par with Joni Mitchell, a post–Woodstock colossus of a genre called "self–rock" if you liked it, and "drip–rock" if, like *Melody Maker*'s Allan Jones implied in a scathing article, the lyrics made you embarrassed to be alive, and you were left with the impression of an artist so bound up in herself that every emotion or occurrence in her life seemed worth turning into a song.

So it was that sounds of gunfire, spoken passages by Yoko and Sean, and a sleeve depicting Lennon's blood–stained spectacles were among the fascinations that assisted *Season Of Glass*'s passage to the edge of the US Top Fifty.

The following September's *It's Alright (I See Rainbows): An Air Play By Yoko Ono* embraced a milder shock tactic on the back cover, whereby a spectral John stands via trick photography, next to Yoko and Sean in what looks like a recreation ground. This particular collision of art and commerce was meant to stress Ono's belief that Lennon remained with her spiritually.

Another self–production, *It's Alright* tended to receive critical attention less for the intrinsic content of its ten tracks than its use of state–of–the–art layers of treated sound. "Instead of using a guitar, I tried to create a guitar sound out of a synthesizer," elucidated Yoko, "I did things like put a 'cello sound and a xylophone sound together – or I would mix a harp and a violin. When you heard the final track, there were all these sounds and it was impossible to work out what they were – but I found it impossible to get a good raw guitar sound. That was something I really missed a lot." (10)

As she'd discover too with the passing years, the day–to–day mundanities of selling records always boiled down to Lennon and The Beatles – which was why *It's Alright* missed the chart, and *Milk And Honey: A Heart Play* – with remaindered *Double Fantasy* items sung by John its chief selling point – came within an ace of Number One in Britain and elsewhere. Even the associated *Heart Play: Unfinished Dialogue* – forty minutes of Yoko and, crucially, John chatting to *Playboy* magazine – harried the lower regions of the US list late in 1983. (13)

Lennon was kept before the public too via Yoko's compilation and marketing of 1986's *Skywriting By Word Of Mouth*, a slim volume of his latter–day prose. If less directly involved, her imput had left its mark on a television film, *John And Yoko: A Love Story*, which tied–in with the fifth anniversary of his passing.

She was to have a far more pronounced hand in *Imagine: The Movie* and its soundtrack from her exploratory soliciting of Warner Brothers to her frame–by–frame scrutiny of hundreds of hours of footage, familiar and otherwise, from the Dakota archives such as the early 1970s sequence from Tittenhurst Park that would be used every time the utopian title song was repromoted as a chartbusting single, most recently during 1999's Christmas sell–in.

Notes

1. *New York Daily News*, 12th December 1980
2. *Six O'Clock News*, BBC 1, 9th December 1980
3. *Chicago Tribune*, March 1981
4. New York press conference, March 1981
5. *Yoko Ono* by J. Hopkins (Sidgwick & Jackson, 1987)
6. *The Guardian,* 15th December *1980*
7. *New Musical Express*, 11th December 1980
8. *The Guardian*, 3rd May 1988. At the time of his death in 1994, Goldman was, purportedly, in the throes of a biography of Yoko Ono with the ominous title, *Black Widow*.
9. *The John Lennon Encyclopaedia* by B. Harry (Virgin, 2000)
10. *Record Collector*, June 1992)
11. *New Musical Express*, 24th June 1981
12. *A propos* nothing in particular, Kate Bush bid £4,000 for a perspex statue of John and Yoko as the Two Virgins in a London rock 'n' roll memorabilia auction in December 1981.

2. The Shareholder

"Put a lot of sunshine in a large bowl. Mix it with the dream of your future. Spice it with a pinch of hope and laughter..."

As the 1980s got out of neutral, Yoko's instinct for commercial and economic manoeuvres seemed to be failing her. In April 1982, a lawsuit for fraud against Jack Douglas, co–producer of *Double Fantasy* backfired, and he received millions plus interest deemed to be due to him in unpaid royalties as well as a piece of the *Milk And Honey* money.

There'd been another fiscal debacle the previous year when Paul McCartney was presented with the opportunity to acquire the Beatles' catalogue, Northern Songs, from ATV as Lord Grade's company had had its fingers burnt by *Raise The Titanic!*, a movie that had cost forty million dollars but had taken only seven. Over the main course one expensive lunch–time, McCartney had persuaded Grade, against his better judgement, to sell Northern Songs as a separate entity from the rest of a huge ATV job–lot. Over dessert, his Lordship said Paul could regain his and John's compositions for twenty million pounds – with a week to make up his mind.

Determined upon the utmost correctness, Paul telephoned Yoko to emphasize that, as he didn't want to be appear to be stealing Lennon's half of the portfolio, Yoko ought to be in on the deal too. In any case, he wasn't sure if he could lay his hands instantly on the full amount. Yoko, however, thought that twenty million was too much. She'd consider the proposal if it was a quarter of that.

Grade wouldn't wear it, and thus the wheels were set in motion for Michael Jackson, the precocious youngest member of The Jackson Five and now solo star, to outbid McCartney, Ono and all other interested parties for the publishing rights to Northern Songs in 1986. "He snatched them from under Paul's nose," chuckled Adam Faith, then writer of a weekly financial column in a national newspaper. (1)

Paul might have been less upset if he could have been able to like Yoko, who seemed to perceive McCartney as the Salieri to his ex–songwriting partner's Mozart. There'd be revisions of this opinion, and personal reconciliations over the decades, but, while there'd be no successor to Lennon as self–appointed Beatles *paterfamilias* – who'd purportedly, chastised George Harrison for the 'incest' of a fling in 1972 with Ringo

Starr's first wife – Yoko would remain to the group roughly what the embarrassing 'Fergie', the Duchess of York, is to the British Royal Family.

Moreover, whether Paul, George and Ringo wished it or not, she was also a *de jure* equal partner in Apple Corps – as she'd been a *de facto* one as John's business representative throughout his house–husband years. Indeed, Lennon had so washed his hands of such matters that he couldn't bring himself so much as to put his head round the door the last time his three former colleagues were head–to–head with Yoko in the Dakota.

With him unavailable physically as well as spiritually, the first major discussion over the division of the empire took place in January 1984 when the four financiers locked themselves away with champagne and a continuous running buffet in an eighth–floor suite at the Dorchester, overlooking Hyde Park. One of Yoko's gofers observed that "nothing was accomplished" (2), and that when she wasn't around, the three who'd travelled a longer road with Lennon loosened up with matey abuse, coded hilarity and selective reminiscences about the struggle back in Liverpool and Hamburg when the world was young.

The next day, Yoko cleared her head by taking Sean to see the Changing of the Guards, but on the 24th the two flew to Liverpool airport, which droned by the windswept mudbanks of the Mersey. On this, Sean's first visit to the Holy City, they were driven by limousine along the A561, lined with chimneys belching the chemical waste that fouled the air and waterways, and slum overspill estates including the one in Speke where George Harrison had grown up. By contrast, Menlove Avenue, where self–styled "working class hero" John had been brought up by his Aunt Mimi, was along the main thoroughfare of Woolton, a village–like district that had more to do with rural Lancashire than Merseyside, embracing as it did mock–Tudor colonies, golf clubs and boating lakes.

Elsewhere too, Sean, after checking in at the Adelphi, the city centre's plushest hotel, was now old enough to feel pangs of received nostalgia for locations to which he'd hitherto only drunk in second–hand as germane to his sire's legend during a walkabout accompanied by a camera crew as if he and his mother were visiting royalty. Chaperoned too by a record company executive, they were seen seeing Penny Lane, Quarry Bank school, the art college and the patch of unofficial countryside along Mathew Street where a 'Cavern' was to be reconstructed next to the Cavern Walks shopping mall, and opposite the John Lennon pub where Charlie, Sean's great–uncle, John's late father's brother, was to regale tourists on the Beatles' scent with endless reminiscences about what John got up to in nineteen–fifty–forget–about–it.

If not as conspicuous, the principal flag–waver on John's mother's side of the family was frail Aunt Mimi, who happened to be staying with a sister in Rock Ferry on the other side of the wide, bleak Mersey. This was convenient for a duty–call from Yoko and Sean.

The pilgrimage to the north–west concluded with a gift from Yoko of a six–figure sum to Strawberry Fields Orphanage. Then she and Sean settled into their seats for the long–haul flight back to the States where Yoko could bask in the afterglow of *Yoko Ono Then And Now*, a black–and–white television documentary, which was as respectful as one of her calibre deserved, an avant–garde artist of sufficient importance to have warranted an entry in the sixteenth edition of *Who's Who In American Art*. While Lennon hoved into view now and then, and McCartney and his wife were among the talking heads in *Here And Now*, the stronger emphasis on the likes of 'Cut Piece' and the 'Bottoms' movie demonstrated that, at least as far as her adopted country was concerned, Yoko Ono was moving into an orbit separate from that of her more famous dead husband.

In Britain, however, *Then And Now* was broadcast on ITV on 8th December 1984 – the fourth anniversary of Mark David Chapman's crime – at the lonely hour of 11.46 p.m. Yet, if there wasn't much mainstream interest in her artistic output, Elvis Costello, one of the first post–Sex Pistols musical ambassadors to triumph over the Atlantic, found much to praise. Indeed, that autumn, his revival of 'Walking On Thin Ice' had been a highlight of *Every Man Has A Woman Who Loves Him*, an Ono tribute album which also featured tracks by, amongst others, Harry Nilsson, Rosanne Cash, Roberta Flack and The B52s, acknowledging her influence with a gripping "Don't Worry Kyoko."

On the horizon was Yoko's similar salaam to John Cage on the *A Chance Operation*, a compilation album on which respects were also paid by Frank Zappa (who bagged '4' 33"'), The Kronos Quintet, Laurie Anderson and Meredith Monk.

As an elder statesperson of modern art, Ono had also been invited onto the panel of the sixth annual New Music Seminar in 1993. Held in New York, it was, ostensibly, a forum for independent record companies and makers of 'alternative' music, but many major labels were present too and reggae megastar Jimmy Cliff and Debbie Harry, the face and voice of chartbusting Blondie, were among the other luminaries passing comment with Yoko.

How swiftly she'd become a vogue. One day, she'd been a ghost of dubious distinction from the recent past, the next – or so it appeared – she was bringing much of the aura of a fresh sensation to those young enough never to have heard much of her before. No time was better for a new album, and Yoko obliged with *Starpeace: An Earth Play For Sun And Air*. Sales were modest, but the spin–off single, 'Hell In Paradise', with soul star Nona Hendryx on backing vocals, was to peak at Number 16 in *(Billboard's)* disco chart, and remained a much–requested spin in associated clubs.

However, while a North American public looked as if it might have been receptive to a coast–to–coast tour, Yoko chose instead a water–testing thirty–two date trudge round Europe's concert halls in 1985 it didn't even break even, not even out of sympathy or morbid inquisitiveness. While a night in Budapest closed on an emotional high with a jubilant fifteen thousand – almost all of them Beatles diehards – blasting up a rowdy singalong finale of 'Imagine', in Vienna, the auditorium was less than half full. That was typical – as was the painfully transparent fact that the older you were, the louder you clapped, and that all the customers wanted was some ersatz Beatles magic.

Yoko seemed to have gone off the boil in the States too. In the light of 'Hell In Paradise', perhaps she should have worked the clubs rather than attempt to fill venues that were the domain of those in the higher league of the 'adult–orientated rock' hierarchy – such as the Universal Amphitheatre in Los Angeles, which shifted only a quarter of the tickets. In the twenty–thousand seaters in the mid–west too, while Yoko was received with some affection by those whose life had been soundtracked by The Beatles, turn–out was so poor that cancellation of the remaining shows was the only way to staunch further financial haemorrhaging.

"I was totally discouraged," gloomed Ono, "Not as a composer, but by the fact that there was no kind of demand for what I was doing to put it mildly. I thought that it was just impractical for me to focus my energy on getting my music out. I had so many responsibilities with business, and with issuing John's work." (3)

There was also another matter to address in the wake of Tony Cox's resurfacing via an article based on an interview with him in glossy *People* magazine in January 1986. Nine years earlier, it read, he and Kyoko had been roped into the Church of the Living World in Los Angeles. Cox then pledged himself to The Walk, an extreme 'prepare–to–meet–thy–doom'–type sect, that preached that Yoko, John and their sort were "the personification of evil."

If unsettled by her former spouses's disobliging remarks in print, pragmatism was the watch–word as Yoko appealed through an open letter in *People* – signed "Love, Mummy" – for Kyoko, now twenty–three, to make contact.

It was to be almost a decade before Kyoko deigned to reply. Disappointment flooded the estranged mother's already overloaded mind, but, as she had after the aborted *Starpeace* trek, she coped by burying herself in work – which was then dominated by The Beatles' long shadow.

Purportedly, she'd given her blessing for the use of a 1968 B–side by the group in a TV commercial for Nike's "revolution" – get it? – in footwear. Solicitors' advice was sought by Starr, McCartney and Harrison because, predicted the latter, "If it's allowed to happen, every Beatles song ever recorded is going to be advertising women's underwear and sausages. The other thing is, even while Nike might have paid Capitol Records for the rights, Capitol certainly don't give us the money." (4)

To begin the redress of alleged royalty grievances, a legal battle had been instigated by the injured parties against EMI in 1984. Four years later, the group and Yoko also slapped a writ for damages against Dave Clark's video company for Beatles clips shown on Channel Four's re–runs of ITV's *Ready Steady Go!*, the mid–1960s pop series on ITV. There were also allegations that Clark, once drummer–leader of The Dave Clark Five, was selling video compilations of Beatles material, from *Ready Steady Go* footage, without permission. Minor matters included an injunction to stop an English label from issuing an album of the Beatles' failed 1962 studio audition for Decca.

Sometimes, it appeared that Ono and the ex–Beatles were being cheated by each other too during the perpetual unscrambling of Apple lucre. In August 1987, Yoko, Ringo and George filed a lawsuit directed at Paul for a deal he'd made whereby six post–Beatles albums he'd delivered to Capitol had rewarded him with what could be interpreted as an increased slice of the company's Beatles cake. Though dismissed by one Apple employee as "a storm in a teacup," the plaintiffs complained also that Capitol's delay in releasing Beatles material on CD has cost them millions in lost income. Acting for the three, lawyer Leonard Marks claimed the hold–up was

Capitol's way of punishing them for an eight–year battle over disputed monies from *Abbey Road*, and an attempt by the firm to force the group to drop the action.

The ongoing litigation was at the root of Paul's non–attendance on a January Wednesday in 1988 at the gala where The Beatles were to be inducted into the third Rock 'N' Roll Hall Of Fame. Amid the murals and mosaics in New York's deluxe Waldorf–Astoria Hotel, what was left of the group was represented by George, Ringo, Julian Lennon – and Yoko who was coaxed to the podium's microphone to say a few words, *viz* "I am sure that if John was alive, he would have been here." Her presence also prompted a piquant comment about institutional sexism from Mary Wilson of The Supremes: "It seemed so symbolic of the record industry and rock 'n' roll in general that the only two women onstage were Yoko Ono and me." (5) Neither Wilson nor Ono were to make their way onto the boards, heaving with celebrities, for the "impromptu" jam session at the end.

It was regarded as more 'womanly' perhaps for Yoko to contribute a cameo recipe for an intangible dish called 'Dream Soup' to a Christmas stocking filler entitled *Rock 'N' Roll Cuisine*. This was not, however, amongst merchandise purchasable at a Lennon art exhibition, supervised by his widow in London.

A retropective of Yoko's own work was shown in galleries across the globe, reaching London's Riverside Studios in May 1990, when she herself was present in England to lend monetary assistance to Olivia Harrison's appeal for the Romanian earthquake – which could be felt as far away as Moscow and Istanbul. Mainly, however, she was there to compere a televised and international concert spectacular for charity she'd arranged at Liverpool's Pier Head that, if several months in advance, was to mark what would have been John's fiftieth birthday. But a relatively minor landmark on rock's road to respectability, it still attracted the likes of Ray Charles, Lou Reed, Roberta Flack, Kylie Minogue, Christopher 'Superman' Reeve and other disparate big–names–in–good–cause, even if some bickered over billing.

While they declined to show up in person, Paul and Ringo each sent a filmed piece, with Starr's 'Hi, Liverpool!' and 'supergroup' overhaul of a Beatles track from 1964 – bridging a gap between Philadephian duo Hall and Oates and Welsh guitarist Dave Edmunds' John Lennon Tribute Band. George, however, elected to have nothing to do with an event he considered to be "in poor taste." (6)

At least Harrison had been approached by Ono to participate. No Merseybeat groups "who'd got drunk with him" (7) had been requested even to warm up for her star turns or to muscle in amongst the assembled cast for the big finish with 'Give Peace A Chance', lately re–made by Yoko and Sean with lyrics revised as a Searing Indictment of the Gulf War between the USA and Iraq.

On the recording front too, *Onobox*, a six CD box–set (included hitherto unreleased items), embracing the music she produced between 1969 to 1984, was in preparation for eventual release early in 1992. To promote it, she gave the media – from *The New York Times* to *Record Collector* – unblinking copy, endeavouring, not always successfully, to clarify the collection's obscurer byways, and retelling the old, old story about her and John for the trillionth time.

A less–publicized opportunity to keep herself in the public eye was to arise the following autumn when she sanctioned an exhibition in Los Angeles entitled 'Family Blood Objects' and containing bronze casts of Lennon's bullet–ridden shirt , and replicas of his shattered glasses. These could be bought for, respectively, $25,000 and $18,000 each.

Notes

1. *Acts Of Faith* by A. Faith (Bantam, 1996)
2. To Jerry Hopkins
3. *Record Collector*, June 1992
4. *Q*, January 1988
5. *She's A Rebel* by G.G. Gaar (Blandford, 1993)
6. *Sunday Times*, 6th May 1990

3. **The Indweller**

'I've finally learnt to live with myself exactly as I am'

At January 1994's Rock 'N' Roll Hall Of Fame extravaganza at the Waldorf–Astoria, Paul McCartney was the only ex–Beatle to show up. He was there to make the induction speech when his late and most famous songwriting partner received a lifetime achievement award. As the ovation unfurled, the widow climbed the podium for the statuette. She and Paul then obliged hovering snap–shotters and the cream of the US music industry with a seemingly conciliatory, even affectionate embrace as if all their feuding and furies of the past twenty–odd years were spent.

It gets better. When Yoko and Sean visited England the following year, they sampled hospitality *chez* McCartney in Sussex for a weekend that might have seemed more like a fortnight for some members of the household. The stay culminated with a session at Paul's home studio in which he, Linda and their children accompanied seven minutes of Aunt Yoko's screech–singing of a one–line lyric entitled 'Hiroshima Sky Is Always Blue' (1), a remembrance of the fiftieth anniversary of the nuclear bombs falling on Japan.

The creation of this hitherto–unreleased opus was, smiled Yoko, the final confirmation of a new understanding between her and McCartney: "It was a healing for our families to come together in this way. That feeling was very special." (2) While she – and Paul – may have insisted that there was no ulterior motive, for the more cynical amongst us, the sub–text of this and the more public all–pals–again encounter at the awards ceremony might have been McCartney oiling the wheels of Ono's co–operation on a planned CD anthology of Beatles tracks from the vaults to be supplemented by her donation of stark voice–piano tapes of latter–day Lennon compositions for Paul, Ringo and George to use as they thought fit.

As "Keeper Of The Wishing Well" – her phrase – Yoko had opened these archives, which also embraced several hundred hours of out–takes, in–concert performances, alternate mixes *et al*, a few winters earlier for broadcast as *The Lost Lennon Tapes* for a US radio series that stretched out for four years.

The items handed over to McCartney were sifted by himself, Harrison and Starr with the net result of their superimposing fuller accompaniment and grafting entire new sections onto 'Free As A Bird' and 'Real Love', the spin–off singles to *Anthology*, issued over the period of a year on nine albums (in packs of three) as appendant commodities to a six–hour documentary film to be spread over three weeks on ITV, and presented likewise on foreign television.

Predictably, *Anthology* sold millions, affirming that 'Free As A Bird' almost–but–not–quite reaching the top in the UK chart was but a surface manifestation that the ceaseless fascination with the wretched group, making even this abundance of leftovers as much of a joy forever as similar if less commercially viable boxed produce from around the same time by The Zombies, The Beach Boys and The Doors.

Yet business between Ono and McCartney was by no means concluded. Indeed, the weather vane of rapprochement lurched back to the old thinly–veiled antagonism when it came to Yoko's attention that, wherever he could, in tour programmes and on disc, Paul ensured that composing credits read "McCartney–Lennon" rather than, as it had been from 1963 up to and including *Anthology*, "Lennon–McCartney."

This was nipped in the bud by Yoko and her legal team, but you could understand Paul's attitude. On the basis of mostly song–by–song break–downs by Lennon during one of his last interviews, Spencer Leigh figured out that, statistically, McCartney was responsible for approximately two–thirds of The Beatles' output of originals, including 'Yesterday', subject of over a thousand cover versions.

This was borne out by implication too in John's remarks to an aide in 1979: "Paul never stopped working. We'd finish one album, and I'd go off and get stoned, and forget about writing new stuff, but he'd start working on new material right away, and as soon as he'd got enough songs, he'd want to start recording again." (2) McCartney corroborated this twenty–three years later in a weighty and widely–circulated press statement, grousing too that "Late one night, I was in an empty bar, flicking through the pianist's music book when I came across 'Hey Jude' written by John Lennon." At one point, Yoko earned more from 'Yesterday' than I did. It doesn't compute – especially when it's the only song that none of the [other] Beatles had anything to do with."

Was it ever thus? It would be pleasant to think that any number of black bluesmen with a lackadaisical regard for business received, if not royalties, then acknowledgement due to them from white rock bands like Led Zeppelin, who rewrote Howlin' Wolf's 'How Many More Years' as 'How Many More Times'. More to the point, a typing error attributed a version of The Yardbirds' 'Shapes Of Things' on an album by The Jeff Beck Group to bass player Paul Samwell–Smith alone rather than drummer Jim McCarty and singer Keith Relf too. Then there was the case of The Animals' 'House Of The Rising Sun'. This joint overhaul of a traditional ballad topped international charts, but as there wasn't sufficient room on the single's label to print all five Animal names, only one was used – that of organist Alan Price, who according to drummer John Steel, had least to do with the arrangement of the song. The others were placated with the promise that it wouldn't make any difference to shares in the royalties, but insists drummer John Steel, "We never saw any of that money. Alan still earns on it today."

Just as Price was ostracised by the other Animals, so Yoko Ono wasn't invited to a memorial service in New York for Linda McCartney, who had died of cancer in 1998. "Paul was saying, 'Well, we're not friends'," sighed Yoko, more in sadness than anger, "Probably he was very upset about his wife's death as well." (3) She also took the first of many opportunities to praise McCartney's abilities as a composer.

Ono was also to be embroiled in another Beatles–related dispute. In 2002, she was able to purchase 'Mendips' and present it to the National Trust. She also helped finance its restoration, operating costs and the salary of a permanent live–in custodian, but a BBC Channel Four series about the Trust was to include a feature about 'Mendips' and a complaint that "Yoko Ono interferes – through her advisors – with every decision while failing to cough up much in the way of funds." (4)

Nevertheless, she'd shown willing by being conspicuous at the official opening and unveiling of the honorific plaque in March 2003. That same month too, she'd been there to view a seven–foot statue of John in the presence of the Queen when Liverpool displayed its pride in him by renaming its principal air terminal 'John Lennon Airport' in the teeth of certain civic objections that Lennon, though an admirable young man in many ways, had had his share of young man's vices. Yoko was also pragmatically supportive of the John Lennon Memorial Scholarship at the University of Liverpool, which was to benefit talented local youngsters, just as the Jimi Hendrix Memorial Foundation had been doing for boys and girls in seats of learning in and around his home city of Seattle since 1971.

Yoko had become, therefore, a fully–integrated member of the ruling class of a pop establishment containing the likes of Eric Clapton MBE, Van Morrison OBE, Sir Cliff Richard, Sir Paul McCartney, Sir Elton John and Sir Mick Jagger. There'd been mutterings about a knighthood, albeit posthumous, for John Lennon too with its consequent spotlight on Yoko as a next–of–kin with mixed feelings about the honour, but not quite the same as those John had experienced when he and the other Beatles had set the ball rolling by accepting an MBE each in 1966.

It's likely that I've got Yoko all wrong but, to me, she gives an impression of hurrying her duties by John out of the way in as bombastic a manner as possible while simultaneously using him as leverage to further her own artistic ends: kind of "Yes, he was quite a guy but listen..." While she gave her blessing to a Broadway musical based on his life in 2003, Yoko allowed a John Lennon watch to be marketed for 1996's Christmas sell–in – but rather than his face, it portrayed his naked buttocks.

"Faces can lie. Backsides can't," (5) Yoko had explained two years previously when the burghers of Langenhagen wondered what to do about the seventy thousand posters of someone else's bare bottom she'd had plastered around the German town, chosen, apparently, at random for this visitation. The citizens' reaction was akin in macrocosm to those of the ordinary New Yorkers who'd read about the first excursion for 'Cut Piece' way back when.

Yoko would be at it again on Monday 15th September 2003 when her seventy year old self stripped in protest at the international political climate at the Ranelagh theatre in Paris in a one–woman show cultural light–years from the *Star Peace* tour. During a slow–moving eighty minutes, it was the old strategy of inviting individuals in the audience to snip away pieces of her clothing – though specifying that each bit was to be no bigger than a postcard, and suggesting that they "send the scrap of fabric to someone you love." Two hundred obliged, removing her T–shirt and black silk skirt, but stopping short of the knickers and matching brassiere. Yoko herself prevented one adventurous wielder of the scissors from starting on her black suede shoes before donning a white *kimono* and retreating into the wings to sustained applause.

During the proceedings, some had exchanged nervous glances. Who'd have thought the old girl still had it in her? Nevertheless, the next morning's newspapers reported rather than analysed a performance that had had a certain period – not charm exactly, but a period something about it. Yoko seemed to agree: "Recently, I saw 'Cut Piece' performed by a guy in New York. There was no tension in the audience like there used to be, and the atmosphere was much lighter. After thirty years, it's probably not avant–garde any more." (6)

Far less so had been Yoko's renting of giant billboard space amid the flashing neon signs of Piccadilly Circus to declare in stark black print on white background, "Imagine all the people living life in peace." As the build–up to war in Iraq intensified, this was followed by full–pages in major broadsheets for the more succinct 'Imagine Peace...Spring 2003'.

Yet Ono's less costly precedents of confrontations, passive and active, a lot of them pre–Lennon, as well as an all–new exhibition, 2004's *Odyssey of a Cockroach*, have been debated seriously in media discussions about, say, Damian Hurst's dead sheep, Tracey Emin's unmade bed and similar controversial 'Britart' works nominated for Turner prizes in the late 1990s. Conversely, the publicity blitz prior to a retrospective in September 2003 at Venice's Biennale festival of contemporary art drew from Ono the amused comment that the offerings of Emin, Hirst *et al* were "Very bad. Bad in the sense of good." (7)

Not so ambiguous had been a subjective preface she penned to *She's A Rebel: The History Of Women In Rock & Roll* by Gillian G. Gaar: "I could not put it down, even though it was a somewhat painful process as it reminded me of my own unresolved hurt. It also uplifted my spirit to realise that I was not alone." (8)

While her connection with Lennon may have brought Yoko to an incalculably wider record–buying public than might have warranted in the usual course of events, she was, on the strength of chart statistics, as recognised a pop star as many that tripped off Joe Average's tongue more readily. In June 2002, once–*risqué* 'Open Your Box', the self–composed B–side to 1971's 'Power To The People' was remixed in electro–pop fashion, with an undercurrent of dub–reggae, in an attempt to re–invent Yoko as a disco diva. A poster campaign infiltrated underground train stations in London, New York and other major cities, and the disc found its way onto club turntables with almost mathematical precision. Not quite a year later, an overhaul of 'Walking On Thin Ice' by The Pet Shop Boys eased to Number One in *Billboard*'s dance charts, thanks in part to its association with Larry Levan, disc–jockey at New York's celebrated Paradise Garage, who plugged the original vinyl version heavily before his early death in 1992.

Yoko had also breathed the air round Adrian 'Tricky' Thaws, once rapper with British hip–hoppers, Massive Attack, but now the toast of the Big Apple's club scene – and Cibo Matto, a duo of expatriate Japanese feminists – singer Miho Hatori and general instrumental factotum

Yuka Honda, who happened to be Sean Lennon's girlfriend. Quite an accomplished musician himself now, Sean went on the road with Cibo Matto as bass player, having formed Ima (9), a trio that backed his mother on both her new album, *Rising*, and the 1996 tour that promoted it. The stock Oldest Teenager In The Business, Yoko remained as *au fait* as Sean and Yuka with the latest sounds, dancing away the night of her seventieth birthday to The Strokes, Moby and, of course, Cibo Matto and Ima.

Her joy was completed by a card from thirty–nine–year–old Kyoko, whose permanent reunion with her parent had started with a guarded conversation from Denver, Colorado, in November 1997, a few days after the birth of Emi, Yoko's first grand–child. Encouraged by her husband, a devout Christian, Kyoko was amenable to a face–to–face meeting, which took place in New York a few months later. An underlying, if brusque, fondness that absence had not erased had infused further telephone calls, and Kyoko and the baby's visit was, therefore, relatively undramatic and free of trauma.

Joint heirs to Yoko's multi–million dollar estate, Kyoko and Sean are as different vocationally as a brother and sister could be. She's a teacher while he continues to plough the same furrow as his father. Though possessing a degree in anthropology from Columbia University, Sean secured a recording contract partly on the strength of his talismanic surname, thus furnishing his pop career with the same best and worst start as half–brother Julian, whose 1998 album, *Photograph Smile*, was in the shops the same month as Sean's thirteen–track *Into The Sun* debut. Produced by Yuka, it was, he reckoned, "about the happiness of being in love and the craziness that goes with it." (2)

Conducting himself with observed good humour when Sean's effort was deemed by most to be a more profound critical success than his own, Julian said he liked *Into The Sun*, qualifying this with "He knows he's comfortable for the rest of his life. It's not like he feels a hunger, but he's talented." (2) He laced this with a flavouring of sour grapes so piquant that a story persists still of Yoko pulling strings to have *Photograph Smile* dropped from radio play–lists.

The edge was taken from Yoko's euphoria at favourable reviews of *Into The Sun* by her mother shuffling off this mortal coil on 23rd January 1999, aged eighty–eight. Dutifully, Yoko attended the funeral in Tokyo, sitting next to the ailing Eisuke, who'd been driven from his and Isoko's final home in Fujisawa, nearly forty miles away.

Yoko jetted back to the Dakota where, in September 2003, post–Woodstock singer–songwriter Carly Simon joined a growing list of celebrities, among them Mariah Carey and Madonna, to be turned down by the residents' committee when they submitted bids for newly–vacant apartments in a block theoretically as protected as Howard Hugues's Las Vegas penthouse had been.

Yet a blithe fatalism informed Yoko Ono's daily routines. Like the Loch Ness Monster, there have been unofficial sightings of her now and then. Up by eight, she'd be noticed slipping out to local convenience stores, strolling in Central Park, sipping coffee in a Times Square cafe or emerging from a cinema. Keeping to daylight hours nowadays, she was also retiring early with only "the past" (7) prompting wakeful periods during a cossetted but hard–won retirement in which another headline–hogging outrage would be a mere sideshow.

Notes

1. Also known as 'Hiroshima, It's Always A Beautiful Sky'
2. *The John Lennon Encyclopaedia* by B. Harry (Virgin, 2000)
3. To Paul Trynka
4. *The Times*, 1st November 2003
5. *The Beatles After The Break–Up: 1970–2000* by K. Badman (Omnibus, 1999)
6. *Record Collector*, June 1992
7. *Daily Telegraph*, 24th August 2003
8. *She's A Rebel: The History Of Women In Rock & Roll* by G Gaar (Blandford, 1993)
9. Japanese for 'now'

WOMAN

Barb Jungr

1. Yes: An Overview of The Art Of Yoko Ono

It is not possible to travel back in time. Of course, in our progressive world we have access to many records; photographic, film, televisual and text. Many of them now also accessible on the Internet. But in terms of understanding the effect that something had at a given point in time, we are all in the hands of memoirs, diarists, and newspaper and magazine archivists. And ultimately, all that they can do is serve to alert us to what was in the media mind set at a given point in history. It cannot be for us what we most seek: real experience. And this makes an understanding of the effect of Yoko Ono's work on the world most interesting and most elusive. I asked a friend in New York, who'd had another friend who had known Yoko, Tony Cox (Yoko's second husband) and their daughter Kyoko when Yoko was producing her early works amongst that city's burgeoning avant–garde scene, for an impression, some opinion about her work, at that time. When it was all just beginning. He said, "it was unusual in those days for someone to say she was doing a work of art which consisted of sitting in a large paper bag and waiting for someone to join her in it. Of course he didn't realise she was simply being seminal." Yes. She was seminal.

There's little doubt about that now. Love her or hate her – and she still has detractors by the score – it cannot be denied that Yoko was ahead of all sorts of ideas which later became current practices. So seminal is certainly one way of thinking about what Yoko was doing with those early performances and pieces. Seminal is defined by the Collins English Dictionary in the following ways: Potentially capable of development. Highly original and important. Rudimentary or unformed. Of, or relating to semen: seminal fluid. Of, or relating to seed. In these definition,s Yoko's work fits all five in one way or another and is perhaps a good way to begin to think overall about her art before diving more specifically into some of the pieces which include films, writings, exhibitions, songs, poems, scores, performances and sculptures.

The emergence of the avant–garde in New York was concurrent with Yoko's creative flowering at Sarah Lawrence, the prestigious college just outside the city at which she first heard of Cage and serial music, and where she had begun to realise that no one art form properly allowed her the expressive palette her emerging creativity and sanity demanded. The potential for development was twofold. Yoko developed through the avant–garde scene, and the avant–garde scene benefited enormously from her contributions, which provided an exotic mix of the ancient Japanese arts, post war Japanese thinking and a uniqueness of vision which, to this day, retains a freshness and a quality of almost cleanliness of thought.

There's a clear connection between all of Ono's works and the early foundation stone studies that she imbibed. From her piano playing and vocal training, through philosophy (which clearly influences all the works with their focus on 'the idea' and the participative response/completion of the observer's imagination), and the poems, drama and expansive creatively driven arts courses at Sarah Lawrence, Yoko Ono found a way of making art–as–communication. As John Cage, one of Ono's profound early collaborators, has said of his own work "When I wish as now to tell of critical incidents, persons, and events that have influenced my life and work, the true answer is all of the incidents were critical, all of the people influenced me, everything that happened and that is still happening influences me."(1)

Perhaps all artists might admit this, certainly looking now at the range of canvasses Ono covers, there's always a connection to the past. In her fusion of her experiences of American and Japanese cultures, in the effects of the war on her early life and subsequent political stances, throughout all, the essential ingredients can be found in her past. This is a prevalent feature also in the kind of artist Ono was/is, where the actuality of experience forms the basis of the art being produced; the artist is the art. In the practice of conceptual art wherein the concept embedded within the artwork is more important than the piece itself, the notion that the observer contributes to the event or experience of the artwork reduces the distance between the artist and the product to such an extent that the artist's life and work are in may ways inseparable and the artist's response to their life is to turn it into their art. As Ono herself said of her early life and her drive to create art in interview with Melvyn Bragg "I was not feeling too much part of a circle, wherever the circle was...the only way I can really communicate is through my art and also that's where I am free." (2)

When Yoko left college and entered the world of the avant–garde herself, she became part of what would be seen later as a highly influential group of artists whose collaborations would stimulate and whose importance would be seen to have had a profound effect on several major art forms. the Fluxus Group, a loose collective of like minded artists breaking barriers and exploring the new territories of conceptual art provided an entrée for Yoko, as she did for them when she offered her own loft as a performance and gallery space for their mutual events. She has said of this that they thought she was a rich man's wife, they didn't see her as an artist like themselves. Not at first. But before long George Maciunas realised her potential and soon her own early 'Instruction Pieces' were part of the 'happenings' eventually leading to her collaborations with a group of cross and multi discipline artists who would come to define a contemporary art movement.

It may have been obvious to the high art world that Yoko was at the forefront of what was to be seen, eventually, as a historically charged moment in the history of conceptual art in the western art world, but that message has taken some time to filter down to the rest of the hoi polloi. Without doubt this has been part of the double–edged sword that Yoko's marriage to John Lennon became in terms of her place in the pantheon of super stardom. On the one hand, through her association with Lennon she had on tap funding, the best publicity and a creative partnership with a very 'like minded' other. But all of these things came with a price tag the size of Paris. The funding would be perceived by many as gold–digging. The publicity she received was not in the potentially more receptive broadsheet newspapers but in everything from the tabloids (in whose hands she undoubtedly suffered racism and sexism of a most egregious nature) to the electronic media.

And that creative partnership – well, that gave her some stupendous works; the 'Bed' and 'Peace' campaigns, the advertising billboards, and perhaps most importantly, the music. But the music was often heard as both unfashionable and, more to the point, unmusical, delivered as it was direct to the palettes of pop fans mostly raised on the 4/4 beat and the sixties radio platter of two and a half minute pop tasties. Yoko was serving aural sushi when the listeners were eating salt–in–the bag crisps. But what is increasingly evident to art lovers, conceptualists and those born late enough or far away enough to have missed the battering she took from the British and North American press (male and female, they all had their say) is that Yoko was doing something no–one else was doing.

And whether you like what she was doing or not, she was doing it first. It probably goes without saying that historically there aren't many prizes for 'doing it first'. Most people 'doing it first' seem to die in penury. So highly original, absolutely. And important? Yes. To the conceptualists Yoko was combining elements and introducing ideas which would long be taken up by other artists and she was doing so in a refreshing way, bringing concepts of the organic, the numinous and the spiritual together. Many of her peers would study Buddhism and find solace and fascination in the Eastern, but Yoko embodied that in her experience and 'herstory'. And in terms of her creative partnership with Lennon, musically Yoko was hugely influential on many vocalists who superseded her in a wide variety of other popular music genres.

If one looks at Yoko's work from the earlier pieces whether performance based, musical or textual to the more recent works there seem to have been many stages of development. At the time that Yoko eased her way into the art consciousness (not an easy ride), her work was finding itself. As time has passed and she, amongst others, have discussed the works and their values have been accepted. She has moved on astonishingly, particularly beyond Lennon's untimely death. Her recent exhibition in Paris at the Musée D'Art Moderne contained some works made in the last ten years alongside older pieces reinvented or represented. They seemed to have an awareness, a wit and a substance that was more clearly enunciated, more immediate perhaps, than evidenced previously. But as I began by saying – we cannot go back, and so who knows, perhaps had we stood in front of 'Smoke Painting' –

"Light canvas or any finished painting
with a cigarette at any time for any
length of time.
See the smoke movement.
The painting ends when the whole canvas or painting is gone."

(Yoko Ono)

– in an under– heated loft in the early 1960s in New York we might have felt similar resonances. Effectively, the work of most artists begins unformed until the public know enough about the artist to frame the work in a space that includes the psychology of the artist and until the artist, pushed to talk about it, forms answers, and there is enough of a body of work for a pattern to have emerged. And Yoko has always been exceedingly coherent about her work. More to the point, Yoko has said on all occasions that her work is 'participatory' – that it is completed by the onlooker. This is especially true of her 'Instruction Pieces', which depend on the onlooker's imagination to be complete, through to the current 'Peace' exhibit in Liverpool in 2003, where the viewer is invited to stamp the word 'Peace' onto a world map on an area which would benefit from it.

In that Yoko's work might be arguably proto–feminist, feminist and post–feminist, it can be argued that it is seminal in this much wider sense.

Where to begin on the multitude of steps Yoko took with these explorations of her work? Perhaps at 'Cut Piece' which even today has the capacity to engage the attention, to shock and provoke. Witness the publicity surrounding the Ranelagh Theatre in Paris' performance in September of 2003. At the Paris exhibition running in 2003, on the 'Wishing Tree', a man had written a short statement on a piece of paper. It said "we are enriched by the experiences of this woman laid bare for us here." "The experiences of women," he added, "have been largely denied us, and they are a necessary and essential part of humanity."

That her work elicited such a response from a viewer, such an honest and utterly heartfelt communication, speaks volumes. Another wish said, "I wish galleries would stop showing shit." There are certainly those who would argue with the political stances (particularly the feminist) and with reason, but whatever in–depth analysis of Ono's life and work might reveal, she embraced and discoursed with passion, and, for whatever the time scale, commitment. Her influence on Lennon's understanding of the skewed relationships between men and women, particularly during the sixties, had an effect on his work and inspired him to comment extensively on these issues, and indeed write songs about them. We shouldn't underestimate the ripples spread by this and nor should we expect either John or Yoko to live every second of these commitments. North Americans allowed Clinton, and the British, Prince Charles, much more rope than anyone ever allowed either of these star–crossed lovers.

There is a piece Yoko made. Coffins lie in lines. Through each a tree emerges. Her understanding is evidence. Living and dying. The Shinto connection between the human and the animate world. Her early life in a Japanese home where the door opened right out into the garden. The garden/outside world and the home/inside world were as yin and yang, mutually interconnected. Seeds fall from dying flowers. Trees, wind, air, fire, water and plants fill Yoko's work. They are as significant as the sky, the moon and the sun. They form part of her/our imagination play and they are real. They frame us and embrace us.

At the Temple in Tokyo in an early event, Yoko gathered her audience and they watched the sky through the night, surrounded by the trees, as dawn broke the watchers took a bath together, then the monks served them breakfast. At the temple she was inspired to make her 'Wishing Tree' piece. At the temple the seed of belief grows into understanding within the individual's psyche and soul. Yoko's work seeds into the onlooker ideas and possibilities which grow into all manner of changing landscapes.

WOMAN

Speaking of why the humble citrus held significance for her, Yoko said she liked grapefruits when she was a child, and they seemed to her like a hybrid of oranges and lemons. She titled her first self–published book of instructions in Japan in 1964, naming it Grapefruit. The notion of Yoko as a 'hybridisation' (a botanical term wherein two genetically unlike species are cross–bred) "appeals". We see within her two cultures, Japanese and North American. Her work exhibits a deep relationship to Zen Buddhist concepts and to Japanese poetic and artistic art forms where minimalism is an aesthetic. This is expressed by Zen Master High Monk Mr Sugunaga succinctly "The idea of Zen art is to create beauty using the absolute minimum."(2) But she makes her home in New York and returns there with Lennon, and her art is though rooted in Japanese philosophical thought seeded and grown amongst, and in, the American avant–garde.

So how to understand the effect of this exceptional woman's work on an unsuspecting American public? In London the early exhibitions certainly caught the 'in crowd's' imaginations. She was in Berlin, in Paris and on stage with Cage and Coleman. Screaming for all she was worth. Lennon, in the story he must have told a thousand times about their meeting through her work at the Indica Gallery in London, makes clear exactly what it was that captured his imagination. On climbing up a stepladder to view through a tiny eye glass that allowed the participant to see a piece of paper on the ceiling on which was written the word, "yes" Lennon remarked that everything else in the art world seemed so nihilistic. Yet here was someone saying "yes". Regarded now as a landmark artist who helped to define the conceptual art movement, Yoko Ono has come a long way. She has experienced pain and aggression at a level that would have broken most creative souls. But she used her art to move herself through these attacks and to become strong. It was her saviour on a personal level during those early days, and it has clearly been a staff when the road was hard indeed. Yoko Ono's work is still saying 'yes'. And that's perhaps the easiest way to begin to grapple with her immense contribution to the creative history of the last sixty years.

Notes

1. John Cage, An Autobiographical Statement. *Southwest Review*, 1991. Whole statement displayed on Web Permission of The John Cage Trust, New York.
2. Mr Sugunaga interviewed on *The South Bank Show*, Granada Visual SM 699.
Grapefruit, Yoko Ono, Book, Simon and Schuster, 1964.

2. **From Scream to Singing**

"I wanted to throw blood"

It is already enshrined in the story of the love affair that shook the pop world to its core that when Yoko and John finally got it together they were in his house, and his wife was away, and they'd done the dance of courtship which, whether you believe Yoko's detractors and their biographers or not, had taken some months. They went upstairs to the attic studio and made their first musical collaboration whilst off their heads and then made love. For the first time.

That this is probably more information than any thinking person needs is shot into the shade by the product of that first creative – in all senses of the word, union. The album *Unfinished Music Number 1: Two Virgins* was recorded on May 20th, and released in 1968 by the Apple label. Its fair to say I think, (and I speak here as a fan of Yoko Ono's musical and vocal works), that only because Lennon part owned Apple did they get this out of the studio and onto the eager spinning decks of anyone else. But this is more to do with the relationship that would alter Ono's artistic and creative processes and life forever, than the content of the record. For Yoko Ono was well versed in ground breaking musical concepts long before meeting Lennon and if anything, what is becoming increasingly clear, is that her effect on him was easily as profound as his was on her.

But her effect on him was manifested through the influence of her personal identity as an artist and her ideas. It seems fair now to say that his on hers was perhaps much more to do with his being one of the earliest and perhaps most iconographic of the sixties musical figures, a Beatle, and the effect of the wealth, fame and notoriety that conferred. Note Yoko's contribution to the *Unfinished Music* title of the album with its subtle reference to the sub–heading of her Indica Gallery show (sometimes billed as 'Unfinished Paintings') because the work had to be completed by the onlooker/listener. Ono had trained as a composer and was familiar with and had collaborated with some of the most contemporary musicians of the time. They may not have been household names, but at high art altitudes they were pushing musical boundaries into unmapped territory and are today regarded as pioneers of modern classical and jazz music.

In the beginning, there was a young girl, trying to impress daddy by playing the piano superbly and failing, failing, because of her small hands. That young girl grew up and on the way studied singing at her

Japanese college. She absorbed the Japanese musical influences of her surroundings; the Zen and Shinto philosophies, she breathed them in, they entered her as on the very air, alongside her taught Western classical models. Her well–born mother was skilled in the Japanese cultured arts, she studied and was excellent at ikebana (flower arranging) and understood and read Japanese singing and musical scores, playing the shamizen and koto (traditional Japanese instruments). Yoko later remarked that her own musical compositions in their bare notations and instructions resemble the minimal musical Japanese scores her mother read. Of her studies at her American University Yoko has said

"My heroes were the twelve tone composers – Schoenberg, Berg, those people – and I was just fascinated with what they could do. I wrote some twelve tone songs, then my music went into (an) area that my teacher felt was really a bit off the track and....he said 'Well, look, there are some people who are doing things like what you do and they're called avant–garde'." (1).

It wasn't just music. No one field of art allowed her expression, the soil it needed to blossom. The discipline needed to develop classical compositional skills, or coloratura soprano was so not featuring in Ono's vision though she was an adept student of lieder before studying philosophy at Tokyo's Gakushuin University. But no one art form embraced her. This is not to imply that as an artist she lacks discipline, far from it, in terms of her output and of her dedication to her work she is clearly an extraordinarily hard working and serious person. But rather it draws attention to the need for expressions of freedom that run like veins through many of her works, and which in the years just prior to and after Lennon's death, were severely curtailed by the needs of the business empire she managed on behalf of their joint estate. The fearlessness with which Yoko attacked vocalising, and, for the listener, what that exposes psychologically expanded vocal horizons exponentially.

Long before *Two Virgins* there were collaborations in New York with another student of Cage's, LaMonte Young – who is regarded by many as the seminal creator if minimalism in music. He and Yoko attended lectures hosted by the then famous *enfant terrible* of contemporary classical music, John Cage, at the New School in Manhattan in Greenwich Village with her then classical pianist husband, Toshi Ichiyanagi. In the wonderfully extensive book and testament to her creative position in the art world, *Yes*

Yoko Ono there are photographs of Yoko against a wall, her trademark black flowing hair framing her porcelain face, screaming her way into and out of the free improvisations that are being made around her. In 1992 she said, "It was all just a head trip. The avant–garde boys didn't use the voice. They were all just so cool, right? There was also (a) very asexual kind of atmosphere in the music. And I wanted to throw blood." (2)

"I wanted to throw blood."

How much clearer could she be? The intention in Yoko's early vocal works was not to please, or to sell records or move units. This was not the world from which she was emerging. It was to create, to express something from the inside to the outside. To externalise the inner psychodramas that were seeking release. In the wider picture, Yoko's emergence as a musical figure parallels similarly 'dissident' creators whose works are now, like hers, recognised for the overall impact they have had on their musical genres since. Like Ono, they travelled lonely roads at first, creating outside the mainstream. But they stayed outside the mainstream and were judged by the criteria and aesthetics of their peers, whereas Yoko's work suddenly found itself in the glare of a spotlight, which judged her and her music through an entirely different cultural lens. It is only in the last few years that she has been recognised and assessed as an avant–gardeist and her works acknowledged and assessed more fairly.

At the time Yoko hit New York and hung with LaMonte and composer Richard Maxfield, Ichiyanagi and the Fluxus Group (whom she invited to perform in her cold water loft), the musical boundaries of jazz and contemporary classical music were under siege. The tonal works of Berg and Schoenberg, the explorations into uses of tapes and repetition of Boulez and Stockhausen, the free jazz movement liberated by Ornette Coleman from the previous conventions of harmony and melody, blowing his trumpet and the jazz community into a new sea entirely; all these musical and compositional storms raged around Ono. She was a part of a musical movement, and like those counterparts she was using a very particular, and for her a deeply personal, medium, the voice.

She was also experimenting with tape–recording, and overdubbing. Respected by 'serious' musicians, (the classical Juilliard cellist Charlotte Moorman was a friend and lifelong promoter of Ono's musical works, often performing them herself) and artists, and married to a respected pianist, Ono returned to Japan with her husband in 1962. There they arranged for David Tudor (one of the leading avant–garde pianists of our time, composer and later MD of Merce Cunningham's Dance Company) and John Cage to come and perform with them and participated and co–created the Tokyo Fluxus scene.

In 1964, Ono returned to New York and became increasingly active making work which fearlessly crossed barriers fusing recordings with film and performances. Fluxus mainman George Maciunas encouraged her and she found acceptance at last from the other avant–garde artists, which must have helped her confidence enormously. Finding a metaphoric and creative 'voice' through which she could express the interior landscape and fear she had experienced allowed her to use her actual voice more and more. The 1968 *Two Virgins* collaboration with Lennon affords a first recorded experience of Yoko's use of vocalising and soundscape. Lennon had also experimented with tape loops and unusual recording techniques prior to meeting Ono and their mutual concerns coincide on this, for both, seminal recording. Although Ono had worked as a solo artist, she had consistently collaborated in her work in New York and Japan. She was used to defining her own artistic vision amongst similarly strong–minded creators, and Lennon for her was just another artist. It must have been a breath of fresh air for him to find a like–minded soul for, as many critics and indeed Cynthia Lennon have noted since, the art world was also where Lennon began his creative life.

"Filled with unorthodox music, Yoko's inimitable screaming and snippets of conversation and bird song (long before sampling and ambient music), the album was controversial and unpopular – as was its cover."(3) As Ono herself remarks in interview with Paul Trynka in 2003 "it was totally misinterpreted, like saying 'Yoko's screaming'. When you really listen to it, you know that its very kind of musical – musical is a very strange word – but adding a kind of dimension in music, rather than just some Oriental woman screaming." (4) In a discussion of muses, Prose is far less kind, and represents exactly the kind of judgmental misunderstanding that dogged Ono's work pretty much from this point onwards until its recent renaissance.

"The recording features whistling, caterwauling, groaning, wailing, moaning, shrieking, samplings of old records, the sound of guitars being tuned and strummed, background noise, scraps of conversations. The result is so dull that only incipient passion and the promise of sex (that is, some approximate re–enactment of the circumstances under which it was made) could persuade someone to listen to the end, for the chance too hear Yoko cooing, in a ready schoolgirl's voice, a simple ditty about remembering love." (5)

But it's all about aesthetics. If you listen to this recording expecting a Lennon and McCartney melodic sing–a–long with jolly harmonies, then yes, you are going to be sorely disappointed. But it isn't just that. Ono is expressing vocally in a way that is both provocative, disturbing, affecting and vitally contemporary. She was very clearly 'doing her own thing'. It's no wonder it made some people angry. And Ono is right when she says defensively that Hendrix was also breaking barriers, but people coped with that, no problem. There again, Hendrix wasn't married to a Beatle. Nor was he a Japanese woman with attitude and a belief in herself at a time – the sixties, when good girls put out and shut up and looked pretty.

This was pre–feminism, but Yoko had already taken steps with work like 'Cut Piece'. She was used to the company and understanding of other avant–garde artists and audiences. Not the average tabloid reader, or worse, journalist. In a revaluation of their first four experimental albums Andy Davis declares, "From its cover inwards, the album was an astonishing manifestation of The New.... *Two Virgins* should be seen as a document of obsession, set against the backdrop of the late '60s underground art scene.... As a defiantly non musical, intense personal work *Two Virgins* is separate from any of The Beatles, John Lennon's, or indeed Yoko's "proper" recordings." (6) Davis notes the relationship of some of Lennon's Beatles work to this recording, citing Lennon's musical wit and its relationship to '50s radio humour before adding, "to expect an enjoyable listen is to miss the point."

The album indeed begins with noise and bird song, samples, whistles and echoes. Yoko's first vocalising is spoken. She answers Lennon, and responds to his guitar slides with a whoop. As he begins to strum she widens her voice and sings open syllables in falsetto. She's light and sweet. Then she screams. The effect is frightening. It is unreserved. Returning to the gentle singsong and whoops, then her voice extends into a single point of pain, a grief filled cry as Lennon's guitar grows increasingly discordant and he speaks and shouts. Yoko floats across the top of this, the voice soaring birdlike and descending into a wail of pain. The piano crashes. She opens the voice out and the operatic quality makes a fleeting contribution. The 'screaming' is a much more complex sound than the word suggests. In fact she draws on many elements of the sound palette within that rubric. Sometimes animal–like, child–like at points; passionate, grieving, desperate, open, closed, higher, lower. Weird yes, but never, ever dull. In fact, she's increasingly resourceful with her instrument. She begins to shout and Lennon responds, she makes tones of great beauty, sings 'yes' and he responds 'yes', her 'yes' extends from all woman into banshee. Then like a scratch on a blackboard, eerie, echoed by his guitar. Sometimes the voice is free of vibrato, sometimes it shakes. "Who's that?" she cries. He responds. He laughs. They interact. Then like a buzzing bee (a sound that characterises the soundtrack of the film *Fly*) transforming into a harpy Yoko continues.

The contemporary vocal practice of leading Voice work students incorporates archetypes, and the use of voice outside the 'usual' parameters of 'singing' (particularly given the restricted timbral uses in western classical and popular music). It also includes therefore a much wider ethno–musicological model of the voice incorporating the vocal practices of other cultures.

We are more open now to these aural qualities Ono explores. She begins to sound like a child crying, but we know she's a woman. It's distressing to listen to. We now know that the effect of vocalising can put us, the listeners, into emotional places we might otherwise avoid. She becomes playful. There's a childlike joy in their mutual exploration. They are making love before they actualise it. They are giving each other 'who they are'. But not with words.

For Ono, who found the New York avant–garde men asexual, this must have been a wonderful union. As Lennon plays the organ, she sings. Almost modal, she develops a church like melody. Her voice passes from woman to child in one leap. Lennon roars. She becomes feline. He riffs, she repeats, she mews. Then Lennon plays a quiet guitar tune and Ono sings a song. "Remember love" she sings, in the voice of almost a teenage girl. For the last twenty years our charts have been full of this kind of vocal tone. It's not a million miles from Marianne Faithfull's early voice on record. Breathy, girlie, gentle, reassuring; this song ends the record. It could be a private anthem for Yoko, one half of the most famous love story of my generation, and a woman who has spent the years since Lennon's death remembering love privately and publicly.

Notes

1. Ono quoted in 'Interview With Yoko Ono' 173.
2. Gann, *Village Voice*, 11th October 1992.
3. Clerk, *Uncut,* September 2003.
4. Trynka, *Mojo*, May 2003.
5. Prose, *The Lives of the Muses. Nine Women and The Artists They Inspired*, Aurum Press, 2002
6. Davis, in *Record Collector* 215, July 1997.
Unfinished Music No. 1: Two Virgins, John Lennon/Yoko Ono, CD, RCD 10411

3. The Sixteen Track Voice

In an often quoted interview with *Rolling Stone's* Jonathan Cott in early 1971, John Lennon enthusiastically refers to Yoko as having a "sixteen–track voice."(1) By this time the world had come to know Yoko and John as a couple, and had opportunity to hear much more of their joint work. After the debacle over the nude photographic cover of *Two Virgins* more joint musical output was to come and in November 1968 Apple released *Unfinished Music No 2: Life With The Lions*. The title punned on a well–loved 1950s radio programme, but this cover featured Yoko in a hospital bed with John at her side. It documented, however, much more than just the miscarriage of their child. As Edward Gomez says of their second release together, "The documentary, life–as–art character of Ono's collaborations with Lennon was rooted in the avant–garde aesthetic that she knew well."(2)

The album explored further aspects of Yoko's music, and also contained a two minute track of silence. There was a live recording titled 'Cambridge, 1969' on the second side which was of a performance in Cambridge with Yoko vocalising, Lennon playing guitar, the 'free jazz' drummer John Stevens (of Spontaneous Music Ensemble) on percussion, John Tchicai (one of Coltrane's contemporaries) on saxophone and Mal Evans on 'watch'.

The remastered CD's first track, 'Cambridge 1969', is introduced slightly hesitantly by Yoko, who then lets rip with a tight sound of intense, laser like precision. The guitar accompanies with customary feedback, alongside Yoko's voice the two like tram lines of insane sound. Andy Davis describes it as an exorcism of their "collective demons."(3) Yoko extracts tiny melodies, then returns to her focus of demonic sound. The guitar echoes. Her pitch rises, then suddenly there's silence and she returns. Escalating, the guitar builds and slowly Yoko opens out the timbre, she alters her vowel sounds. The voice begins to oscillate in pitch, resembling the glottal shake variations of a Quawali singer. Nusrat Fateh Ali Khan comes to mind. Of course, his was a deeply religious singing at the service of greater power.

Ono's expression shares something of that quality. It's like a volcanic explosion from within her. Time seems suspended in this unformed, unrestricted vocalising. Then she screams. The timbre changes again. The guitar timbre alters with her and from that Yoko changes her timbre and pitch again. There is absolute communication between Lennon and Ono.

They are joined in this music making in the same way that they appear to be joined in the many photographs of them taken at this time, staring into each other's eyes. The guitar riffs and Ono's voice alters again, into a celebratory 'oo'. Is she begging without words? The range of her vocal imagination and sound is exhilarating and sometimes shocking. Much of what is happening for her is illuminated by some of the comments she made to Cotts in that 1971 interview.

"The older you get, the more frustrated you feel. And it gets to the point where you don't have the time to utter a lot of intellectual bullshit. If you were drowning you wouldn't say: 'I'd like to be helped because I just have a moment to live.' You'd say, 'Help!' but if you were more desperate you'd say, 'Eioughhhh,' or something like that. And the desperation of life is really life itself, the core of life, what's really driving us forth. When you're really desperate, it's phoney to use descriptive and decorative adjectives to express yourself." (1)

The desperation Ono talks of refers to the enormous sense of isolation she lived with from her early childhood through her student years and in those first projects in Manhattan. The lack of acceptance by other artists during those times caused her much distress. This was followed by the isolation she began to feel after she was accepted when her film *Bottoms* became something of a cause celèbre receiving accolades and creating for her a degree of fame within her circles and the art press. All served to create this individual of immense inner strength and resilience with accordingly equal vulnerability. Meeting Lennon changed that. In 1971, despite her problems with Cox and her daughter Kyoko, coupled with the infringement of motherhood on her work and time, Yoko had found someone with whom she could collaborate, who would open her musicality into another landscape, and her expressive uses of the voice correspondingly expanded. She said to Cotts;

"I'm starting to think that maybe I can live. Before, it seemed impossible; I was just about at the vanishing point, and all my things were too conceptual. But John came in and said, 'All right, I understand you.' And just by saying that, all those things that were supposed to vanish stayed." (1)

Near halfway through the *Cambridge* piece, which is 26 minutes long, it almost feels as though Yoko is trying to exorcise herself, to free herself of

147

the demons who, if she can give them voice, might fly free from within her heart, soul and mind. The voice settles. Playful, it becomes a flying plane circling around and over the guitar sound. Whoops like the ritual spitting out of some internal illness and then a wail, extended like the lines she asks you to draw in her artworks. The voice is high in pitch; it's the song of a deranged soul wandering a lonely landscape, dipping as the guitar takes its place. Again Yoko takes flight. She is, as a palmist once described her, a very fast wind. Percussion surrounds the lovers in their extraordinary musical dance. The saxophone joins them. Yoko seems desperate to communicate, near words form, do we hear what we think we hear? Then the mewling of a kitten, some animal on a wild plain, a cat on heat calling into the African night until the sound of the sax dies away.

'No Bed For Beatle John' is Yoko in the tiniest, saddest voice. A voice of the girl inside herself. This girl singing, is pregnant, hospitalised and under observation. She will loose her child. Perhaps somewhere within her she already knows. Lennon sings faintly in the background. But it is Yoko who, although soft, is leading. She sings her press release, telling of the cover of the *Two Virgins*. Her voice sometimes with vibrato, sometimes without, always melodic and soft. As though by singing these words somehow she can release the inner pressure. Lennon sings of his upcoming divorce. It's a very odd piece. Moving, and yet also cold.

The next track is a recording of the heartbeat of this baby, who will never see life in the world outside. Yoko is using her art and Lennon's access to recording and production to document their relationship as surely as she documented her own development through her paintings, pieces, performances and films. The difference is that this is now very, very public.

There follows two minutes of recorded silence. Cage had long worked with the concept of silence, and Yoko had explored this too in her Carnegie Hall Recital Rooms performance in 1961 with George Brecht, La Monte Young, Jackson Mac Low, and with help from Richard Maxfield. She wanted to discover "the sounds you hear in silence. You would start to feel the environment and tension and people's vibrations. Those were the sounds I wanted to deal with, the sound of fear and darkness, like a child's fear that someone is behind him but he can't speak and communicate this." (1) This silence reiterates Yoko's contribution to the recording. These early recordings of Yoko's and John's feel very much driven by her conceptual musical praxis.

Maintaining their closeness and joint creativity, in October 1969 Yoko and John released their *Wedding Album*. Calling out their names to each other "across the entire range of human emotional responses: in love, in fear, in pain, with longing, with worry, in desperation, in anger. Beneath all this, the visceral throb of the couple's heartbeats can be heard, recorded, once again, through a stethoscope. It's a claustrophobic, painfully personal recording, and it leaves the listener agog at the frenzy with which Lennon and Ono seemingly devoured each other." (Davis, 3)

There is a recording of their 'Bed In For Peace' at the Amsterdam Hilton wherein Lennon explains the campaign/art event they are constructing. In his retrospective view of their early work, Davis finds this album the least interesting except perhaps for its packaging. The album, designed by Apple art director John Kosh, was packaged with their drawings, a gate fold sleeve, a doily, a copy of the marriage, photo of their wedding cake (!), certificate and a 'bagism' bag. Yoko's presence is tangible. The inclusion of these wedding accoutrements suggests a reaching out through her artworks; its as if she/they want the world to participate in their wedding. But new plans were already afoot.

Yoko was beginning to feel the need for another conceptual framework, and Lennon had committed himself to supporting her musical work and her talent and so the Plastic Ono Band was born. The first advertising slogans for the band said "You are the Plastic Ono Band" playing both on the audiences' participation in the concept of the band and also referring to the notion that band line–ups need not be 'fixed' in the way of the supergroups. There's an almost polar opposite in band concept to that of The Beatles in Ono's description of the kind of band Plastic Ono would ideally be. She wanted "a band that would never exist....that didn't have a set number of members...that could accommodate anyone who wanted to play with it." A band whose members could change according to the requirements of the music. Lennon said "Plastic Ono Band was a concept of Yoko's."(4)

Their first release *Plastic Ono Band: Live Peace In Toronto* (now remixed and re–mastered and available on CD) was also released in 1969, and recorded at the band's performance at the Toronto Rock'n'Roll Revival in September of that year. Band members included Eric Clapton on guitar, Voorman on bass and Alan White on drums. Their joint but separate *John Lennon/Plastic Ono Band* and *Yoko Ono/Plastic Ono Band* were released in December 1970. Some of Yoko's tracks were jam sessions from the rehearsals for John's release but all were her compositions. Lennon's recording cites Phil Spector as a producer while Lennon and Ono are joint producers of her record.

She enjoyed this process enormously and began to relish the opportunities that commercial recording could creatively offer. Although critics were on the whole, dismissive, Bill McAllister in *Record Mirror* said "Yoko breaks through more barriers with one scream than most musicians do in a lifetime."(5) These recordings were concurrent with the Ono–Lennon's pursuit of Janov's Primal Scream Therapy, Yoko finding less in Janov's work than John, (obviously, since she had long been exploring the scream vocality far beyond Janov's remits). But John embraced the vocal delivery as Yoko began to learn through him an understanding of commercial recording practice in the form of a more structured rock 'n' roll rhythm. Yoko's 1970 release is unsurprisingly very much more rock oriented. But that doesn't lessen the music's impact or indeed hold back her vocalisations.

In 'Why' she screams the question; enraged, barking, howling at some far–flung moon. Driven by Starr's direct drumming and Voorman's solid, unrelenting bass, Lennon's guitar and Ono's voice interplay as before, Ono is almost speaking in tongues. Andy Davis finds that the track "seethes with a confrontational menace not heard again in Britain until 1976 punk." with "Lennon's scratchy, razor–wire guitar is harder and more experimental than anything he ever managed for his own recordings."

'Why Not' begins with Ono twittering, a sound like paper stuck in a fan, a ghostly Japanese priestess walking across an almost bluesy musical backing. The voice fills with breath, becomes childlike, floats and mewls, chops and stutters. The stuttering, the 'breaking up' of words is something that Ono has talked about in terms of the process of speaking which begins in the head, in the mind, as a series of broken pieces of sound before emerging as connected speech. The disengaged nature of the stutter is uncomfortable, particularly as it sits against the gentle backing.

Yoko's singing is unusual in the western context, and when judged by a western aesthetic. Generally, in western popular music, timbres define particular singing styles to an extent. It is unusual for any commercially successful singer to display too many timbral changes. To rock the aural boat. But Yoko is singing from inside herself. In exactly the way she makes her art works, or her films, indeed all of her creative output is about herself. She is her source material. When she makes her various sounds on these early records they are mostly non–verbal. Where they are verbal her voice sounds more 'usual'. It is when she works without words that something else happens in the range of sounds produced. Such sounds can be regarded as the most archetypal expressions of emotion.

Newham suggests that before language "To communicate anger, fear, sadness or revenge, people had to represent both vocally and physically the essence of these emotions, which involved a spontaneous translation of affective experience into acoustic and kinetic expression." (6) This expression demanded a complete commitment of voice and body, the dualism we would come to enjoy and the subverting 'civilising' effects of language and postures that societies and cultures would encourage and enforce would create psychic tensions which might effectively be released by sounding these 'voices' and their correspondingly buried associated feelings. Early societies, Newham suggests, would use these sounds not only to express emotion but also to identify features of landscape and experience, and would communicate solely through them. Ono herself emerges from a spiritual background which incorporates the animate and inanimate, her Shinto and Zen background and her experience of war as a child all take part in her liberating 'screaming'.

"In the absence of words, the body and the voice had to assume a thousand different shapes in the course of describing a single day's events. The people of pre–verbal cultures therefore had to be great performers, sculpturing and orchestrating their bodies and their voices like singing acrobats, representing a child, an animal, performing fire and rain, expressing triumph and defeat. It is from these essential and primal vocal utterances that the act of singing originates." (2)

At the time when Primal Scream Therapy was developing, Alfred Wolfsohn was training his students to release their voices and free themselves from the shackles of their own somatic and psychic limitations. He had already shocked the European psychological community with his students' performances. By the time he died in 1962, he had proved the fundamental connection between the voice and the psyche. Wolfsohn too had found his creative path through the free expression of the voice. He too had experienced the effects of war first hand as a young man. He had fled the Nazis in Hitler's Germany. He sought to liberate his own inner demons through liberating his voice. In an article by the psychologist Eric Weiser Wolfsohn said,

"Man has for many centuries failed to appreciate his voice; he has underestimated it and neglected it and allowed it to waste away; he has virtually strangled it, chained it up and confined it in a straitjacket; as he has so often done before, man has once again turned his sinning against nature into dogma; the dogma of tightly restricted, neatly labelled categories – male and female voices, high and low voices, children's voices and adult's voices; the dogma that maintains that every human being has been assigned a particular register from birth, or at least from the moment the voice breaks, that covers no more than around two octaves; soprano, mezzo–soprano, and alto for women, and tenor, baritone and bass for men. The truth is that natural human voice, freed from all artificial restrictions, is able to embrace all these categories and registers – indeed, it is able to go much further."

Yoko goes much further. With the track 'Greenfield Morning I Pushed An Empty Baby Carriage All Over The City', the guitar sets up a recurring riff and Yoko intones the title words. Now we have language but with a use of extensive echo and the opening of the vowels she releases torrents of sadness on notes of falling glissandi like snowflakes in a blizzard in a downtown city street. There is no child in this voice. This is a mother's loss. The voice is thicker timbred. In the lower register, utterly embodied. The sounds seem as though they emanate from Yoko's abdomen. Even the higher register notes have a much rounder, much more 'motherly' timbre. Sounds of birds remind us of the sweetness of life, set against the panoply of pain that is 'Greenfield Morning'. The birdsong increases, until it is a veritable forest of music. An empty baby carriage. Yoko mourns her lost child and again seems to be presciently tuning in to what will become one of her and John's most painful shared experiences, the tracking down and estrangement of her daughter Kyoko.

'AOS' is from a rehearsal tape for the show at the 1968 Albert Hall show with Ornette Coleman. It begins with a wall of sadness against Ornette Coleman's tragic trumpet accompaniment. The guitar wails and after a pause, Yoko makes the sounds of a woman trying to rise, attempting to come up, to surface. She is in the lower register, the voice sighs, resignedly, "No, no, not yet" she says. Now the sounds of a woman in approaching ecstasy of orgasm breaking forth into the screech of a wounded peacock. Coleman and Edward Blackwell's drums encompass Ono as she folds her harpies wings' voice back, down, down. She breathes, the breath hugely audible, in the background someone coughs.

'Touch Me' is a collection of howls, suddenly interrupted by another rhythm, another set of vocalisations. A train running past introduces 'Paper Shoes', and a collage of sounds opens into a vision of the world of movement and travel, of distance and presence. Waves of interweaving sounds, rain falling, vocals coming back and forth, rhythms of sound; voice and effects play together in this damaged vista of her world. CD bonus tracks were a version of 'Open Your Box', 'Something More Abstract' and 'The South Wind.'

The inclusion of the 1968 Coleman piece served to demonstrate to the world that Yoko's work had a history and that she had had other musical collaborations of note before those with Lennon. The record is a surprising amalgam of Yoko's compositional and performance skills incorporating contemporary recording techniques and rock and pop musicians. Yoko said that she would start to scream and Lennon would play and she would improvise and he would respond. But she was forced to work physically very hard to be heard against the amplified instruments and sometimes in the studio technicians and engineers simply couldn't cope with the sounds and demands of her extemporising.

She found solace in the heartbeat of the 4/4 rhythms of rock which she had at first rejected as an avant–gardiste, as being simplistic. She came to think that the loss of the 4/4 beat by the art music composers had set them up at the top of a building, whereas for her the beat gave back the heart to the music, brought it down into the ground of human experience. She had recorded the heartbeat of the baby she would loose. Nothing would go to waste in the process of making sense of the world through the creative process of making and expressing art. Nothing of Yoko's life was not transformed through creativity. Everything was in the work, and the work was in everything. And through her released and uninhibited vocalising, she was indeed able to exhume, reexamine, release and strengthen herself. For soon she would need all that strength and more.

Notes

1. Cotts, 'Yoko Ono and her Sixteen Track Voice' in *The Ballad Of John and Yoko*, Doubleday/Dolphin 1982, first published in *Rolling Stone* Magazine, March 18th, 1971.
2. Gomez, in 'Works', *Yes Yoko Ono*, Japan Society New York and Harry N. Abrams, 2000.
3. Davis in *Record Collector*, 215, July 1997
4. Coleman, *Lennon, The Definitive Biography*, Harper Perennial, 1992.
5. McAllister quoted in Gomez, *Yes Yoko Ono*, from *Record Mirror*, 19th December 1970
6. Newham, *The Singing Cure, An Introduction To Voice Movement Therapy*, Rider, 1993.

Unfinished Music No 2: Life With The Lions, John Lennon/Yoko Ono RCD 10412, Zapple 01, 1969

Plastic Ono Band: Live Peace In Toronto John Lennon/Yoko Ono, LP, Apple CORE 2001, 1969

Yoko Ono/Plastic Ono Band Yoko Ono RCD 10414, Apple SAPCOR 17, 1970

4. Fly and The Infinite Universe

In 1971, Apple released Yoko's double album *Fly*. The cover included collages by George Maciunas of Fluxus, pictures of Joe Jones' machines and daughter Kyoko's and Yoko's own drawings. The musicians (with John Lennon of course) were Eric Clapton on guitar, Ringo Starr on drums, Klaus Voorman on bass, Jim Keltner on drums and percussion plus a plethora of terrific session players. Between them they contributed flair–filled jams and imaginative musical frames for Yoko's ideas. Billed as 'Yoko Ono and Plastic Ono Band' (with Joe Jones Tone Deaf Music Co.), for Jones was a longtime Fluxus collaborator with his music making machines, performances and work with Maciunas and George Brecht. The recordings included the use of machines that Jones and Ono created which could be manipulated by switches.

With the work of Maciunas on the cover and Joe Jones' contributions the album drew together these various old and new strands of Yoko's creative/personal life. Her conceptual pre–Lennon art, composition and performance and her with–Lennon commercial music making. Commercial in the sense that the recording processes, 4/4 driving rhythms, use of high–ranking and prominent rock and pop musicians and access to substantial funding for sleeve design and production techniques reflect the more mainstream music industry to which Lennon had introduced her. The album was recorded on downtime whilst Lennon was making *Imagine*, and, rather like the cover, it features many of her vocal and compositional/conceptual facets. It also begins to reveal what she could be capable of musically and is a profoundly interesting record of her process as musician/composer/vocalist and poet/lyricist.

"Wake up in the morning....caught in fear, Midsummer New York my heart shakes in terror, my heart, hands, my legs, my mind, everything I touch is shaking, shaking....wake up in the morning, the bed's wet in sweat.....shake shake"

The band plays a rock 'n' roll as Yoko sings to the melody reminiscent of the opening part of the verse of "Heartbreak Hotel", playing on the old blues "wake up in the morning" lyrical entrée to what seems to be a juddering emergence from a drugged night before. "The bed's wet in sweat....everything you see is shaking shaking." When she sings 'Shake" like a furious addict denied a fix, she growls as she sings "aching, aching" and we have a very different Ono. With *Fly* Ono sings with the rhythm, letting herself be part of the rock picture. Even the timbral interplays sit with the beat, the improvisations tied to the drum and guitar riffs. Yoko found a new form and worked with it. The way she plays on the standard blues lyrical intro but brings it into the present tense, the use of "shake" with the melodic resonance of Elvis's hit, calling on both his movement and the sound of his voice in the lyric "shake" and reinventing the melody. All these point to Yoko's ability to tap into cultural ideas and subtly reframe them, calling us to readjust our way of listening, to question ourselves, to participate actively in the act of listening.

'Mindtrain' begins with a howling guitar train whistle and a rattling drum and percussion moving vibe. It's evocative and sets a musical idea which is immediately overturned when Yoko begins to vocalise. Here, Yoko's voice is like a rhythmic, bleating sheep. It's completely incongruous with the musical frame, calling us to both hear the voice against the music as almost separate entities. And there are words and again there are the stutters overlaid with wailing *glissandi*. Her voice is speech inflected, and we question whether we are hearing words, or fragments of words. "Shining down" Yoko sings, "past many towns," "train" spoken between whoops and growls, squeaks and vocal noise. The 16 minute track builds the layers and layers of Yoko's vocal 'licks'; words interact with one another as sound collage over the flowing 'mind train' of the music.

'Mind Holes' begins with a wail over a gentle descending guitar pattern, North American landscape of twanging country blues guitar is overlaid by the many voices of a ghostly oriental wail, crying into a Paris Texas dreamland. Plucked guitar strings and slides underlay the sighing and animal crying of an unhappy spirit. The juxtaposition of the Americana soundscape and the frailty of Yoko's sad eastern lamenting evoke a sense of the loss of an ancient world. Do we mourn for some landscape flattened for a shopping mall? Is Yoko vocalising her chase across America for her daughter? The open–endedness of the tracks always leaves the listener guessing/participating.

Beginning with a screech of pain 'Don't worry Kyoko, (Mummy's Only Looking For Her Hand In The Snow)' places the voice is front of the mix with Yoko speaking over and over "Don't worry" before stretching a syllable and shouting "Don't worry" as the 'ee' of 'worry' is stretched like a piece of piano wire about to break. All this over John's recurring, angry, angular guitar pattern. Taking many timbral sounds over the pattern, sometimes her voice judders and shakes. The vocalisations become extreme and drift in and out of speech through vowels. The link between pain and suppression of pain sitting somewhere in this tension between non verbal speech and pre verbal sounds. The effect is disconcerting, misaligning. Always playing with texture, exploring emotion and provoking response, the track in its way totally conforms to Yoko's life/art.

Lyrically exploring the notion of being of being John's wife and a mother, (both in the personal and general senses in which all women are 'mothers' in this world), and struggling with her preoccupations with the notion of 'peace' and 'war', (themes she explores throughout her life to the present day), and our responsibilities as people to comfort and to try to articulate the mysteries of life and death, the track 'Mrs Lennon' is curiously, extraordinarily prescient. When Yoko later released the substantial collection of her recorded work *Ono Box*, she omitted this track. Over a beautifully lyrical backing of gentle and flowing acoustic guitar, keyboard and bass and in the softest voice, like a woman adrift, Yoko sings:

"Mrs Lennon, oh Mrs Lennon, checking the sky to see if there's no cloud, there's no cloud
oh then, I guess sit must be alright.
Mrs Lennon, oh Mrs Lennon, making the tea and watching the sea,
there's no waves, oh then, I guess it must be alright.
Silver spoon, oh silver spoon, I lost my silver spoon.
And our children all our children if they have to go to war,
yes my love, its ok, half the world is always killed you know.
Husband John extended his hand, extended his hand to his wife,
and he finds, and suddenly he finds, that he has no hands
they've lost their bodies, yes they lost their bodies
neither of them, oh neither of them ever left each other
yes my love its ok half the world is always dying you know"

Herein are many of Yoko's themes; the sky, the sea; the overwhelming capacity of nature to subsume, to inspire and to enfold us. The sense of loss in the missing silver spoon. Is Yoko talking about the career trajectory she might have had had she continued as a solo artist and never met John? "They lost their bodies." Is this the compromise we make in marriage? To lose ourselves in the 'other'? "Neither of them ever left each other" but that doesn't matter because we all die a little every day. There's an unending sense of that 'line' that Yoko draws on the gallery walls, asks us to draw, from ourselves out into the world. As though umbilically connected to events, objects, emotions; as artists we string ourselves along, linking, changing, explaining, denying, surprising, and above all, imagining.

'Hirake' begins with Yoko demanding that we "open your box, open your legs, open your ears, open your nose, open your mouth, open." Contemporary funk underlays her extemporised theme. "Open the world!" she shouts. 'Toilet Piece' begins and ends with a flushing toilet to develop into the percussion intro of 'O' Wind (Body Is The Scar Of Your Mind'. Yoko's distinctly melodic exploration sits beautifully over this quasi Hindi backing track.

The original record of *Fly* offered the theme track of their film *Fly* and indeed the reissued CD offers this on disc two along with the tracks 'Airmale', 'Don't Count The Waves', 'You' and 'Telephone Piece'. 'Airmale' is a vocalisation over percussion and noise, rattles and wire–like sounds with loops and echoes. It's exciting and expressive, though in a way Ono's vocal territory here is becoming more familiar. Beginning with an almost Oriental vocalisation of the title 'Don't Count The Waves' with an atmospheric soundtrack, a Doctor Who theme gone awry on a strange planet, sonic expression embraces Yoko's negative command. Strings and Yoko's voice take 'You' in the talons of a bird over a plain of plucked strings, voices shine and decay, flare up and die away, the birds of her voice call to the other birds, overlapping air waves. Again the aural expression of sky and sea is present. The voices build, one upon another, lower in pitch then raise, the dynamic outpourings thrill and excite.

'Fly' is Yoko and guitar, and is best experienced alongside the film, where it is evident that Yoko's voice exhibits the inner landscape of the filmed, silent woman and expresses also the movements of the flies over her body. A phone rings and 'Telephone Piece' gives us Yoko answering her phone. "Hello, this is Yoko." The CD features 2 bonus tracks 'Between The Takes' and 'Will You Touch Me'. The first has a scratched backing with a very present Yoko vocal track. The second begins with Lennon's voice, he counts her in and she begins to sing a simple Lennon–esque melody over his acoustic guitar. He stops her. She begins again. Her voice is small, like a little girl's, as she sings: "Will you touch me, will you hold me when my mind is full of tears, will you kiss me when my mind is so dark. All of my life the doors kept closing on me and nothing in the world can open my heart but some kindness. Will you touch me when I am shaking in fear, will you reach me when I am trembling with tears." There's a slowing down and she sings syllables and then he whistles, before stopping to tell her about the structure. The track ends abruptly. They disappear.

As Peter Doggett notes of Yoko's next major release *Approximately Infinite Universe*, "While Lennon slumped into creative ennui, Ono borrowed his Elephant's Memory band for another double album. No scream–fests here: this was a full–blooded exercise in militant but compassionate feminism. Fuelled by equal doses of anger, humour, despair and love. this is her strongest collection of songs." (1)

On the sleeve of the now available CD, framed by photographs of Lennon and Yoko in deep 'togetherness', a portrait of Ono musing, and a profile portrait cover shot of her in her full beauty, is an essay titled 'The Feminisation Of Society.' Originally written in '71, it is abridged from the *New York Times* article published in February in '72. She acclaims the 'feminisation' of society, a society based on love rather than reason. In recent years there's been an increasing questioning of the mapping of human behaviour onto gender, for example emotionalism onto the female. There has been increasing awareness that this has been detrimental to both sexes and in the anthropological, philosophical and political debates expanded by feminist, gay, lesbian and developing world disciplines things have moved along. Ono's essay is both of its time in terms of the agendas she confronts but its also pretty prophetic. But the world of pop and even progressive rock was unable to function well with political statement. It's hardly surprising this work received mixed reviews since the critical network surrounding the music industry was, and remains, predominantly male.

It is par for the course that biographer Jerry Hopkins entirely misses the point of this and, indeed, most of Yoko's albums. Reluctantly however even he notes that for the first time much of the popular musical press recognised Yoko's work positively. That the albums made little impact on the national charts – a fact Yoko's detractors erroneously deem important, serves only to show how much of music is judged, not on its merit or artistic value, but by its sales. Aesthetic judgement and the relevance of groundbreaking work is best not confused with commercial activity. On those grounds many great musicians and acts would be found wanting. The recent reassessment of much of Yoko's music in the thinking music journals is testament to the longevity of her work though its true to say it was missed by many at the time.

Tosche in *Rolling Stone* reviewed the release of the album thus: "It is indeed a shame that the vocals on this album have been allowed to dominate the music, for the boys from Elephant's Memory have rarely sounded better. Yoko, however, in her role as lyricist, is, as they say, laughable. ....Since when does the staggering, ever–expanding universe have anything to do with some rich kid sniveling about the turmoil within her run–of–the–mill soul or crooning philosophical and political party–line corn that went out of style with last season's prime–time TV?" Yoko's work was rarely if ever reviewed for itself rather it was framed within the misconceptions abounding about her past and intertwined inextricably with received views about her relationship with Lennon. *Approximately Infinite Universe*, like most double albums, could have probably been shaved down to one better collection. More is most often found to be less, let's face it. Having said that the recording production, the band, and Yoko all sound fantastic. Her vocals are imaginative and her singing – now text based – has moved somewhere else. She's tight with the band, and 'Yang Yang' opens the album with muscle and attitude.

"Yang yang's soft voice goes on and on,
I hate you, I hate you, where did it go wrong?
Yang yang goes talking to himself on the phone.
Yang yang sends his men pebbles and stones,
Yang yang rips his women down to the bones.
I own you, I own you, so give us a song,
Yangyang goes talking to his world on the phone.
Yang yang's born with a phone cord 'round his neck,
Yang yang never fails to stick to his kick.
I want you, I want you, you're making me sick.
But yangyang, the chord's never long enough
To reach your mommy's trick."

With a chorus urging us to "join the revolution!", Yoko begins a two album exploration of what's 'happening'. And what's happening is politics, she's mixing with the Jerry Rubins of the world, she's talking feminism and she's framing her thoughts on peace and war amongst the personal understanding she's getting from being John's chick. Because, make no mistake, however the avant–garde New York intellectuals might have felt about women's equality, those feelings were not reflected across their society. American women were reading the *Women's Room*. Gloria Steinem was raging and Greer's *The Female Eunuch* had been out barely a couple of years. The debate was only just beginning. And Yoko brought it into her work, and tried to frame it for herself.

Ono's problem often was that she sounded like a little girl, and the 'singing' quality of her voice sometimes sits at odds with the statements. Maybe if she'd sounded like a soul diva she might have been taken more seriously. But so much of the critique of her text based work seems to be dominated by a response to her vocal tone which often sounds light, airy, Oriental, frail, earnest and sometimes strident. None of these tones were 'en vogue' at the time in the popular charts. Singers with frail and delicate voices sang sugar songs of love and broken heartedness. They didn't tell you to go out and smash up a phone box. And why take such issue against her lyrics? Here's a snippet of Candi Staton's hit 'Young Hearts Run Free' "What's the use in sharing this one and only life, waking up just another lost and lonely wife, my mind must be free to learn all I can about me." None of it was Dylan, or indeed Dylan Thomas.

There's a lot to be interested in on this album, not least of all because it speaks of the confusion that most thinking women felt at that time denied the intellectual debate and mentality of Greer. Sometimes Yoko becomes pedantic, sometimes she's less than poetic. But her recurring themes are there. Peter Doggett is unreserved in his praise when he says that this was "musically at least – more orthodox. Backed by New York bar band Elephant's Memory, Ono delivered some fiery rockers, elegiac ballads, and even straight pop tunes like 'Waiting For The Sunshine'. The core of the album though" he writes, "was its strong lyrical content, making it the first fully–fledged feminist record in rock."(3)

Yoko released a single from these sessions in her motherland. The record was vilified for its feminist content but more importantly she stood for her beliefs and released in, of all places, Japan – where hierarchical ideas about the position of women in society were very rigid. There has been recent academic criticism of her 'feminist' stance and debate about whether she fulfilled her commitment. But Yoko was not a 'feminist artist', she was an artist who embraced some feminist ideas, and whose entire career was about the discovery and appropriation of themes which at the time were pertinent to her. To accuse her of letting down feminism is tantamount to accusing her of being a bad Buddhist and is to miss the point of her creative process.

Alongside the rhetoric are the familiar sunrises, questions, imaginings and that revealing title, *Approximately Infinite Universe*. Ono attends to that interplay between the dualities of western thought and Japanese sensibility, whose world view and philosophy gave us the movement between yang and yin, the understanding of the one within the other. John and Yoko, Yoko and John. It/she confused people. The title track speaks of Sapporo, in Japan, "where the men talk rough and never sing. Two bottles of loneliness patching the holes in her dream." Yoko sings "the wind of the future blows through her head saying there's no point of return." How lonely it must have been with what seemed like the whole world sitting in judgement of her. There are some beautiful tracks on this album, as the people who bought *Onobox* or the now available CD have discovered. And she kept on putting the work out there.

Notes

1. Doggett in *Mojo*, May 2003.
2. Tosches in *Rolling Stone*, 1972
3. Doggett in *Record Collector*, 154 June 1992.
Fly, Yoko Ono, Apple SAPTU 101/2, 1971
Approximately Inifinite Universe, Yoko Ono, Apple SAPDU 1001, 1972

5. **Double Fantasy and Season Of Glass**

In the early 1970's Yoko Ono released *Feeling The Space*, collaborating with guitarist/producer David Spinozza and superb session musicians while Lennon and she endured their separation, (the 'lost weekend' of eighteen months). Peter Doggett finds this to be "arguably her weakest album" as it lacked Ono's originality which seemed subsumed by the music which he found "failed to match her lyrical passion."(1) But there is a growing confidence in her singing voice, which with text rather than sound, previously often sounded frail.

Yoko tried on this record to move herself into a more jazzy vein; her preoccupying themes once again were women and their survival in patriarchal societies. As a thinking independent Japanese woman, it's not in any way surprising that these notions should preoccupy, particularly in the early 1970's when they were current debates and feminism was entering academia as a force which would irrevocably transform many disciplines. Power and retaliation, oppression and sexual response, all ideas which Ono had been exploring for some years, appeared in these lyrical stances. She then recorded the album *A Story*, shelved after her reconciliation with Lennon until some tracks were included on *Onobox* in 1992, and which was later released in full in 1997.

In the years that followed, she took increasing responsibility for Lennon's fortunes, at which she proved excellent, rescuing and 'husbanding' their mutual assets which subsequently became highly productive. She became pregnant and gave birth to their son Sean, continuing to run their businesses whilst Lennon stayed at home, for a time creatively (at least in the sense of making art) unproductive. Then Lennon began to write again, and in 1980 the husband and wife (ironically with some sense of exchanged gender roles) returned to the studio fired with renewed musical, emotional and spiritual commitment to make what would be their last recording together, *Double Fantasy*.

In ten days, they recorded some twenty two tracks, from which the album selection of fourteen was finally made. The structure hinged on their alternating (mostly) compositions, and the album was named after an orchid John had seen in the tropics. Their previous collaboration had been the heavily political *Sometime in New York City*, released in 1972. That double album had expressed their sympathies for radicals Black Panther Angela Davis and John Sinclair (the imprisoned manager of Detroit's now legendary MC5). Frank Zappa and Eric Clapton appeared on the

163

albums, as did the track 'Woman Is The Nigger Of The World'. The new album's concerns were much closer to their hearts; themselves and their commitment to one another, the terrain of their marriage and the effects that had on their individual emotions and consequently their responses to life.

It's evident from a comprehensive look at Ono's work that the move from avant–garde composer/performance artist/film maker to popular songwriter happened across a series of her albums. By *Double Fantasy* she has found her feet with a very different form of artwork, one in which Lennon excelled: Popular songwriting. Robert Palmer summarises well the changes rung by the time of *Season Of Glass*, the record she released after John's death which he describes as the work of a "mature pop craftsman." Partly he ascribes this more positive critical response to her contributions on *Double Fantasy* as being due to a growing tolerance of what he calls her "vocal mannerisms." This is attributable to the pop mainstream having absorbed acts from punk and New Wave whose vocals were at least as hard to handle as hers had been (and could be). Audiences had, therefore, become more acclimatised to hearing unusual voice work in popular music. Also the record itself is a finely crafted, highly technically produced and arranged adult album with a mainstream sensibility and Yoko's writing was regarded significantly as "more up to date and emotionally compelling than Lennon's." Palmer recognised that

"Ono had changed, too. She had learned to say what she had to say in songs that were telegraphically urgent but also finely crafted, with instrumental riffs, lead lines and solos that sported an attractive lyricism and were well suited to her more conventional but still distinctive singing. In effect, Ono and the popular audience had met each other halfway. Songs like 'Give Me Something', 'I'm Moving On' and especially 'Kiss Kiss Kiss' did not sound dramatically different from much of the music that was popular in rock discos, and these songs were heard frequently in the discos, while Lennon's songs conquered AM and FM radio, as expected." (2)

John opens the album with '(Just Like) Starting Over'. This Tin Pan Alley piece of crafted song on the theme of lovers reinventing their love is followed by Yoko's 'Kiss Kiss Kiss'. The track has a conventional structure undercut by effects and sounds and overlapping voices. Yoko's vocal effects are controlled to provide a foreground and a backdrop to a main vocal melodic line as the track builds to an aural orgasm along the lines of Gainsbourg and Birkin's 'Je T'aime, Moi Non Plus' but with less of the sentimentality of that 'sex Parisienne'. The track demands that the singer be touched, in the verses this is expressed firmly but gently, a break of despair "Why me Why you" interrupts and all the while there's a geisha like moaning slowly intensifying finally opening into unrestrained vocal release.

John's 'Cleanup Time' details their mutual life role swaps;

"the queen is in the counting home
counting out the money
the king is in the kitchen making bread and honey
no friends and yet no enemies
absolutely free
no rats aboard the magic ship
of (perfect) harmony"

Referring to oracles and Gods in heavens, the song is short and optimistic and is followed by Yoko's 'Give Me Something'. Again a demand. A warrior's cry begins the track. Everything's cold and hard, there's a shout in the background, as Yoko's lead line sings "Give me something better" – something, she tells us/him, "that's not hard." Tight and sharp and focussed, with a guitar solo, and slow but effectively punchy ending. The song sits in such contrast to Lennon's happy snappy track, providing a counterpoint which clearly expresses something quite deep in male/female relations. Something's gone wrong, it's been fixed, we are happy again now, says the man. I have been hurt and I demand redress and change and I will not throw out the reality of my experience until I know I am given something new, says the woman. It's not uncommon particularly where there has been a sense of betrayal. And in a sense Ono was betrayed. Not in fact by Lennon, for she knew all about his sexual escapades, but by life and love and the reality of all those structures she had felt tying her hands during the *Approximately Infinite Universe* period. Ono had swapped expressing these deep feelings with non–verbal sound for a tight poetic attack on the reality of her/woman's existence in lyric and music; in song.

The song 'I'm Losing You' speaks of Yoko's memory for what has gone down, and John's inability to deal with it all. Yoko answers with 'I'm Moving On'. "I want the truth and nothing more" she sings, "I'm moving on it's getting phony." A startling noise and stunning riff opens the track. Yoko's work on the album is so strong and she seems to have a control of her vocal sound she's never had before. She sounds less girlie and more woman, less frail, more strong; to use the feminist term, empowered.

John's 'Beautiful Boy' and 'Watching The Wheels' are answered by 'Yes, I'm Your Angel', which begins with a sonic soundscape of what seems like a New York Ballroom, taking us into some forties ditty complete with tra la la's. "I'll give you everything in my magic power" sings Yoko, and even though this is softly sung, it has a body to this range of the voice that wasn't exhibited before. There's a sense of change having happened in the viscerality of the sound. In feminist terms 'voice' has come to mean much, much more than the sounded voice. In freeing her songwriting voice, Yoko seemed also to have freed her singing voice.

The track 'Woman' seems to speak directly to Yoko and although it has a generality which raises it out of the particular it is clear that it is a peaen to Lennon's soul mate, to the woman he clings to as almost a foetal child in Leibovitz's famous photograph taken during the promotions for *Double Fantasy*. In 'Beautiful Boys' Yoko expands her lyric towards the end of the song, opening out from her own 'beautiful boys' to the beautiful boys of the world. Haunting, with its slightly Oriental melodic inflections and flute like sounds, gentle string sounds, it's a whole new Yoko singing "Don't ever be afraid to fly."

John sings 'Dear Yoko' making his message clear to the whole world. The response? 'Every Man Has A Woman Who Loves Him'. Again, Yoko's feelings are more complex. "Oh Yoko, I'm never ever ever gonna let you go" sings John, but for Yoko its just not so simple anymore, and over a reggae feel we hear "Why do I roam when I know you're the one, Why do I run when I feel like holding you?" It's a two section song, with harmonies, beautifully constructed, building slowly. Her tracked voices almost choral. Then Yoko develops her themes in 'Hard Times Are Over' but this Yoko is a woman. She's perhaps the 'Woman' of John's song, but she's also much more. Maybe the time spent away from art and on business, the strain of John's time away and his ennui, have affected this change. But there subtly throughout it's expressed as "Hard times are over, over for a while." A rolling almost gospel sound with a big chorus. Again the tracking of the vocals strengthens them. The harmonies on the chorus sweet, and sad.

'Help Me To help Myself' sings John to his 'Lord'. The album ends with the track that Yoko and John were mixing the night he was shot. It's also the track he recognised would bring Yoko the chart attention he wanted for her. And it got there. Hitting the dance charts earlier this decade it was, in a remixed version, stonking. It is pretty incredible in the original form. Dipping into disco culture, it takes from Yoko's soundscape period, and taps into the future in the way art can/does.

"I may cry someday
but the tears will dry whichever way
and when our hearts return to ashes
it'll be just a story"

The yells that punctuate the backing, these repeated aching shrieks as the track pumps along through an instrumental to a percussion breakdown over which it seems Yoko is being sick, throwing everything up. Then groaning before she speaks, her spoken voice is filled with knowing. The voice of a woman who has met the Gods and knows their power, knows the risks, but still cannot see what is coming....what is ahead.

"I knew a girl
who tried to walk across the lake
'Course it was winter and all this was ice
That's a hell of a thing to do, you know
They say this lake is as big as the ocean
I wonder if she knew about it?"

The repeated screams take the track away as guitars pierce the sonic landscape. Its the most stunning piece on the album and is utterly contemporary. The CD closes with John's voice and a slight giggle from Yoko. Would that they had left us with 'Walking On Thin Ice'.

The world and its wife know what happened. En route back into the Dakota, a man stepped from the shadows and shot Lennon. He died that night. Yoko was there. She was there when he was shot, she was there when he died, and she handled all of it with a dignity, strength and courage rarely known in celebrity circles. All that high–born Japanese background, all her quality as a human being, were called upon and emerged. Even those who had dismissed her could not fail to see how courageous she was. Never condemning, she took herself and her young son and moved through her grief and pain whilst remaining loyal to Lennon's memory in every way, to this day.

And since we know all her work is autobiographical – she has said so many times, it is not surprising at all that her next release, *Season Of Glass*, attempted to take her through that worst stage of grief, the ghastly realisation of being alone. Yoko went into the studio weeks after the event that had torn her world apart, because as any artist knows, that is the only way you can get through it. Work. The work takes you through it. On the track 'No, No, No' she uses real gunshots at the head of the track. She later wrote, says Joy Press, "that she had finally learned what musique concrete really meant."(3)

Doggett's assessment is that the album provides "an unsettling portrait of grace under tragic pressure." for the world's fascination. The striking cover photograph shows a pair of bloodstained glasses beside a glass of water on a table in front of a window which looks out over Central Park on what appears to be a gloomy day indeed. Light, water, air, blood. On the back of the CD cover a poem, which ends "there is a season that never passes and that is the season of glass." Produced by Yoko and Rob Stevens, the opening 'Goodbye Sadness' has taken Yoko's voice into the spaces she inhabited before John. Like the defenceless child within, grief is barely concealed as she hopes for release from this sad space she inhabits. A mournful saxophone interjects and solos. The sleeve contains a thanks, "music was my salvation" and dedicates the album to John, whose presence she had in the studio with her. In her portraits on the sleeve she is now alone, one with her son asleep on the bed, her arm and gaze protecting him. There's a telephone call. Yoko answers. Its a thousand light years away from the phone calls on the earlier records, from two minutes of recorded silence, and its followed by the song 'Mindweaver'.

Originally Yoko had worked with Phil Spector but his trademark sound was not right for her vision and whilst remixing she found the stark sonic world she had wanted for these songs. When Robert Palmer wrote about Yoko's work on this album, he didn't have the benefit of knowing as we do that Yoko would be back in the charts in 2002 with Orange Factory's remix of Plastic Ono Band's 'Open Your Box'. But he did register clearly the change of opinion that over that next twenty year period, albeit with its career ups and downs, would filter across the media and the world, resulting in Yoko Ono's music finally achieving recognition.

"The rest of the record is a report from the frontline of grief and delirium, though most of the songs were written some years before the tragedy. What emerges is a songwriter who has finally learned to channel her anxieties and frustrations – her cultural schizophrenia, the strictness of her father, her years as an artistic rebel – through finely modulated pop–song forms. Parts of the album are positively brilliant – the sweet cooing of 'Nobody Sees Me Like You Do', the dirty edge of 'Dogtown', the forthright treatment of sexual revulsion in 'No, No, No' – and it is never less than gripping...It seems strange, but Yoko Ono is a forty–eight year old pop singer and songwriter who may be just beginning to realise her full potential."(2)

That was twenty–one years ago, and lots more happened to Yoko in the meantime. Works of art she had made years before would emerge in galleries all over the world as the art cognoscenti ran to embrace their Fluxoid conceptual heroine. Her films would be recognised as a body of work and part of the experimental film movement which would inspire the works of video and installation artists. And Yoko would grasp the Internet, speak out on peace and national events, and make more records.

Notes

1. Doggett in *Mojo*, May 2003.
2. Palmer, 'The Other Half Of The Sky: The Songs Of Yoko Ono', in *The Ballad Of John and Yoko*, Doubleday Dolphin/Rolling Stone Press, 1982
3. Joy Press interviews Ono in *The Wire*, Issue 146, April 1996.
Sometime In New York City, Apple PCSP716, 1972
Feeling The Space, Yoko Ono, Apple SAPCOR26, 1973
Double Fantasy, John Lennon/Yoko Ono, CD, Capitol 7243 5 28739 0, 1980
Season Of Glass, Yoko Ono, CD RCD 10121, 1981
Onobox, Yoko Ono, Rykodisc RCD 10224/9, 1992
2717
A Story, Yoko Ono, Rykodisc RCD 10420, 1997

6. Rising: Starpeace, Onobox and Blueprint For A Sunrise

In the aftermath of loosing John and after *Season Of Glass*, there were some UK releases on Polydor; *It's Alright, I See Rainbows*, ('82) *Heartplay: Unfinished Dialogue* ('83) and *Milk And Honey* ('84), before *Starpeace* was released in 1985. *Milk And Honey* again united Yoko and John with alternate tracks and but the ideas stayed in the same lyrical ballpark as those on *Double Fantasy*; the nature of their lives and love. Clerk tells us the album contained six unreleased tracks recorded as demos during the *Double Fantasy* sessions to which Yoko added six originals, five of which were recorded after the tragedy.(1) The album explored their relationship, with a couple of curiously prescient Lennon tracks; 'Grow Old With Me' and 'Borrowed Time'. The new edition contains one of the last interviews recorded with the pair before Lennon's death.

Yoko's own work *It's Alright, I See Rainbows* was an attempt to push recording and studio techniques to their limit, and Yoko was imaginative in her use of sound and instrumentation. She used eighty one tracks on the track 'Never Say Goodbye', which was as Joy Press remarks, "a Herculean task in the days before mixing desks were computerised."(2) She developed these techniques on *Starpeace*, but it performed only poorly, commercially. Titled as an ironic comment on the Reagan administration's 'Starwars' Treaty it is Yoko in far lighter vein. On the re–released CD, many tracks are remastered and remixed and there is the bonus track of Yoko singing 'Imagine' at her show on the *Starpeace* world tour in Hungary.

But Yoko was understandably disappointed at the responses to the work and although the reviews were good, and the press at last were warming to her style and sound, she said "After *Starpeace* I was totally discouraged – not as a songwriter or composer, but by the fact that there was no kind of demand for what I was doing, to put it mildly! I thought that it was just impractical for me to focus my energy on getting my music out. I had so many other responsibilities with business, and with issuing John's work. Forget Yoko Ono, there were lots of things I had to do as Yoko Ono Lennon." (3) The *Starpeace* tracks all have an intense disco feel, with some wonderful and varied reggae and dance vibes, (given the time of the recordings and the prevailing dance culture that's hardly surprising).

But Yoko was becoming more and more interested in recording techniques and the creativity that they engendered in her. And she needed to work, as process, as catharsis, and to find herself again in the world as Yoko Ono and as Mrs Lennon (without John). Which must have been astonishingly hard after the intense togetherness they had shared, for even during their separation they spoke daily, they never stopped being the most important people in each other's lives. She said of that period in her life; "In the 80s, after John's passing, I really fell into music in a way that was like a security blanket; I needed to hold onto something. Doing something elaborate, like elaborate harmonies or instrumentals, was a way of getting into a more complex place, which was therapeutic. It made me feel there was a whole new world I was delving into." (2)

The list of musicians on the album is, to say the least, impressive and reads like a who's who of groove supremos of the time including, as it does, Bernie Worrell (keyboards), L Shankar (violin), Island Records' kings of rhythm Sly and Robbie on bass and drums, Nona Hendryx on backing vocals, the late Tony Williams (drums) and Eddie Martinez on guitars and electric sitar. The Sly and Robbie influence is palpable, and the grooves carry everything in cool style as indeed they had done for disco queen Grace Jones. The songs sit together as a coherent whole. Lyrically there's a sense of Yoko growing and moving on. Its a substantial recording and no wonder after making this she was disappointed that it didn't excite the record buying world.

So time passed, and Yoko dedicated herself to the managing of Lennon's creative and their commercial estate. She continued to go into the studio writing and recording and becoming more and more involved with the growing remix dance culture. Her artwork was increasingly in demand at prestigious galleries and Biennales, and she raised her son.

In 1992 she released the ambitious *Onobox* through Rykodisc, which reinstated her in the music world as a recording artist. It also served to provide the catalyst that was needed for newer and fresher ears to visit/revisit her work and to see it as a through line which of course didn't happen at the times of release, particularly of the earlier and more demanding work. The public perhaps still regarded Yoko primarily as Lennon's widow, but she was becoming increasingly admired her for her dignity and attention to his legacy.

But *Onobox* caused the music industry and press to renew their interest in her work. *Onobox* was a turning point. Dedicated to her son Sean, it was a collection of her work sometimes remixed and remastered (though not heavily) and collated through six CDs to provide an overview of her recorded musical history. The packaging, including pictures and lyrics, rapidly became a collector's item and was subsequently reissued later in the decade due to popular demand. As Press notes in her *Wire* interview,

Yoko was rediscovered at just the time that 'women in rock' were becoming the subjects of investigation, and *Onobox* received rave reviews bringing it to the attention of younger musicians who were less concerned with her history *vis à vis* Lennon and The Beatles and who listened up. Courtney Love was so enamoured of Yoko that she sang 'Twenty Years At The Dakota' for her. But *Onobox* was essentially retrospective. It was near ten years since something new had been commercially released, and in 1995 on Capitol Records when the time was right Yoko unveiled her new and exciting recording, *Rising*.

While the work was hitting the decks Press interviewed Ono and found that she "has made a return to her avant–garde roots with *Rising*, her most uncompromising album since *Fly*. She is accompanied by IMA, a group of ace teenage musicians spearheaded by son Sean Ono Lennon." Yoko was genuinely surprised at the number of dance mixers who wanted to work with her material, and said "I didn't know there were so many brothers and sisters out there thinking in the same directions as me." But there were. At sixty two Ono was returning to her roots with the vigour and success of a returning, once exiled queen. Rising? She was indeed.

The CD packaging is uncompromising in black and white. The cover shows Yoko's face emerging from blackness, her one visible eye looking straight ahead into the world. Her cheeks are edged in the darkness and the title *Rising* is pale yellow as are the names, Yoko Ono/IMA. Lyrics are printed over Yoko's bespectacled face (looking unnervingly like Lennon). Her eye alone framed by a keyhole looks out. She is photographed standing on some windswept forest wasteland in a kimono and she and the band stand together against a New York wall and alleyway on which the word 'Rising' is scrawled amongst the graffiti.

There's a statement too, 'When Molecules Rise, They Converge.' It describes how the playwright Ron Destra approached Yoko to write songs for his play 'Hiroshima.' The process of entering the studio to record songs for the play brought up for Ono latent memories of Japan, her mother, and the relationship between them and that of hers with Sean.

Her childhood bombing experiences in Tokyo make harrowing reading, as does the description of the times she spent starving with her mother and brother in the countryside of rural Japan. Many of these themes are explored in her touching 'Women's Room' exhibition, including her abuse at the hands of the doctor, and her and indeed the Japanese people's experience of living through the deaths of those cruelly bombed with the first nuclear warheads in Hiroshima and Nagasaki. Ono makes the connection between personal memory and present experience in New York, where AIDS is devastating the city, remarking finally on the quality of creative process to purge the soul of "pain, anger and fear."

The CD opens with 'WarZone', a high energy attack with tight focussed lyric; "Skin peeling, Bones melting, Hold your heart, Hold your life." The album is produced and mixed by Yoko Ono and Rob Stevens, and they do a terrific job of creating a spontaneous sounding live band feel which sits in complete contrast to the studio dominated albums immediately preceding *Rising*. Many critics viewed it as a return to form and more importantly a return to earlier vocal experimental work.

Whilst without doubt the tracks are punctuated to a greater or lesser degree by Ono's free vocal extemporising, there is a substantial difference in the voice work here. On earlier albums, the voice simply attacks each track leading and often working in call and response with Lennon's guitar. On *Rising*, Ono has learned where and how to use these soundings, these creations and purgings within, and with, a musical framework. The result is to make them much more difficult to hear. Much more painful. And much, interestingly, less easy to dismiss as simply 'screaming'. They are used to highlight and express alongside text, they sit much more firmly within the rhythmic context of the tracks.

It is as though a bound woman is freeing herself of the past as her mummy bandages unravel. Sounds of birthing sit alongside sounds of grieving and the lack of multi layering, the effect of them being more 'live', brings a very different immediacy to the music. Almost a companion to Galas' 'Plague Mass', Ono's performance, particularly on the track 'Rising', is suffused with an emotional content that for me feels absent from the earlier Cagean–inspired experimental work. 'Wouldn't' has a spikey groove, with a speech sung text. There's a maturity to this lyric/poem, offset by Yoko's fresh voice. She seems to have a control of her singing voice and a sense of singing that again is not evident in the earlier work where the text based vocalisings often tend to girlie breathiness. 'Ask The Dragon' is a testament to being, and begins with the slightly sexual vocalising that characterised 'Kiss Kiss Kiss', but this seems more playful particularly set against the harsh gorgon voice that Ono uses to speak sing the lyric.

With its hard rock New York Dolls–Velvet Undergrounds guitar thrash opening, 'New York Woman' could have been an early Blondie track. David Fricke's four–star review of the album in Rolling Stone says a lot about the change in responses to Ono's position in the American music marketplace.

"There are times when nepotism makes sense. The ardent patronage of her husband, John Lennon, enabled Yoko Ono to record and release some of the most fearless and prophetic music in avant–rock: the 1970 shriek feast Yoko Ono/Plastic Ono Band; the proto–New Wave bedlam of her '71 double album, *Fly*; the immortal 1981 serrated–boogie thang 'Walking on Thin Ice'.Based on the corrosive vigour of his guitar playing and IMA's strong minimalist rumble, Sean Lennon is the most sympathetic collaborator Ono has had since his father was killed. He, bassist Timo Ellis and drummer Sam Koppelman let Ono's rippling yelps and raw lamentations roam free over the fat clang of a rhythm guitar in 'New York Woman' and the brute rain–dance pulse of 'Turned the Corner'. 'I'm Dying' sounds like the Plastic Ono Jesus Lizard: one grinding chord progression cranked up to a crowd–surfing frenzy with Ono going into the kind of death–warble overdrive you usually don't expect from a sixty two year old millionairess.....In 'Kurushi' – Japanese for 'tormented' or 'suffocating; – she loses herself vocally in the huge spaces left by Lennon's austere piano figure and in the word itself, drawing out the syllables with emphatic desperation.....Like the Stooges' classic mantra 'We Will Fall', 'Rising' draws on the base element of howling rock & roll expression – fourteen minutes of crawling through shit to get to sunlight. That's not avant–garde. It's just music as real life." (4)

Ken Ficara, drawing comparisons to the work of current contemporary musicians and signifying as did Fricke that neither Yoko's age nor her financial standing are acceptable reasons to reject her ground breaking contributions and indeed this release, writes:

"Yoko Ono's new album, *Rising*, is simply outstanding.... She was tearing her guts out when Courtney Love was in diapers; she was doing industrial music when there was still industry in the US; she was doing strange spoken word pieces when Laurie Anderson wasn't old enough to drink; and at sixty–three, she is still out ahead of the crowd and kicking some serious ass. Yes, some of these songs go off into the sort of wordless screaming that characterised some of her extreme 60s work, but with a solid groove underneath that make you want to turn it up instead of turning it off. Despite years of abuse by ignorant Beatles fans who neither like nor understand her work, she's still a fascinating and dangerous musician who will not let you off easily." (5)

For Ono the work represented the closing of a circle, and speaking to Press she said of rising "I felt that Sean was very supportive of me, just like John. So there were no silly questions – you know, 'Why are you screaming, Yoko?'" The first live performance of *Rising* was at a memorial event at a shrine near Hiroshima. The music was rewritten for ancient instruments; didgeridoo, Japanese drum, Chinese gong and tabla. Certainly there is a link from Yoko's first Plastic Ono recording. It is more a spiral, it hasn't closed, the line has moved somewhere else, somewhere present (even with its evocation of the destruction of Japan and its play on Yoko's memories) whilst resonating utterly with that earlier work.

In 2001 Capitol Records released *Blueprint For A Sunrise* with Yoko playing fully on her Japanese 'dragon lady' reputation photographed/ graphically designed with long red pointing fingers and nails, a red headdress and ceremonial kimono as Chinese Empress Tz'u–hsi, a woman who sold her country to British colonialists and killed her son. Now near seventy, Doggett noted that Yoko's "artistic palette – brazen, bare, fuelled with daredevil spirit – remained totally modern, and uniquely individual."

Her opening track stands spoken/spat text against her vocalisations over a driving beat track. It seems as though on these two albums, Yoko is releasing vocally all the pain and horror of her early experiences in the clearest manner. 'Mulberry's' spoken introduction takes the audience to her early mulberry hunting ground. She uses the word mulberry to work through these reminiscences, stretching the voice through time. The voice now forges bridges across the pain rather than failing to cross the gap between there and now.

Where her earlier vocalisations suggested the vast chasm between her and her country, her and her mother and father, her and the public, her and her art, her and the man in her life (as though she was trying to heal some kind of inner wound by screaming across it), this seems to be the controlled anger, the directed gaze of a woman who has come to terms with her memories and can channel her focussed feelings through her unrestrained voice. 'I Remember Everything' is the woman celebrating her love, the love she has lost. The frailty that the voice once had is still there but with age it has resilience and a character it previously lacked. The range is lower, but that clarity remains. A power chorus celebrates the importance of memory, and the individual possibility of transformation through recall, while the certainty of 'Are You Looking For Me' recounts Ono's personal themes through the voice of fear.

The album ends with bird song, for as always Ono returns to nature, to hope, to dawn and new possibility. Whether she is really a singer, or a songwriter, becomes an irrelevance. She has struggled to assert herself as an artist, and in these days of musical collage/remix/montage this is an entirely acceptable view of her recordings. Once again David Fricke gave the album a four star review in *Rolling Stone*, once again he commended and understood the work.

"Misunderstood, even reviled during her first decade as a rock & roll singer, Yoko Ono, at sixty–eight, is in the curious position of being taken for granted as a punk godmother... in a new age of fear, Ono's keening wail and choked–breath seizures now seem prescient, the sound of life during wartime from someone who, as a child in Japan in the 1940s, knew the real thing.... Women are beaten, and beaten down.... Yet what distinguishes Ono as a singer is not her shriek but the stubborn joy inside.... An uncanny echo of recent trauma, 'Mulberry' attests to the best and worst in humanity: our ability to visit disaster on one another, then to transcend it. Blueprint for a Sunrise is Ono's way of saying we never learn from our mistakes – and that we should never stop trying."

Finally, it seems as though Yoko Ono has found, at least within the music industry, a recognition and celebration that perhaps she never knew she would or could have received. Finding in herself and in the collaborations she has made with the young musicians and remixers and her stalwart studio associates a new palette on which to express her words, her vocalisations and her experiences. The use of art as catharsis is always a double–edged sword. There is a strong argument that the effect is best received by the audience and that the performer's lack of control distances response rather than engendering empathy/sympathy.

In Ono's early work the catharsis seems to be for her, and it correspondingly separates us from her. In these two recent recordings her use of voice is much more affecting because of that new control. The audience is brought in, invited. Even though the soundings seem similar, their effect is quite different. It is not surprising that this work allowed audiences unfamiliar with her earlier pieces to re attend to them, nor that younger journalists were able to appraise the work more fairly. There are critiques to offer of the material, and indeed various writers note that whilst the work is indeed ground breaking and fantastical, it sometimes seems to them to lack listenability. Nonetheless they argue that the work has a place and do not resort to racism, sexism or just plain misunderstanding in order to decry Ono's artistry. At last, on record, that appears to be no longer in question.

Notes

1. Clerk in *Uncut*, 76, September 2003
2. Joy Press interviews Ono in *The Wire*, Issue 146, April 1996.
3. Yoko Ono speaking to Doggett in *Record Collector*, 154, June 1992
4. Fricke in *Rolling Sto*ne URL: http://www.rollingstone.com/reviews/cd/review.asp?aid=46799&cf=
5. Ficara on the internet, URL: http://www.ficara.net/writing/yoko–rising.html
6. Doggett in *Mojo*, May 2003.
7. Fricke in *Rolling Stone* issue 882 November , 2001
It's Alright, I See Rainbows, Yoko Ono, Polydor POLD 5073
Heartplay: Unfinished Dialogue, Yoko Ono, Polydor 817 238–1
Milk And Honey, John Lennon/Yoko Ono, POLH 5, 1984
Starpeace, Polydor 827 530–1, 1985
Starpeace, RykodiscRCD 10423, 1997
Onobox, Yoko Ono, 6 CD set with book, Rykodisc 10224/9, 1992
Rising, Yoko Ono, Capitol 7243835817 26, 1995
Onobox, Yoko Ono, 6 CD set with book, Rykodisc RCD1022429, 1997
Blueprint For A Sunrise, CD, Capitol 7243 5 36035 2 6, 2001

7. Cut Piece and The Performances

"'Being an artist' (then) means not doing different things than others do, but doing things differently. Modern Society undoubtedly needs creativity, critical imagination and resistance more than it needs works of art. It needs artists with their ways of doing things more than it needs the things that they make. It needs them for what they are rather than what they do – and if it does need them for what they do, then it is in the sense in which artists are producers of culture rather than of discrete artifacts that characterise that culture. The society relies on artists to be agents of culture who provide an index of human experience as well as a critical support for social practices and ideologies from which the concepts of culture are developed. And here again, it is the work of art, the actions and consequences of art, rather than the works of art, that is the active ingredient of culture." (1)

Pavel Buchler makes a convincing stance for the argument often used in the definition of the work–as–art that the conceptualist produces; "It's art because I say it is." And for the realisation of being 'an artist' as the *raison d'être* of art in contemporary western culture rather than the material/physical work itself. Yoko Ono's work is herself; her life experience, her intuitive understanding of the nature of communication framed through her sense of isolation and the use of her art as communication.

When she displayed her collection of wooden coffins with trees growing out of them in Israel, and referenced her own loss through violence or with her Peace Map in Liverpool wherein the observer stamps the word peace on the map where it is perceived as absent, Ono provokes us to remove ourselves from the sense of disempowerment we feel in our contemporary society. Separating neither life from death nor art from politics, welding them together she asks us to respond to, and with them. Resonating with the Zen and Shinto philosophies she imbibed as a child in Japan, she refuses even now to bow down, to give up. Working for peace, she asks us to think of a larger objective, of more than ourselves. Furthermore, Ono's work has the capacity to do more than provoke ideas and discussion, or elicit participation; notions that she often put at the forefront of her earlier works.

When attending the 'Women's Room' exhibition in Paris, I discovered for myself that her work has the capacity to move, to elicit deep and profound emotional response. The many hundreds of floating offerings hanging from her 'Wishing Tree', on which people hung tiny pieces of paper with their wishes written on them by hand, are a testament to the popular response to her work. As I sat in the gallery, I observed every single person who came through the door write something (either positive or negative) on a piece of paper. People wanted to make that communication with the piece. Based on the tradition of placing prayers on trees in the temples of her childhood, once more, Yoko drew on a Zen past which has illuminated all of her work, and which also attracted the attention of the Fluxus collective of artists in New York with whom she first found allegiance.

Although many of those early Fluxus meetings in Yoko's flat simply made her feel even less like the artist she knew she was/wanted to be, eventually her work had its effect. George Maciunas recognised her quality. She shone with an originality and a drive to communicate from the despair of her personal demons and isolation, about which she has spoken in depth on many occasions. To all artists, the work is the point. Everything else, life, relationships, feed the work. The artist is a strange sort of vampire, living off, feeding off these experiences. And perhaps this was the biggest burden Yoko Ono carried for all her early years in the public eye with Lennon. She always asserted herself as an artist. She behaved, effectively, like a man. She put her work first. She held her head up.

And speculating on the way her life might have been had she simply pursued her conceptual art and performances out of that excessively devouring public eye, what course could her life/art have taken? In interview with Melvyn Bragg, she said she thought, looking back, that she should have been more assertive. Certainly there's been the dichotomy of the feminism and the rhetoric of women's liberation set against the "stand by your man" Tammy Wynette–ian behaviour at the Beatles sessions where Yoko sits quietly in the corner. Lord, she might as well be knitting! Her togetherness with Lennon was taken to the point that he actually wrote, "Yoko and me, that's all I believe in." Theirs was in many ways a classic example of *folie à deux*, or the love we know as Eros, where the two simply gaze into one another's eyes searching for themselves, reassuring themselves that they are real, that they exist. But there was another history to her, a herstory that involved leaving her daughter with her second husband to go and make her art.

In 'City Piece' (1961 winter) she already faces these dilemmas: "Walk all over the city with an empty baby carriage." That baby carriage appears again after Yoko's miscarriage of her and Lennon's child and the ongoing battle for custody of her first child Kyoko on the Yoko Ono/Plastic Ono Band recording of 'Greenfield Morning I Pushed An Empty Baby Carriage

All Over The City'. Hers is a story that brought her to a stage in Tokyo; sitting and offering up a pair of scissors and inviting the assembled audience to cut her clothes from her, a performance she recently re enacted in the name of Peace in a theatre in Paris. But that first time, the younger Yoko had no idea what would/could happen. She just offered herself to the event and proffered the scissors to the audience. As an act of submission, in that highly stratified highly gendered Japanese society, it was supreme. It was also very Zen. What would be left of a person when all was stripped away? The search for the formless self.

In a repeat performance in New York, as her bra strap was cut and she for a second betrayed an emotion, she was berated by some other Fluxus members. Calling attention to the very nature of women's experience 'Cut Piece' is one of the many Ono performances that lend her work a feminist stance. But it is mistaken to assume that her work was directed at or for a particular nexus; at the core of her work was philosophy. The choice of study she made in Tokyo, was the study of ideas. She spills over with ideas, like a fountain shooting so violently from a tiny cup that the cup is overturned. And her ideas are unlike anyone else's.

Sometimes she is also part of the zeitgeist, as with 'Amaze' where there was a prevailing interest amongst artists for the fascination of labyrinths or with her vocal extemporisations used to liberate held and deep emotional trauma, as with the works of the Roy Hart Theatre and African American soul, blues and gospel singers. But her ideas had germinated long ago in the pre–war Japanese society in which she grew and the American society to and from which she travelled following her mysterious and absent father. The path/line she tremulously walked from young, disturbed, war traumatised girl to acclaimed visual, performance and pop music artist grande dame is easily visible in the spotlight of hindsight. She wrote in her (at first) self–published book of drawings and instructions 'Grapefruit' in 'Line Piece 111', "Draw a line with yourself, Go on drawing until you disappear." In the song 'I Want You To remember Me', on *Blueprint For A Sunrise*, she says

"My one eye
searched for the sky
My pillow
hung over the window
Months passed by
Years passed by
No shadow was left of me."

Moving in and out of shadow, working with light, nature, the changes that are wrought daily by the passing of time and clouds, the music in bird song, how the mind receives information, film, photography, installation, sculpture, poetry, music, performance, video, internet, advertising and the daily experiences of her own world. Yoko Ono's need to communicate has driven a unique, long and winding road through all, although she did of course come in through the bathroom window.

Consider the wonderful conceptual photographic 'Vertical Memory' piece. A picture repeated twenty one times, the computerised amalgamation of three men's faces central to Yoko Ono's life; father Ono Eisuke, husband John Lennon and son Sean Lennon, is frame by frame accompanied by title and sometimes text. Each text documents the stages of a woman's life from the experience of birth through to death. At the first picture, 'Doctor 1', the text reads "I remember being born and looking into his eyes. He picked me up and slapped my bottom. I screamed." The young woman meets a series of doctors, who take out her appendix, her tonsils, try to kiss her, perform abortions until her life completes it's cycle and under the title 'Attendant' we read: "I saw a dark hole in the shape of an arch. I saw my body being slid into it. It looked like the arc I came out of at birth, I thought. I asked where it was going to take me to. The guy stood there looking at me without saying a word, as I lay down, It all seemed very familiar. What percentage of my life did I take it lying down? That was the last question I asked in my mind."

Lars Schwander suggests that "The words establish connections to the common lines of female destinies and the succession of conditions, but it is not an exposé of the artist's privacy." But Ono has always had the ability, (sometimes better expressed than others), to be successful in what artists do. To make of their own experience such particularity that the onlooker/listener/observer/audience absolutely resonates with exactly that particularity through the instrument of their own emotional response. Ono has always exposed her privacy, quite deliberately. Otherwise what exactly are John Lennon's bloodstained glasses doing on the front cover of *Season Of Glass*? To say nothing of the recording of her soon–to–be miscarried baby's heartbeats on 'Life With The Lions'. Through so doing she allows the participant of her art of whatever media to join with and recreate that art personally. The conversation begins with her experience. We share with her our primeval dread of the dark in 'Light Piece' and her need to constantly re–light a match for fear she/we will disappear. We share the existential reality of existence in the 1961 piece 'Painting In Three Stanzas'.

Let a vine grow.
Water every day.
The first stanza – till the vine spreads.
The second stanza – till the vine withers.
The third stanza– till the wall vanishes. (2)

In the Plexiglas 1971 piece 'Amaze' Ono invited participation as people tried to solve their way in and out of a complex sixteen foot square transparent walled maze at the centre of which was a cubicle containing a toilet. Occupants of the cubicle could see out but from the outside were largely invisible to observers. Sometimes people became so distressed at their inability to traverse this maze that they had to be talked out by a caretaker. Existence may cost us our sanity. "To date, 'Amaze' is the physical culmination of Ono's long–standing interest in light as a sculptural material that is intangible, temporal and colorless." says Schwandler in *Yes Yoko Ono*. "Amaze adds a layer of meaning with its partially enclosed, but not private, space of the toilet. The predicament of being simultaneously hidden and utterly exposed links Amaze with the 1971 Plexiglas box 'Hide Me' as well as with Ono's infamous performance event 'Bag Piece'." (3)

In the 1964 'Bag Piece' one or two people went inside a large black muslin bag and took off their clothes. They might then perform a series of activities. Ono and Cox performed 'Bag Piece' in London as part of the Destruction In Art Symposium, and spectators found the piece oddly gripping. John Lennon embraced the bag concept completely. As he also embraced Ono's disrobing/desexualising of the human body; in the sleeve of *Two Virgins*, in the disturbing inanimate body violated by free wandering insects in the film *Fly*, in the geometric fascination of 'Bottoms'.

Together they coined the term 'Bagism' and used the performances to draw attention to their promotion of peace. In 1969 Yoko and John performed 'Bed–In for Peace' at the Amsterdam Hilton Hotel. Yoko's pieces here were transformed using the media access she had acquired though her association with Lennon and with his collaboration into huge statements and instruction pieces on a scale hitherto unimaginable for her, moving her art out of the gallery and right into the home in newspapers, on television and radio broadcasts. More than this, "Drawing upon the philosophical and phenomenological aspects of Ono's Bag Piece, they publicised the intimacy of the nuptial bed as a metaphor for cultural transformation, demonstrating the essential relation between private beliefs and public behaviour. In this way Bed–In For Peace wedded erotic love and an intellectual desire for world peace with the ideological goal of ending the Vietnam War." (3)

Then they launched their musical anthem and advertised, 'War Is Over!/If You Want It' on billboards in urban entertainment centres and major capitals (Times Square New York City, Piccadilly Circus London, Sunset Boulevard Los Angeles, Hong Kong, Athens, Berlin, Port–of–Spain Trinidad, Rome, Toronto and Tokyo). The work confronted a new level of international audience instantly. This was a binding together of ideas and actions which linked personal, public, political and artistic interests while questioning the very nature of how, where and what we see and hear and what we do/make with that knowledge. They struck at the heart by exposing the body. They struck at the body by exposing the machine. Art and politics were one.

Ono's contribution to, and use of, this art form is regarded by Kevin Concannon as widely under recognised. She continued this work on a grand scale after Lennon' death, in 1983, with a full page ad in the New York Times proposing a national peace poll. In 1989 she recreated the 'War Is Over' campaign but developed it further. Concannon concludes "Ono has stated that all her work is a form of wishing, and this might be what lends her advertising works their special power. For advertising too, works from the premise of desire. The difference, of course, is that conventional advertising operates by provoking desires that can be fulfilled by their clients' products, whereas Ono's faith in the power of wishing is freely shared." (4)

Come to the wishing tree. Write your wish on piece of paper. Hang it there amongst the many others. Take a second and read what they have written. Look at the possibility of freedom. And then, walk to the window, and fly.

Notes

1. Pavel Buchler, *Art: What is it Good For?*, Institute Of Ideas, Hodder and Stoughton, 2002.
2. *Yes Yoko Ono*, Japan Society New York and Harry N. Abrams, 2000.
3. Rothfuss and Yoshimoto, *Yes Yoko Ono*, Japan Society New York and Harry N. Abrams, 2000.
4. Concannon in *Yes Yoko Ono*, Japan Society New York and Harry N. Abrams, 2000

8. **Legacy**

The other evening in a television advertising break there was an advertisement for Sony Ericsson. The sound track was obviously contemporary. But immediately it was apparent that this was a piece of music which could have been made by Yoko Ono twenty or more years ago. There were the oft heard repetitive loops, the snatches of half–words amidst groans and sexual soundings, the rising and falling of Ono text vocal voicings over a driving and insistent rhythmic track combining strange sonic elements, at once unrecognisable and yet strangely familiar. Yoko's influence at that moment was as prominent and synchronous (for I was writing about her that very evening) as would have been a superimposition of her face on the screen. It was so forceful. I shared that significant moment of recognition with Lennon through time and space. We had heard and identified something similar.

There's a moment in the history of John and Yoko's lives which Lennon reports in interview, of how he hears the B52s whilst on one of the directional trips he was taking with Sean. And instantly realises that Yoko's musical influence has stretched into and beyond punk, that she has been a catalyst. We know that now, too.

The B52's were/are an Atlanta based four–piece whose art punk sci–fi glamrock thrash sensibility caught the imagination of the record buying public through supreme recordings like 'Rock Lobster' and whose rise to fame didn't include (interestingly considering the vocal similarity John noted), massive radio play. John's clear devotion to Yoko included his support of her musical work to a level to which the rest of the world at the time was somewhat less attuned, as many reviews of their joint musical efforts and beyond revealed. However in Davis' 1992 reassessment of Ono's early work he recognises that,

"Considering the pedigree of its protagonists *Yoko Ono/Plastic Ono Band* is a staggering album. Featuring half the Beatles, Manfred Mann's bass player and a Japanese performance artist, the sound is as bleak as anything recorded by the post–punk Industrial Movement, and its soundscapes of pain and isolation unfold with a steely grey realism reminiscent of early Public Image Limited. Lennon had every right to have confidence in Yoko Ono as an artist. She was ahead of her time and remains a true original." (1)

In retrospect, it appears that most serious journalists were baffled by all aspects of Yoko Ono at the time. However, nothing exists in a vacuum, and indeed Yoko was part of a much wider picture emerging during the 1960s musically, particularly in the genres outside the mainstream, but also in its own murky and darker waters.

The sixties provided the exactly right social and cultural conditions for the meeting of the avant–garde art world with popular culture. The Beatles explored art and design, George Martin was a classically trained arranger, the media was exploding and the notion of celebrity was being created in front of our eyes. John and Yoko didn't just make art, they were art. In their white suits walking in the glare of the cameras, Lennon pirouetting and Yoko holding her white hat over her flowing hair, they took their love and lives and made films of themselves at a white piano, or making love, or of John's erections, John's smile melding into Yoko's. They blazed a trail at the end of which it is our great fortune to have now, not an avant–garde artist and a superbly gifted songwriter, but Posh and Becks. In the paucity of our current social and cultural landscape John and Yoko seem like a knight in shining armour and the very essence of a beautiful Louis Carroll Queen (full of grit and surprises).

Influence always suggests that the artist has listened to and taken inside themselves somehow something of that which has affected them. It's possible that many more people were aware of Yoko's music, but on the whole it seems to have existed in a sort of post–Beatles vacuum for the greater listening world, although certainly the music press and Beatles fans collected, examined and some even loved her work. In terms of the contemporary conceptual art world, Yoko is now recognised as a founder of the movement which began somewhere with Dada in Europe and filtered through the New York artistic fraternity to emerge finally at the Turner Prize in Britain.

New art celebrities Damien Hurst, Rachel Whiteread and Tracey Emin stimulate the public's imagination and owe their freedom of expression in some ways to the founders of the movement that spawned them. With that ancestral blessing of ideas. Concepts. But what separates Ono is the quality of both a type of femininity which we might characterise as 'yin' through an action of 'yang' suffused with a deep sense of that somewhat overused and misunderstood word, spirituality. Which is, I think, justified in her work inhabited as it is with the profound philosophies of her childhood. What Yoko offered beyond that was twofold. The belief in the act of art as communication and participation alongside the use of self as the basic putty from which all might be sculpted.

In those early years Ono was working at the cutting edge of the cake with Fluxus in her cold water loft, the thick end of which we eat now at Tate Modern, The Saatchi Gallery, The Whitechapel Gallery and the many other international contemporary museums and spaces. There is far more a complete connection between Ono's 'Women's Room' and Emin's 'Unmade Bed' and various other pieces through which Emin celebrates her sexuality and acclaims her self, her right to 'be'. She too shares Ono's direct gaze and unrepentant demeanour, however she might be perceived to be transgressing.

The Guggenheim's recent exhibition of video and photographic art pays homage to the early Fluxus work and to Yoko's film and photographic explorations. Viola's pieces are in the National Gallery as I write. Ono's early film work was deeply unsettling and also rather humorous. Paglia accuses her of taking away John's wonderful sense of Scouse irony and replacing it with a political correctness which lends support to the somewhat dodgy and erroneous belief that Ono has no sense of humour. Apart from the number of journalists who note that they expected this to be the case and found it not to be so on meeting her, there are many examples which suggest that just because Ono often looked impassive she could be anything but.

In her interview with Melvyn Bragg for the South Bank Show, she says of her experience of starvation "of course, I was fashionably thin" adding "but we didn't care about that at that time." Hey folks, she's joking. Let me know when any of our current celebs manage a sentence let alone a joke. 'Bottoms' is simply hysterical. Its not just that the film is funny; its that people queued up to walk along with their bottoms wiggling about while Ono filmed them, very seriously. I'm sorry, but this to me suggests that Ono has a cracking sense of humour, and rather drier perhaps than imagined (no pun intended). Certainly no–one could have lived with Lennon and not known a laugh when they heard one. I don't think he would have stood that, give the man some credit, after all, he announced Yoko's contribution to the Toronto Peace Concert by saying "And now Yoko's gonna do her thing....all over you!"

During those early years and before the ennui, drugs and life's tragedies took their toll there is a mischievous look to Ono often caught in photographs or on film. *Fly* is an unnerving and captivating visual experience. The combination of the soundtrack and the flies, wandering over the impassive almost comatose body of a supine woman. The soundtrack, the repeated images, slowed and sped up film frames, surrounding the observer with the work, coccooning them within it. Yoko played with that power, and with these media, mixing and matching and paving a way for many other, later pieces and artists.

In terms of her lyrics, there is a personal core of experience that informs the heart of, not only Ono's, but, of that era, also Joni Mitchell's work. Both can be seen to have had a direct effect on the trajectory of the self–confessional writings and independent stances of singers Alanis Morissette, Tori Amos and Ani De Franco amongst others. Courtney Love has publicly acknowledged her debt to Ono. Ono's 'soundings' are part of a of larger picture that encompasses response to war (Wolfsohn's work), the growing awareness that the voice is capable of much more expression (The Roy Hart Theatre, Grotowski, compositions such as Twelve Songs For A Mad King) and the use of the voice as metaphor for gender, race and experience (the novels of Toni Morrison, the voices of Diamanda Galas and Oscar Brown Jr).

In the vocal vision of Diamanda Galas, another uncompromising singer and woman, whose political and personal ancestry is contained within her art form and whose work also provokes and disturbs, there is a resonance of Ono. Galas also performed with free jazz players before dedicating herself to the voice. She too was a highly trained classical pianist who had studied composition. She was also highly influenced by the AIDs epidemic and associated loss and often appeared as proud and strong through her work.

In Meredith Monk's floating ethereal vocal weaving, and her work with timbre and repetition there is a softness, a quiet, feminine finesse that Ono sometimes exhibited. The tape loops, electronica and vocal sounds and humour of Laurie Anderson, another New York avant–garde–iste, bring to mind some of Plastic Ono Band. In 1973 *'The Exorcist'* soundtrack terrorised audiences. The other worldly vocalisations were not a million miles from what Ono was trying to exorcise with her own voice. It's fascinating to listen to Bjork and look at her stance as a woman musician, and see how far we have come. Bjork's relentless individuality, her vocalisations, her mix and match of musical forms and art in her videos and photographs all lend her the air of a young, Icelandic Yoko.

We have come a long way, we no longer make racist slurs publicly (without severe recrimination) but someone was first in that firing line, and that someone was Yoko Ono. Scott Walker's recent recordings have attempted the same sonic landscape work that Yoko was a pioneering force in forging though he went the other way, from pop to art, whereas she went from art to pop – and back again. David Bowie has openly acknowledged Ono's work, Brian Eno too. Nothing operates on its own in our tapestry of life and art, and a lot was going on whilst Yoko moved through her world and life which she picked up on probably subliminally, as do all artists. What makes her works 'landmarks' is her capacity to construct them all in/through her experience.

As Yoko and John developed their recording ideas, La Monte Young began to bring together what would eventually become The Velvet Underground. Free Jazz curled the edges of the jazz world disturbingly and persistently. The rock world encompassed classical music (sometimes hilariously) and the classical world performed arrangements of the Beatles. Through the 1970s punk blossomed in Britain. The vocalisations of leading punk figures such as Polystyrene, Lydon, Strummer, and Siouxsie Sioux sit easily alongside Ono's thrashing, crazed, driven work and her speech–inclined deliveries which sound now completely sympatico when played against some of the bleak post–industrial heroin–heavy music that came out of the northwest of Britain in the 1980s. Ono and Lennon's work, the early Pink Floyd; there were many whose art school, mind expanding music pushed the envelope.

The billboard campaigns with their political stances and focus bring to mind the later Benetton debacles which certainly proved the provocative nature of the combination of advertising and proselytising. The Billboard had proved, whilst seeming utterly derisory to probably the same people who thought the 'Bed for Peace' work risible, to be an extraordinarily powerful medium. As anyone who has stood in front of Yoko's later 'Imagine' campaigns will know. "We don't mind being the clowns for the world," said John Lennon as he and his wife lay in their bed in Amsterdam. Drawing attention to the concept of peace, Lennon commented that there was enough global concentration on war. There needed, Yoko agreed, to be a balance. There needed to be a focus on 'Peace'. The world dutifully laughed, some of that laughter cruel, some simply bemused, amused. The 'Bed Ins', the development of 'Cut Piece' post Lennon's death, Ono's support of gun control lobbyists, Amnesty International, feminism, 'Imagine' billboard campaigns and, most pertinently, her explicit commentaries, although sometimes perceived as inconsistent, reveal an understanding and positive manipulation of the use of media and event to melt the lid off even the hardest cans of worms.

That Ono's media manipulation has influenced is without doubt. Witness the Benetton campaigns which fused politic, image and art in order to sell Europop clothing, and the use of the media by prominent figures to promote ideas. She may not have been the first artist to do this (many other Fluxus artists used similar models) but when she had clout, when she was in a position to be able to 'spend spend spend', she used that capacity to promote Peace. In a world which seems increasingly selfish, placed in the context especially of recent world events, those once apparently naive notions now seem curiously powerful, and rather sad.

One of the people Yoko Ono most influenced – though some would argue for the worse rather than for the better, was John Lennon. To assume that Lennon was going to have had a simple career had he not met Yoko and to continue to write a jolly pop song to keep the status quo and give everyone a laugh seems to misunderstand everything we know about the man. Andy Davis suggests that "Falling in love with Yoko inspired John to take even greater risks than he'd ever contemplated before, and to push back the boundaries of his art. Nothing would be the same again. In Yoko, he discovered someone who not only lived life with the same intensity he did, but also a partner who became his equal in many ways, as well as his teacher in others....Yoko drew him into her anything–goes orbit where conventions of art, music and even public modesty, were discarded like yesterday's newspapers." (1)

In his last interview, Lennon repeatedly paid homage to the woman who had stood by him creatively and personally through perhaps his darkest nights of drug abandoned soul searching, to emerge at the point of *Double Fantasy*. Such a telling title coming as it does after *Imagine*. And indeed, at last Lennon credited Ono with being the inspiration for the song which not only seems to have inspired generations but also recently spawned a documentary about itself, Lennon and Ono. She had long been using the 'imagine' motif; it formed a substantial part of her works and writings. The recording techniques, the release of the *Plastic Ono Band*, the joy she brought to Lennon's not entirely happy life; Yoko Ono's influence reached into the heart and creativity of the most important and loved musicians and songwriters of the twentieth century.

Prose credits her with the power of the 'muse', Camille Paglia berates her for 'infantilising' Lennon. As though he had no will, no mentality or emotional life of his own. Reframed, perhaps it is easier for the world to see him finding in Yoko Ono his mother/lover, goddess/priestess, daughter/ dragon and manager/defender. Whatever the scenario over the time they were together he developed as a person and artist and spoke freely of his dependence on this woman whose work, at the Indica Gallery, had told him, as it repeatedly continues to tell us these many years later: "Yes."

Notes

1. Davis in *Record Collector*, 215, July 1997

9. **Postscript. My Journey**

The world guffawed at Lennon and Ono. Together, they were an item, a couple whose joined–at–the–hipness seemed nigh on dependency. Theirs was the love of a sixties Romeo and Juliet. From different cultures and classes, their hearts engaged and they looked into one another's eyes and saw each other. "I am he and you are he and we are he and we are all together." Lennon had found his soul mate, mother, sister and lover. Yoko had found her partner, her anima creativa, someone who would inspire her to move forward in her own artistic process and engage her as a man, a real man. Not some artsy fartsy emasculated, badly dressed non sexy avant–gardiste. Their vision united around the notion of 'Peace'. Lennon spoke in an interview before his untimely death at the hands of Mark Chapman outside his and Yoko's Upper East Side apartment of how much he had learned from Yoko Ono. She maintained his profile and provided guardianship of his art into this next century.

Currently the Tate Liverpool is hosting Yoko's World Peace Map. Onlookers are asked to stamp the word 'Peace' onto an area in the world where it's most needed. Slowly emerges a world where the word Peace is stamped over and over again, leaving in contrast those spaces which exist in that state of calm naturally.

In 2002 at the Theatre Ranelagh in Paris, Yoko resurrected her now famous art performance during which she sits on stage offering the audience scissors with which they are invited to cut away pieces of her clothing. In this event they were asked to take postcard size pieces of cloth and send them to their loved ones in the name of Peace. Her son Sean himself took part in the event, and indeed the cutting. That a woman of seventy should choose to expose herself in this manner! Even the hardest hearted of tabloid critics found it hard not to be impressed by her demeanour without of course failing also to note her still fine physique. The event certainly garnered column inches through which once again Ono was able to talk about one of life's major preoccupations; peace.

In the early days one of the main criticisms of these events was their apparent uselessness. What good, folks asked, was talking about peace? Lying in bed for peace? Surely one needed to fight for it, to be active. The events seemed utterly passive. Pointless. Ha ha said the clown; for they who laugh last, as we well know, laugh longest. Time has revealed nearly all of Ono's work as rather more than the sum of its parts. Tibetan Monks in exile around the world talk of peace. Mandela talks of peace. In nearby

Battersea Park, a Japanese monk tends the Peace Pagoda, a gift from the sect of Zen Buddhist monks whose entire philosophy is centred around praying for Peace. Yes, that's all they do, they pray on behalf of all of us, for peace.

Yoko 'grew up' in all senses of those words during the American devastation of Japan. As my mother and father's generation of European exiles who survived the abject horror, destruction and torture of the Second World War are fond of pointing out, anyone who has actually experienced a war first hand; experienced the hunger, the fear, the despair and the most desperate urge to live, knows; war is not the answer. The answer is peace. Yoko's plaintive paean to peace begins during her life's extraordinary journey, begins whilst lying and looking at the sky, the perfect sky, imagining menus with which to keep her hungry brother happy, and more to the point, conscious. The work of the Peace Events from lost child to knowing matriarch through naive lover makes complete sense when set in the context of the psychology of survival.

Last night I dreamt that I was at the Edinburgh Festival. We were staging an event and as we sat in the room to plan the days' work Yoko Ono joined us. I was thrilled as in the dream I was already writing about her. She didn't know I was writing about her but was introduced to me as another performer. She was not the Yoko Ono of today. The Yoko Ono of thoughtful intelligence and humour, of controlled passion and anger and liberated imagination. She was the Yoko Ono of years ago. Young and pretty she turned to me in complete calm and took my hand as she spoke. Later in the dream there was blood. It was everywhere. We were chucking it about, wading in it. I awoke and remembered that phrase when, describing her feelings at sessions with her avant–garde musical collaborators, she said she "wanted to throw blood." Of course that was why there was blood in the dream. But why had Yoko Ono's spirit come through at this point, just as I was nearing the end of my journey through her work for this book? I decided to look through my chapter headings and found I had eight. But Yoko's (and my) number is nine. So I contribute this postscript as tribute from one artist to another, and thus I have nine chapters, and the work can be complete.

When I was asked to write about Yoko Ono's art and music, it was on the grounds that my own work in singing and voice had encompassed such a diverse range of techniques both in praxis and research that I might be able to cast some light on her vocalisations and music. Agreeing, I began to research conceptual art about which, at the time, I knew pretty much nothing. Oh, I'd seen some. But I was by no means versed in the subject and the more I enquired the less convinced I was that very many other people knew much about it either. Then I obtained all the recordings, and began to listen to them in chronological order. Read endless biographies of Beatles books and books about Lennon most of which were so vitriolic about Ono that I began to like her more and more. I watched documentaries. I found interviews with her. Devoured everything.

Then suddenly, one day, my patience with her snapped. Furiously I wondered why she had had no prominent women friends. Why there was never any sense that she had relationships with her sister, (actual and in the feminist and metaphoric sense). How could she spout so about feminism and have been so utterly dependent on Lennon? Those dreadful shots of her sitting silent whilst he did his thing. And why was the work so whimsical? And was it really art? Was it just a bunch of old toss which without Lennon's support would have gotten nowhere? Enraged, I booked my ticket to go to Paris to see her then current exhibition at the Musée D'art Moderne.

The daylight had not yet broken as I walked along the silent dark riverside of the Embankment towards Waterloo Station. I met songwriter Des De Moor at the station and we boarded the Eurostar and as we flew towards the Kent coast, dawn broke over London's bewitched skyline, and shafts of golden light showered the downs whilst hares hopped over dew covered fields and idling horses tossed their manes. Paris was bright and sunny when we arrived, and we made our way towards the exhibition along the Seine, the statues and sculptures beaming down upon us. I would not speak of Yoko Ono. I wanted to try to see the work fresh and to see what Des's response to it would be.

We walked into a gallery to hear Yoko's 'Cough Piece' (which so annoyed Francine Prose). It was filling every corner of the room, and one's mind. 'Vertical Memory' spanned the breadth of the room. There were instruction pieces written in tiny black letters directly onto the gallery walls. In a small ante chamber, *Fly* was showing on several screens but on each screen the film was at a slightly different place, the soundtrack played in the darkness as the various flies walked over the inert body of the woman. There were other startling photographic pieces, and there was a well wished upon 'Wishing Tree'. I read wishes for an hour or more. I didn't want to leave that room.

Afterwards Des and I walked slowly back to the Gard Du Nord. The light was fading. We agreed that we had been completely moved. We talked at length the whole way back. I returned to my books and Yoko's records, and I no longer cared about how she had lived her life or what she had or hadn't done in terms of her personal/political choices. In that room I saw the experiences of a woman who had lived through complete and utter desolation. Vanquished. And I recognised in her the need to speak out her own truth and path. I no longer care whether her work is or isn't 'art'. I no longer care how anyone else defines or fails to define conceptualism or whether Ono let the sisters down by taking part in the patriarchy of the art world or whether she controlled Lennon or what she's done with his estate.

She is a courageous human being who somehow, against all odds, made her way to the top of the mountain in an alien and, at times, distinctly hostile culture and society. She got flack because she was an artist who whilst also a woman and Japanese, placed her artistry at the forefront of her existence because without that I doubt she could have survived. I hope that in the history of the twentieth century the western world is capable of embracing Yoko Ono for what she is. A unique and visionary human being, and one of the worlds most famous woman, and I hope that this little book goes some way to redressing that balance.

Epilogue

The extraordinary life of Yoko Ono, whose work and passionate creativity continues today, is best experienced directly, in the galleries that at last recognise her position as an innovative figure in contemporary conceptual art. The woman who for many is most famous as the wife and great love of John Lennon, has forged a life which bookends the Ono/Lennon creative union with superbly inventive and courageous exhibitions. At the ICA's Islington Gallery, in March 2004, her commitment to the issues and ideas, preoccupations and global developments which incense, drive, provoke and dismay her are transformed, as she has shown she is, by the creative process of making work. Encouraging the stamping of peace onto maps of the world, the public's responses to her vision spill out and cover a white wall with comments and designs made from the 'peace' stamps. The participation Ono always sought from her work is here for all to see, provoked by an intensely moving exploration of the inherent violence in western and most particularly North American culture.

Drawing clear associations between present day New York and images of last century's second World War in Europe, the exhibition is characterised by all the interweaving and unique influences of Ono's life somehow coming together. The space contains contains huge photographs, objects, use of media, and the acts of participation which transform us in our experience of her work and which through her art express the urgent demand for peace on this planet. Ono will not turn her face from the destruction of humanity by the inhumanity of war and by random acts of violence, nor will she shy from expressing the exceptional beauty of nature and the calm idyll that promises. Here we find laid bare the powerful effects on her own life of her association with and love for Lennon and her own experience of human tragedy both personal (Lennon's slaying on a New York Street) and political (her childhood in war torn Japan, her experiences of the losses through AIDS in her close society).

Crumpled clothes lie, a bloodstained mess on the floor. Chalk white limbs and torsos, heads, and bodies spew from a corner of the room. Huge rat traps adorned with posters (Your Country Needs You, War Is Over If You Want It) contain books, and sneakers. Lennon's bloodstained glasses on a photograph. A huge photograph of a table setting splattered with blood spills into the gallery as huge pieces of broken crockery. The view with which we are presented and which we assume is that of the humble cockroach, for is it not said that the cockroach will live long after us? And so we become small in that huge space, against the giant blood covered baseball bat, and beneath the huge photographs of the devastation of Europe's cities in the blitz and New York's less salubrious corners. Through mirrors with no glass we stare ahead. We are as Alice, looking through, and seeing anew.

On the top floor, there is a long, black passage. We are asked to walk through an increasingly scary dark, narrow pathway towards a small square of light, on arrival to find there a small, bright photograph of a pastoral and verdant valley over which hangs a double rainbow. One beautiful arc of colour arches over the other. Below are leafy trees and gently waving grasses, that particular bright green colour that happens after summer rain. The passageway somehow speaks directly to that reminiscence of Lennon's, of climbing up that particular ladder and seeing the word 'yes'. Yoko Ono still offers hope. And despite all of the well and less well documented difficulties she experienced in her life, she still believes in the possibility of transformation. Personal, and political. Indeed the exhibition 'Odyssey Of A Cockroach' might well stand as Yoko Ono's artistic apotheosis if it were not for the promise of what is yet to come.

13 Days Do-It-Yourself Dance
    Festival 57

A

A'G Gallery 32
Abbey Road 57, 61, 74, 122
Acorns For Peace 72
Airmale 84, 158
Akihito 20, 22, 24
Alfred Wolfsohn 151
Ali, Tariq 81, 82, 90, 107
All Those Years Ago 113
All You Need Is Love 71, 107
Amaya, Mario 46
Amaze 180, 182
American Society of Independent
    Arts, the 14
AMM 51
Amnesty International 188
Amos, Tori 187
Anderson, Laurie 119, 174, 187
Animals, the 49, 126
Anthology 125
Anti-War Room 75
Antonioni, Michelangelo 48
Apotheosis 74, 83
Apple 61, 63, 65, 67, 68, 73, 75,
    84, 118, 121, 139, 146, 149,
    154, 155, 162, 169
Approximately Infinite Universe
    86, 93, 95, 107, 158, 160,
    161, 165
Are You Looking For Me 175
Art And Artists 46, 50
Ascher, Kenny 95
Ask The Dragon 173
Attica State 89, 111
ATV 117
A Chance Operation 119
A Story 98, 103, 107, 163, 169

B

B52s, the 119, 184
Bach, Barbara 110
Bagism 7, 44, 47, 182
Bag Piece 55, 58, 182
Bartoli, Cecilia 43
BBC 51, 60, 66, 106, 116, 126
Beach Boys, the 125
Beatles, the 7, 55, 58, 61, 63, 64,
    66, 67, 68, 71, 72, 74, 77,
    80, 81, 88, 96, 100, 101,
    106, 112, 113, 115, 117, 119,
    120, 121, 122, 124, 125, 126,
    127, 130, 143, 149, 172, 174,
    179, 184, 185, 188, 192
Beautiful Boy 166
Beck, Jeff 125
Bed for Peace 188
Berg, Alban 140, 141
Bernstein, Leonard 25
Berry, Chuck 40, 91
Between The Takes 158
Billboard 188
Birkin, jane 165
Bitter End, The 39, 40, 45
Bjork 187
Blackburn, Robin 81
Blackwell, Edward 152
Black Dwarf 66, 81
Blake, Peter 36
Blondie 120, 173
Blueprint For A Sunrise 170, 175,
    177, 180
Borrowed Time 170
Bottoms 56, 58, 79, 119, 147, 182,
    186
Boulez, Pierre 141
Bowie, David 187
Bragg, Melvyn 134, 179, 186

Bratby, John 36
Brecht, George 148, 155
Brown, Peter 63
Browne, Earle 29
Brown Jr, Oscar 187
Bruce, Lenny 39
Buchler, Pavel 178, 183
Bunuel, Luis 58
Burdon, Eric 49
Burroughs, William 37, 62
Bush, Kate 116

C

Cabaret Voltaire 40
Cage, John 30, 31, 34, 39, 40, 43,
        50, 51, 57, 119, 133, 134,
        138, 140, 142, 148
Cambridge, 1969 146, 147
Cannes Film Festival 60, 83
Capitol 121, 169, 172, 175, 177
Capitol Records 121, 172, 175
Carey, Mariah 130
Carnegie Hall 33, 41, 42, 148
Cash, Rosanne 119
Cavern 118
Ceiling Painting (YES Painting)
        55, 62
Chapman, Mark David 111, 112,
        113, 119, 190
Charles, Ray 122
Chelsea Girls 37
Chicago Tribune 116
Chordettes, the 27
CIA 92
Cibo Matto 128, 129
City Piece 179
Clapton, Eric 74, 75, 126, 149,
        155, 163
Clash, the 101, 103
Clayson, Alan 8, 9, 108

Cleanup Time 165
Cliff, Jimmy 119
Clinton, Bill 137
Coffin Car 66
Cohen, George M. 32
Cohn-Bendit, Daniel 61
Colby, Paul 40
Cold Turkey 74, 75, 103
Coleman, Ornette 43, 58, 68, 78,
        98, 138, 141, 152
Concannon, Kevin 183
Costello, Elvis 119
Cotts, Cynthia 147, 153
Cough Piece 192
Cowell, Henry 14, 30
Cox, Kyoko 38, 39, 44, 46, 47,
        49, 50, 57, 59, 62, 65, 75,
        83, 84, 85, 86, 90, 91, 95,
        119, 120, 121, 129, 133, 147,
        152, 156, 179
Cox, Tony 35, 37, 39, 40, 41, 44,
        49, 65, 83, 85, 86, 90, 92,
        120, 121, 133, 147, 182
Craig, J. Marshall 52
Creation, the 40
Cut Piece 42, 44, 47, 51, 66, 119,
        127, 137, 143, 178, 180, 188

D

Dadaism 13, 14, 31, 32, 40, 185
Daily Express 102
Daily Mail 102
Daily Telegraph 87, 94, 107, 130
Dakota Building 95, 96, 100, 101,
        102, 105, 110, 113, 114, 116,
        118, 130, 167, 172
Dave Clark Five, the 121
Davis, Andy 143, 146, 150, 189
Davis, Angela 163

Day, Doris 37
Decca 121
Destra, Ron 172
Destruction In Art Symposium 182
Dietrich, Marlene 58
DiLello, Richard 67
Disc and Music Echo 73, 107
Doctor 1 181
Doggett, Bill 177
Doggett, Peter 158, 161, 162, 163, 169, 175, 177
Dogtown 169
Dolls, the 173
Don't Count The Waves 158
Don't Worry, Kyoko (Mummy's Only Looking For Her Hand In The Snow) 75, 156
Doors, the 125
Double Fantasy 103, 112, 114, 115, 117, 163, 164, 166, 169, 170, 189
Double Fantasy (A Heart Play) 103
Douglas, Jack 117
Douglas, Mike 90, 91
Duchamp, Marcel 13
Dunbar, John 49, 55
Dyke, Jerry Van 40
Dylan, Bob 40, 111, 161

E

Edinburgh Festival 191
Edmunds, Dave 122
Edwards, Gordon 95
Elegy For The Walrus 113
Elephant's Memory 90, 91, 93, 95, 159, 161
Elgin Theatre 80

Ellis, Timo 174
Elms, Robert 102
EMI 65, 101, 121
Emin, Tracey 14, 51, 128, 185, 186
Empty Garden 113
Empty Sky 114
Eno, Brian 187
Epstein, Brian 7
Erection 84
Everybody's Weekly 36
Every Man Has A Woman Who Loves Him 119, 166

F

Faith, Adam 117
Faithfull, Marianne 48, 50, 144
Family Blood Objects 123
Farren, Mick 67, 77, 81
Fawcett, Anthony 61
FBI 71, 90, 92
Feeling The Space 94, 96, 101, 107, 163, 169
Ficara, Ken 174
Film No.5 63
Flack, Roberta 119, 122
Flies, the 51, 79
Fluxus 40, 41, 46, 55, 60, 84, 102, 134, 141, 142, 155, 179, 180, 186, 188
Fly 79, 83, 84, 86, 107, 144, 155, 158, 162, 172, 174, 182, 186, 192
Formby, Beryl 112
Fourteen Hour Technicolour Dream 57
Four Seasons, the 40
Franco, Ani De 187
Free As A Bird 124, 125

Fricke, David 173
Frost On Saturday 64
Futurism 14, 40

G

Gaar, Gillian G. 128
Gainsbourg, Serge 165
Gakushuin University 25, 140
Galas, Diamanda 173, 187
Gebhart, Steve 79
Geffen Records 103
Gershwin, George 13
Get Back 66
Ghosts At No. 9 37
Ginsberg, Allen 40, 90, 98
Give Me Something 164, 165
Give Peace A Chance 70, 72, 73,
    75, 123
Glastonbury Festival 83
Godard, Jean-Luc 58
Goldman, Albert 112
Goodbye Sadness 168
Gorman, John 51
Grade, Lord 72, 117
Grammy 112, 114
Grapefruit 33, 37, 40, 57, 84, 85,
    138, 180
Grapefruit in the World of Park,
    A 88
Greaves, Derrick 36
Green, Jonathon 52
Greenfield Morning I Pushed An
    Empty Baby Carriage All
    Over The City 78, 152, 179
Greenwich Village 13, 30, 32, 39,
    41, 43, 44, 88, 98, 140
Greer, Germaine 161
Grotowski, Jerzy 187
Growing (Up) at 37 94
Grow Old With Me 170

Guardian 45, 63, 90, 116
Guggenheim Museum 186
Guthrie, Woody 40

H

Hagiwari 43
Half A Wind 57
Hall and Oates 122
Hamilton, Richard 36
Hammer A Nail In 55, 64
Ham Yard 49
Hancock, Tony 40
Happy Christmas (War Is Over)
    89, 95
Hardin, Louis Thomas 39
Hard Times Are Over (For A
    While) 104
Harrison, George 64, 85, 110, 112,
    113, 117, 118, 121, 123, 124
Harrison, Olivia 122
Harry, Bill 116, 130
Harry, Debbie 119
Hatori, Miho 128
Havadtoy, Sam 114
Heartplay: Unfinished Dialogue
    170, 177
Heart Play: Unfinished Dialogue
    115
Heliczer, Piero 41
Hell In Paradise 120
Hendrix, Jimi 62, 126, 143
Hendryx, Nona 120, 171
Herman, Woody 13
Hey Jude 125
Hide Me 182
Hirake 158
Hirohito, Emperor 20, 21
Hiroshima 23, 75, 124, 130, 172,
    175
Hoffman, Abbie 88

Honda, Yuka 129
Hopkins, Jerry 123, 159
Hopkins, John 51
Hudson, Rock 37
Hugues, Howard 130
Hunter, Russell 49
Hurst, Damian 128
Hurst, Damien 14, 185

I

I'm Losing You 165
I'm Moving On 164, 165
ICA 74
Ichiyanagi, Toshi 27, 28, 29, 30,
    32, 33, 34, 35, 140, 141
IMA 172
Ima 129
Imagine 84, 86, 87, 102, 103, 107,
    116, 120, 128, 155, 170, 188,
    189
Independent, The 14, 86, 107
Indica Gallery 48, 55, 61, 70, 138,
    139, 189
International Times 47, 52, 56
Into The Sun 129
In His Own Write 62
IRA 90
Island Records 171
Islington Gallery 194
It's Alright 115, 170, 177
It's Alright (I See Rainbows): An
    Air Play By Yoko Ono 115
ITV 43, 119, 121, 125
It Was Nice To Know You John
    113
I Remember Everything 175
I Want My Love To Rest Tonight
    95
I Want You To remember Me 180

J

Jackson, Michael 117
Jackson Five, the 117
Jagger, Mick 126
Janov, Arthur 77, 78, 150, 151
Japanese Society, the 32, 33
Jealous Guy 87
John's Children 51
John, Elton 98, 113, 114, 126
Johnson, Robb 8, 53
John And Yoko: A Love Story 115
Jolson, Al 13
Jones, Allan 115
Jones, Grace 171
Jones, Joe 84, 155
Jones, Spike 27
Judson Memorial Church 44
Jungr, Barb 8, 131

K

Kaprow, Allan 30
Karuizawa 12, 14, 15, 22
Keimei Gakuen 21
Keltner, Jim 95, 155
Khan, Nusrat Fateh Ali 146
Kiss Kiss Kiss 66, 164, 173
Klein, Allen 68, 72, 79, 83, 101
Klein, Ed 47
Koppelman, Sam 174
Kosh, John 149
Kronos Quintet, the 119
Kurushi 174

L

Langlois, Henri 58
Lawrence, Sarah 26, 28, 30, 133,
    134
Led Zeppelin 125
Lee, Arthur 48

Leigh, Spencer 51, 125
Lennon, Cynthia 7, 57, 59, 60, 62, 113, 142
Lennon, John 7, 8, 24, 52, 55, 57, 58, 59, 63, 65, 70, 71, 72, 74, 75, 78, 84, 87, 90, 91, 97, 101, 102, 103, 105, 106, 107, 110, 111, 112, 113, 115, 116, 117, 118, 119, 122, 124, 125, 126, 127, 128, 130, 135, 136, 138, 139, 142, 143, 144, 145, 146, 147, 148, 149, 153, 154, 155, 157, 158, 159, 160, 163, 164, 165, 167, 169, 170, 172, 174, 177, 179, 181, 182, 183, 184, 185, 186, 188, 189, 190, 192, 193, 194
Lennon, Julian 113, 129
Lennon, Sean Ono 101, 111, 113, 114, 115, 118, 123, 124, 129, 171, 174, 181, 184, 190
Levan, Larry 128
Light Piece 181
Line 47, 180
Lisson Gallery 57, 58
Logsdail, Nicholas 57
London Art Gallery 77
Los Angeles Times 115
Love, Courtney 172, 174, 187
Low, Jackson Mac 148
Lyceum Theatre 75
Lydon, John 188

M

Maciunas, George 30, 32, 40, 41, 135, 142, 155, 179
MacLise, Angus 30, 41
Madison Square 92, 98, 100, 114

Madonna 46, 130
Maggie May 71
Maharishi 58, 63
Mahon, Gene 47, 50
Mandela, Nelson 190
Manfred Mann 184
Marks, Leonard 121
Martinez, Eddie 171
Martino, Al 27
Massive Attack 128
Maxfield, Richard 30, 141, 148
MC5 89, 163
McAllister, Bill 150
McCartney, Linda 68, 124
McCartney, Paul 7, 55, 57, 66, 68, 72, 77, 110, 117, 119, 121, 122, 124, 125, 126, 143
McCarty, Jim 126
Meck, Nadezhda von 44
Mekas, Jonas 79
Melody Maker 70, 86, 107, 115
Menace, Jacques de 29
Menlove Avenue 118
Men Men Men 66
Merce Cunningham's Dance Company 141
Mercouri, Merlina 59
Metzger, Gustav 40
MI5 90
Middleditch, Edward 36
Midsummer New York 84, 91, 155
Miles, Barry 48
Milk And Honey 115, 117, 170, 177
Milk And Honey: A Heart Play 115
Mimaroglu, Illhan 29
Mindweaver 168
Mind Games 96

Mind Holes 156
Minogue, Kylie 122
Mintz, Elliot 92
Mitchell, Joni 115, 187
Moby 129
Mojo 107, 145, 162, 169, 177
Mona Lisa 56
Monk, Meredith 119, 187
Moor, Des De 192
Moorman, Charlotte 141
Moreau, Jeanne 58
Morissette, Alanis 187
Morris, Adrian 46
Morrison, Toni 187
Morrison, Van 126
Move, the 40, 51
Mozart, Wolfgand Amadeus 12,
    26, 117
Murray, Charles Shaar 103
Musée D'Art Moderne 136
Musée D'art Moderne 192

N

National Gallery 186
Never Say Goodbye 170
Neville, Richard 85
Newham, Paul 150, 151, 153
News Of The World, The 66
New Musical Express 103, 112,
    115, 116
New York Daily News 110, 116
New York Times 32, 42, 91, 96,
    102, 123, 159, 183
Nike 121
Nilsson, Harry 119
Nixon, Richard 73, 93, 94
No, No, No 168, 169
Nobody Sees Me Like You Do 168
Northern Songs 117

Nova 92
No Bed For Beatle John 148

O

Ochs, Phil 40
Odyssey Of A Cockroach 195
Odyssey of a Cockroach 128
Oh My Love 84
Oldenburg, Claes 57
Oldfield, Mike 113
One To One Foundation 92
Ono, Eijiro 11
Ono, Eisuke 12, 14, 15, 16, 17, 20,
    21, 22, 25, 28, 33, 37, 129,
    181
Ono, Isoko 15, 16, 18, 20, 21, 22,
    28, 33
Onobox 106, 123, 157, 162, 163,
    169, 170, 171, 172, 177
Open Your Box 82, 128, 153, 168
Orange Factory 168
Oz 78, 83, 84, 85

P

Paglia, Camille 186, 189
Painting In Three Stanzas 181
Palmer, Robert 164, 168
Pang, May 70, 79, 96, 97, 100,
    103, 112
Paolozzi, Eduardo 36
Paper Shoes 152
Paradise Garage 128
Pearl Harbour 20, 21
Peebles, Andy 60, 82, 84, 100, 105
Peel, David 88, 89
Peel, John 48, 74
Penderecki, Krzysztof 29, 43
Penn, Sean 46
Penny Lane 118

People 57, 71, 73, 81, 82, 88, 99, 102, 120, 121, 128, 179
Pet Shop Boys, the 128
Photograph Smile 129
Picasso, Pablo 51
Pink Floyd 48, 51, 52, 188
Plastic Ono Band, The 72, 73, 74, 75, 77, 78, 80, 81, 83, 103, 107, 149, 154, 155, 168, 174, 175, 179, 184, 187, 189
Plath, Sylvia 95
Playboy 90, 97, 104, 115
Poe, Edgar Allan 13
Pollock, Jackson 40
Polydor 170, 177
Polystyrene 188
Power To The People 81, 82, 128
Prague Spring 64
Presley, Elvis 32, 36, 101, 112, 119
Press, Joy 45, 106, 145, 168, 169, 170, 171, 172, 175, 177
Previn, Dory 95
Price, Alan 126
Prince Charles 137
Private Eye 64, 65
Prose, Francine 192

Q

Q 123

R

Ranelagh, Theatre 127, 137, 190
Ranelagh Theatre 137
Rape 68, 71, 74
Ray, Johnnie 32
Ray, Man 27
Ready Steady Go 121
Reagan, Ronald 104, 170

Real Love 124
Record Collector 31, 38, 45, 116, 123, 130, 145, 153, 162, 177, 189
Record Mirror 150, 153
Record Plant 84, 103
Redgrave, Vanessa 90
Red Mole 81, 82, 90, 107
Reed, Lou 122
Reeve, Christopher 122
Relf, Keith 126
Revolution 9 64
Richard, Cliff 126
Richter, Dan 80
Rising 19, 126, 129, 170, 172, 173, 174, 175, 177
Rivera, Geraldo 92
Riverside Studios 122
Robert Fraser Gallery 62, 63
Rock 'N' Roll Cuisine 122
Rock 'N' Roll Hall Of Fame 122, 124
Rock And Roll 98
Rolling Stone 63, 66, 73, 80, 101, 107, 146, 153, 159, 162, 169, 173, 176, 177
Rolling Stones 66, 101
Rose, Tim 40
Rowbotham, Sheila 66
Rowe, Keith 51
Rowley, Chris 49
Royal Albert Hall 56, 58, 59, 63, 66, 68, 152
Roy Hart Theatre 180, 187
Rubin, Jerry 88, 89, 90, 92, 93, 94, 160
Ruggles, Carl 14
Russell, Bertrand 50
Rykodisc 169, 171, 177

S

Saatchi Gallery 186
Saisho, Atsushi 11
Salieri, Antonio 117
Samwell-Smith, Paul 126
San Francisco Bulletin 13
Sartre, Jean-Paul 61
Schoenberg, Arnold 26, 30, 43, 140, 141
Schwander, Lars 181, 182
Schwitters, Kurt 14
Seale, Bobby 90
Seaman, Fred 112
Season Of Glass 114, 115, 163, 164, 167, 169, 170, 181
Seeger, Pete 40
Sex Pistols, the 101, 119
Sgt. Pepper's Lonely Hearts Club Band 57
Shankar, Lakshmi Narayana 171
Shayler, David 90
Sheff, David 97, 100
Signoret, Simone 58
Simon, Carly 130
Simpson, Wallis 112
Sinclair, John 89, 103, 163
Siouxsie Sioux 188
Sisters, Oh Sisters 89, 91
Skywriting By Word Of Mouth 115
Sly 171
Smith, Mary "Mimi" 113, 118, 119
Smoke Painting 136
Social Deviants, the 49
Soft Machine, the 48, 51
Something More Abstract 153
Sometime In New York City 83, 91, 111, 169
Sometime in New York City 92, 163
Spector, Phil 77, 91, 114, 149, 168
Spinozza, David 95, 163
Spirit Foundation 111
Spontaneous Music Ensemble 146
Starpeace: An Earth Play For Sun And Air 120, 121, 170, 177
Starr, Ringo 62, 78, 106, 110, 111, 117, 118, 121, 122, 124, 155
Starting Over, (Just Like) 107, 112, 164
Staton, Candi 161
Steel, John 126
Steinem, Gloria 160
Stella, Frank 30, 32
Stevens, John 146
Stevens, Rob 168, 173
Stockhausen, Karlheinz 29, 141
Stravinsky, Igor 13
Strawberry Fields 112, 114, 119
Strawberry Fields Forever 112
Strokes, the 129
Strummer, Joe 101, 188
Stuckism 14
Subbulaksmi 43
Sugunaga 138
Sundance 91
Sunday Telegraph 102
Sunday Times, The 77, 123
Supremes, the 122
Surrealism 14, 32

T

Tate Liverpool Gallery 190
Tate Modern Gallery 186
Taylor, Derek 73
Tchaikovsky, Peter 44
Tchicai, John 146

Telephone Piece 158
Temple, Shirley 98
Thatcher, Margaret 104
Thaws, Adrian 128
Thomas, Dylan 161
Tittenhurst Park 72, 73, 74, 77, 84,
    85, 116
Toilet Piece 158
Tomorrow 51
Tone Deaf Music Co 84, 155
Tosche, Nick 159
Touch Me 83, 152, 158
Towers Open Fire 37
True Confessions 36
Trynka, Paul 24, 38, 45, 52, 107,
    130, 142, 145
Tudor, David 141
Turned the Corner 174
Turner Prize 185
Twenty Years At The Dakota 172

U

UNCUT 97
Uncut 60, 107, 145, 177
Unfinished Music No. 1: Two
    Virgins 7, 59, 65, 66, 68, 71,
    87, 106, 116, 139, 140, 142,
    143, 145, 146, 148, 182
Unfinished Music No. 2: Life With
    The Lions 60, 68, 72, 107,
    146, 154, 181
Unfinished Paintings 51, 55, 139
Unfinished Paintings And Objects
    51, 55
United Nations Children's Fund
    75
Universal Amphitheatre 120
Up Your Legs Forever 79, 80

V

Van Gogh, Vincent 35
Varese, Edgard 13, 29, 31, 39, 43,
    52
Vaughan, Frankie 48
Velvet Underground, the 30, 45,
    173, 188
Vertical Memory 181, 192
Villager, The 42
Village Voice 89, 145
Viola, Bill 186
Voorman, Klaus 74, 78, 149, 155
Vostell, Wolf 41

W

Waiting For The Sunshine 161
Walker, Scott 187
Walking On Thin Ice 105, 112,
    119, 128, 167
Wall Piece 47
Warhol, Andy 36, 37, 38, 98
Warner Brothers 116
WarZone 173
Watching The Wheels 166
Wayne, Carl 40
Wedding Album, The 72, 107, 148
Weiss, Adolf 29
Wenner, Jann 63
Whatever Gets You Through The
    Night 98
What A Bastard The World Is 66
White, Alan 149
Whitechapel Gallery 186
Whiteread, Rachel 185
White Album 61, 64
Whitman, Walt 13
Who, the 40, 102, 119, 158, 166
Wildes, Leon 91
Wild Man Fischer 50

Williams, Tony 171
Wilson, Mary 122
Wire 169, 171, 177
Wise, Ernie 7
Wishing Tree 137, 179, 192
Wolf, Howlin 125
Woman 35, 92, 119, 164, 166,
        173, 174
Woman Is The Nigger Of The
        World 92, 164
Women's Room 106, 160, 172,
        178, 186
Wood, Roy 40
Workers Revolutionary Party 90
Working Class Hero 78, 86
World Peace Map 190
Worrell, Bernie 171
Wunderlick, Alfred 39

Y

Yang Yang 160
Yardbirds, the 125
Yes, I'm Your Angel 166
Yesterday 125
Yes Yoko Ono 140, 153, 182, 183
Yoko Ono Then And Now 119
You 158
Young, Lamonte 35
Young, La Monte 148, 188
You Are Here 62

Z

Zappa, Frank 43, 48, 83, 119, 163
Zombies, the 125

ABOUT THE AUTHORS

Alan Clayson

is a writer, broadcaster and musician specialising in music from the 1960's. He's been described by Q magazine as 'The AJP Taylor of pop' who also commented, 'his knowledge of the period is unparalleled'. He wrote the screenplay for the successful British film 'Backbeat', which covered the Beatles' days in Hamburg. Additionally he has written scores of music based biographies including works on Roy Orbison, George Harrison, Ringo Starr, The Troggs, The Yardbirds and his lifelong friend the late Screaming Lord Sutch.

He regularly contributes to Mojo, Record Collector, Folk Roots, The Independent, The Times and numerous other periodicals. In the late 70's he fronted the legendary punk icons 'Clayson and The Argonauts', and still performs regularly. He retains his position as one of the great British eccentrics.

Barb Jungr

has been published by The Institute of Ideas and is a regular feature writer and columnist to the magazine The Singer and has written for Folk Roots and The Guardian. As a singer, performer, songwriter and writer, Barb Jungr has redefined European cabaret in Britain. Her recent CD 'Every Grain Of Sand', was featured in The Telegraph and The Sunday Times 10 best jazz CD's of 2002. She tours internationally and recently won the prestigious New York award for "international artist of the year" from Backstage.

Currently writing the musical The Ballad Of Norah's Ark she has taught singing and songwriting masterclasses all over the world, and is a regular contributor to radio in the UK on the arts and music. When in London, she is visiting voice tutor at London Metropolitan University.

Robb Johnson

is now widely recognised as one of the finest songwriters working in the UK today. He has played pubs, clubs, pavements, pickets & benefits, theatres, arts centres & festivals, local radio, Radio 3 & 4, Belgian Radio, Nicaraguan TV & Channel 4, the Albert Hole in Bristol and, as part of Roy Bailey's 1998 concert, at the Albert Hall in London.

His record label Irregular Records has done much to focus a renewed interest in the chanson genre. He has contributed extensively for the magazine Rock'n'Reel, & contributes a regular column to Folk On Tap. He has written and published one song book, Words and Chords and Journeys Down Denbigh Road, a book of multi-faith stories for children. At present he divides his time between being a musician, a record company, a writer, a Nursery Teacher and a dad.

Robb Johnson should not be confused with Chrome Dreams' proprietor Rob Johnstone.